The Church, the Far Right,
and the Claim to Christianity

The Church, the Far Right, and the Claim to Christianity

Edited by

Helen Paynter
and
Maria Power

scm press

© Editors and Contributors 2024

Published in 2024 by SCM Press

Editorial office
3rd Floor, Invicta House,
110 Golden Lane,
London EC1Y 0TG, UK
www.scmpress.co.uk

SCM Press is an imprint of Hymns Ancient & Modern Ltd
(a registered charity)

Hymns Ancient & Modern® is a registered trademark of
Hymns Ancient & Modern Ltd
13A Hellesdon Park Road, Norwich,
Norfolk NR6 5DR, UK

All rights reserved. No part of this publication may be reproduced,
stored in a retrieval system, or transmitted,
in any form or by any means, electronic, mechanical,
photocopying or otherwise, without the prior permission of
the publisher, SCM Press.

The editors and contributors have asserted their right under the Copyright,
Designs and Patents Act 1988 to be identified as the Authors of this Work

Scripture quotations, unless otherwise indicated, are taken from the Holy Bible,
New International Version, NIV. Copyright © 1973, 1978, 1984, 2011 by Biblica, Inc.
Used by permission of Zondervan. All rights reserved worldwide.
Scripture quotations are also from the Authorized Version of the Bible
(The King James Bible), the rights in which are vested in the Crown, are reproduced
by permission of the Crown's Patentee, Cambridge University Press.
And from God's Word, 1995, 2003, 2013, 2014, 2019, 2020 by
God's Word to the Nations Mission Society. Used by permission.

British Library Cataloguing in Publication data
A catalogue record for this book is available
from the British Library

ISBN 978-0-334-06549-4

Typeset by Regent Typesetting

Contents

Biographies vii
Foreword – David Gushee xi

Introduction – *Helen Paynter* 1

Part 1 From the Coal-face

1. A Norwegian Perspective 17
   Steinar Ims

2. From Prejudice to Pride: Towards an Organized Anti-racist Community 29
   Henrik Frykberg

3. Putting the Semantic Struggle into Practice: A Response to Steinar Ims and Henrik Frykberg 46
   Hannah Strømmen and Ulrich Schmiedel

Part 2 The Interfaith Perspective

4. A Lebanese Perspective on Religion-inspired Political Extremism 61
   Martin Accad

5. Beyond the Far Right: 'Respectable Racism' and British Muslims 69
   Shenaz Bunglawala

6. Contextualizing the Claim to Christianity: A Response to Martin Accad and Shenaz Bunglawala 81
   Hannah Strømmen and Ulrich Schmiedel

Part 3 Politics of the Far Right and the Church

7   Encountering and Countering the Far Right in the UK Today   93
    James Crossley

8   'Stop waving crosses around and making them a symbol
    of hate': Localized Christian Responses to the Populist
    Radical Right in the UK   105
    William Allchorn

9   Probing Challenges and Chances in UK Politics:
    A Response to James Crossley and William Allchorn   121
    Hannah Strømmen and Ulrich Schmiedel

Part 4 Christian Theologians Respond

10 The 'Semantic Struggle' against the Christian Far Right:
    Learning from the Good Samaritan   133
    Nick Spencer

11 Challenging Far-right Claims to Christianity:
    A Northern Irish Perspective   147
    Chris Wilson

12 Taking Theology Out of the Trap: A Response to
    Nick Spencer and Chris Wilson   161
    Hannah Strømmen and Ulrich Schmiedel

Conclusion: The Church, the Far Right, and the Claim to
Christianity: Towards Some Recommendations   173
Helen Paynter

Afterword: Lived Theology   194
Hannah Strømmen and Ulrich Schmiedel

Index of Names and Subjects   201

Biographies

Dr Martin Accad is a professor, researcher, author and activist in the fields of theology, interfaith relations, peacebuilding and political theology. He is on the faculty of the Arab Baptist Theological Seminary and the Near East School of Theology in Beirut, as well as at the Fuller Graduate School of Intercultural Studies in California. He is now also founder and director of Action Research Associates, an institute that puts research at the service of change activism and dealing with the past for the purpose of dialogue, peacebuilding and reconciliation.

Dr William Allchorn is Associate Professor in Politics and International Relations at Richmond American University in London, and is an expert on far-right extremist social movements in the UK, Western Europe and globally. His first book, *Anti-Islamic Protest in the UK: Policy Responses to the Far Right*, was published by Routledge in 2018.

Shenaz Bunglawala, MSc, is a writer, researcher and strategist specializing in policy, media and advocacy relating to British Muslim communities. Her most recent work has been published in *I Refuse to Condemn: Resisting Racism in Times of National Security*, by Manchester University Press in 2020, and *Hidden Survivors: Uncovering the Mental Health Struggles of Young British Muslims* in partnership with the University of East London in 2021. She is a Trustee of The Muslim Institute.

Dr James Crossley is Professor of Bible, Society and Politics at MF Oslo and Academic Director of the Centre for the Critical Study of Apocalyptic and Millenarian Movements.

Revd Henrik Frykberg, MDiv, is Bishop's Advisor on interfaith and integration for the Church of Sweden in the diocese of Gothenburg. He is a long-standing member of the Nordic Nonviolence Study Group (NORNONS), an organization dedicated to the promotion, development and discussions on non-violent actions.

BIOGRAPHIES

The Revd Professor Dr David P. Gushee, Distinguished University Professor of Christian Ethics at Mercer University, Chair of Christian Social Ethics at Vrije Universiteit (Free University) Amsterdam, and Senior Research Fellow at the International Baptist Theological Study Centre. He is the elected past-president of both the American Academy of Religion and the Society of Christian Ethics. Dr Gushee is the author, co-author or editor of 28 books, including the bestsellers *Kingdom Ethics* and *Changing Our Mind*. His other most notable works are *Still Christian, After Evangelicalism, Righteous Gentiles of the Holocaust*, and the recent *Defending Democracy from its Christian Enemies*. With his works read around the world, and an active lecturing schedule on several continents, he has global impact in the field of Christian ethics. A leader in the growing post-evangelical movement, he has also put feet to his faith in several activist campaigns. Gushee and his wife, Jeanie, live in Atlanta, Georgia. Learn more at https://davidpgushee.com.

Revd Steinar Ims, MDiv, works at the Council on Ecumenical and International Relations in the Church of Norway. He is the Senior Adviser on religious and life-stance relations and dialogue, and is currently board member from the Church of Norway in the Council for Religious and Life Stance Communities in Norway (STL).

Revd Dr Helen Paynter is a Baptist Minister with the Baptist Union of Great Britain, and Tutor in Biblical Studies at the Bristol Baptist College. She is the founding Director of the Centre for the Study of Bible & Violence.

Dr Maria Power is a Senior Research Fellow at the Las Casas Institute for Social Justice, Blackfriars, University of Oxford. She has published widely on religion and the conflict in Northern Ireland, most recently *Catholic Social Teaching and Theologies of Peace in Northern Ireland: Cardinal Cahal Daly and the Pursuit of the Peaceable Kingdom* (2021) with her monograph on *The Bible and the Conflict in Northern Ireland* forthcoming in 2025.

Dr Ulrich Schmiedel is Professor of Global Christianities at the Centre for Theology and Religious Studies, Lund University. He has written widely on public and political theology.

BIOGRAPHIES

Dr Nick Spencer is Senior Fellow at the think tank Theos and the author of a number of books, most recently (with Hannah Waite), *Playing God: Science, Religion and the Future of Humanity* (SPCK, 2024).

Dr Hannah M. Strømmen is Senior Lecturer in Bible, Politics and Culture at the Centre for Theology and Religious Studies, Lund University. Her work focuses on receptions of the Bible in the twentieth and twenty-first centuries.

Chris Wilson, MA, is a theological educator working with refugee communities in Ethiopia and a part-time PhD student at the University of Aberdeen with Trinity College Bristol. His research interests focus on constructive theological responses to the challenges facing churches in Northern Ireland and other conflict-affected contexts.

Foreword

by David Gushee

It is distressing to learn that a Christian (or 'Christianist') far-right movement is brewing in many parts of Europe. Having watched it develop in the USA, especially over the nine years of our lamentable era of Donald Trump, I cannot wish anything similar on any other country. But, alas, this movement is transnational – or, to be more precise, even more transnational than I had known before reading the excellent contributions collected here, and the fine work to which they are all responding.

What should we call this movement – Christian or Christianist? The latter term, used by William Allchorn in Chapter 8 of this volume, is one that I myself have used in an article or two over these last years. It has the appeal of separating something like real, true or normative Christianity from a toxic variant deploying the rhetoric of Christianity but utterly alien to it.

But who has the authority to decide what is real, true or normative Christianity? Such a judgement is beyond the purview of sociologists and historians, not that they always remember this. No, considered in theological/biblical terms, this is a judgement that belongs ultimately to God, to whom all will render an account on the last day. But between now and then it is a judgement that belongs to the Church itself. That begs the question, what is the Church, and who speaks authoritatively for it?

Anyone who has studied the work of Dietrich Bonhoeffer, mentioned several times in this volume and highly relevant to its considerations, knows that these were precisely the questions he was asking, and answering with uncompromising radicalism, during the German Church struggle of the Nazi years. His answer was clear – the real, true only Evangelical Church of Germany was the Confessing Church, not the nazified Reich Church. For Bonhoeffer, the authority to make this declaration was established by the ecclesial synods of Barmen and Dahlem. Nazified Christianity was no Christianity at all, but a toxic, illegitimate variant. The way the true Church knew this was by testing Reich Church policies, practices and doctrinal developments against scripture, the historic Protestant confessions and the declarations of Barmen and Dahlem. This was not a matter of opinion or one on which toleration of conflicting 'perspectives' was possible.

That settles it. Right? Well, no. Bonhoeffer's position, though vindicated by history, was (of course) rejected by many distinguished bishops, scholars and church leaders who ended up on the Reich Church side – and also by a neutral group occupying a middle position. Bonhoeffer's view was not even universally shared in the Confessing Church, especially as that Church weakened in the late 1930s. It was not fully embraced by the ecumenical movement of which Bonhoeffer had been a participant for several years. Not even Bonhoeffer could overcome divisions at every level of Protestant church life in Germany, despite his valiant efforts.

Thus the question remains – when some part of the Church goes fascist, is this a Christian phenomenon, or a toxic, obviously sub-Christian variant better described as something like 'Christianism'?

The chapters in this volume are motivated by concern about the rise of a populist, xenophobic, Islamophobic far right in Europe that, in some cases, claims Christian theological grounding and deploys the symbolic repertoire of Christianity. I share the writers' concern related to the exact same development in the USA. In my capacity as a Christian pastor and ethicist whose vocation is to offer statements about real, true and normative Christianity, I have also regularly declared that what I have called authoritarian reactionary Christianity (others use different names) is a toxic sub-Christian variant that must be rejected, even anathematized, by Christian communities, leaders and people everywhere.

But I also recognize, as Hannah Strømmen and Ulrich Schmiedel do in their book *The Claim to Christianity* (2020) and repeatedly in their chapters here, that at a descriptive or phenomenological level many far-right Christians genuinely believe that their politics is well grounded in the authoritative sources of Christian faith, notably scripture. Even if some of us critics might view such claims as specious, these far-right Christians are not persuaded. This is a fact.

Moreover, Strømmen and Schmiedel, and some other authors here, recognize that just about every noxious claim made by the Christian far right has some kind of historical precedent. Thus the term 'Crusader Christianity', with its obvious historical rootage, is more than apropos. This means that as a matter both of fact and of history Christians cannot simply attribute far-right excesses to a perverse, bizarre Christianism. The sources lie deeper than that, most often within the Christian tradition itself.

The reader will be left to wrestle with such matters in the pages that follow. I suggest that the paradoxical tension between these two types of claims – theological-ethical-normative claims emerging from leaders and people within a living Church that is accountable to its Lord for its actions today, and descriptive/historical claims from scholars and journalists about what is going on in far-right circles claiming Christian grounding – must be maintained.

Meanwhile, I commend the authors for tackling a movement that, in my own normative view from within the Church, deeply discredits contemporary Christian witness and reverses crucial lessons learned over many centuries of Christian history. The problem is global. I urge Christians – and others – to close study of the chapters that follow.

Introduction

HELEN PAYNTER

In 2014, members of the British political organization Britain First invaded mosques across the UK with army-issued Bibles.[1] The intruders called it a 'Christian crusade'. The following year, the United Kingdom Independence Party (UKIP) published a 'Christian Manifesto' in preparation for the 2015 general election, with the title 'Valuing our Christian Heritage'. More recently, Britian First released a film of themselves invading so-called 'migrant hotels' to hassle the residents there.[2] The threat posed by such ideologies is very real; as a 2022 parliamentary research briefing shows, recorded hate crimes in England and Wales are increasing year on year.[3] A recent poll by the group Hope Not Hate found that 45 per cent of Black and Asian minority ethnic Britons had either experienced or witnessed racial abuse over the last 12 months, and 40 per cent had experienced or witnessed racial violence (Hope Not Hate, 2021).

In 2008, the British National Party (BNP) membership list was leaked online, revealing that it included individuals listed as priests in the Church of England. The General Synod of the Church of England subsequently voted overwhelmingly in favour of banning clergy from being members of the BNP (Peace, 2016, p. 107). Nor is this the only bold stance that has been taken against far-right movements. In the lead-up to the European elections in 2009, then Archbishops Rowan Williams and John Sentamu advised people against voting for the BNP: 'Christians have been deeply disturbed by the conscious adoption by the BNP of the language of our faith … to foster fear.'[4] The BNP responded to the critiques with a poster featuring a picture of Jesus, citing John 15.20, KJV: 'If they have persecuted me, they will also persecute you' (Peace, 2016, p. 107).

However, in recent years less public opposition has been offered to hard-right rhetoric from official church sources. In the meantime, far-right incidents continue to increase (Hope Not Hate, 2023).

Sadly, this trend is not isolated to the UK. In fact, it is far more developed among a number of our near neighbours. For example, at the time of writing, the Netherlands has just held a general election where the anti-Islam, anti-EU populist politician Geert Wilders and his Party for Freedom (*Partij voor de Vrijheid*) have commanded more votes than any other party.[5] In Hungary, the Prime Minister Viktor Orbán has built a platform upon repelling the threat from an amoral, rootless cosmopolitan elite, which poses an existential threat to Christian Europe, particularly through the movement of peoples. In his own (translated) words:

Europe and Hungary stand at the epicentre of a civilizational struggle. We are confronted with a mass population movement which is an imminent danger to the order and way of life that we have known throughout our lives up until now ... Europe is now under invasion.[6]

Hungarians are an endangered species ... I think there are many people who would like to see the end of Christian Europe, and they believe that if they replace its cultural subsoil, if they bring in millions of people from new ethnic groups which are not rooted in Christian culture, then they will transform Europe according to their conception, and this will make the continent a better place. We utterly reject this.[7]

Under Orbán's government, Hungary has experienced a substantial and concerning wind-back in its democratic freedoms (Gushee, 2023, p. 139).

An equally concerning rise in hard-right politics is also clearly visible if we turn our attention to the West rather than the East. The invasion of the US Capitol on 6 January 2020 was the violent expression of a movement with deep historical roots in racism, especially in the American South. Under Donald Trump, attitudes that had been semi-concealed were brought into the open and given full expression, centring around Making America Great Again, building a wall to keep out migrants from Latin America, conspiracism, white supremacism and gun rights. This movement has been enthusiastically embraced by white American evangelicals, who have bought into the narrative of American exceptionalism (America as God's chosen nation); the restoration of 'biblical values' by revoking LGBTQ rights and restricting or banning abortion; and gun ownership as a Christian duty (Vegter and Kelley, 2020). (It should be noted that the self-identification as 'evangelical' is starting to become more of a political designator than a religious one (Gorski and Perry, 2022, p. 107)).

While hard-right expressions in the UK have not currently reached the level seen in the USA and some other parts of Europe, their evident potential to provoke violence and destabilize democracy should evoke deep concern. And since, as we will discuss below, certain elements of these ideologies appear to invoke certain Christian theological themes, this should exercise the Church.

The Nature of the Hard Right

So far we have used the term 'hard right' without doing more than gesture at its precise meaning. But before we move on, it might be helpful to add some content to the term.

Contributors to this book variously use the terms 'far right', 'hard right', 'radical right' and perhaps 'extreme right'. Depending on their specific expertise in the area of political theory, these may or may not be used with high precision. In any case, there is no consensus on the definitions of these terms. For this reason we consider this imprecision to be a feature rather than a flaw, particularly since – as we shall discuss shortly – the book is concerned less with the specifics of the *manifestation* of hard-right ideology, but rather the Church's *resistance* to it. None the less, some working definitions are in order here, if only to witness to the breadth of hard-right expressions under consideration.

In his book *The Far Right Today*, Cas Mudde defines the far right as 'those on the right who are "anti-system", defined here as hostile to liberal democracy' (Mudde, 2019, p. 7). He then divides that into two sub-groups. The *extreme right* 'rejects the essence of democracy, that is popular sovereignty and majority rule' (p. 7). Classic examples of the extreme right include Adolf Hitler and Benito Mussolini. By contrast, the *radical right* 'accepts the essence of democracy, but opposes fundamental elements of *liberal* democracy, most notably minority rights, rule of law, and separation of powers' (p. 7, emphasis original). This might be represented as in Figure 1.

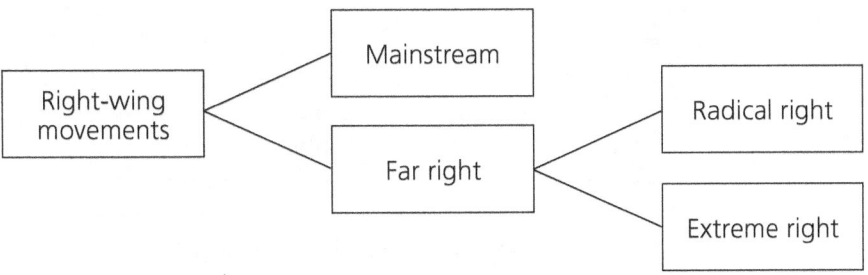

Figure 1

It will readily be seen that hard-right ideologies do not occupy a single point on the political spectrum. In the UK, some groups, such as UKIP, position themselves with varying degrees of plausibility as 'mainstream' organizations. To quote Cas Mudde again:

> Where does Britain's Conservative Party stop and the United Kingdom Independence Party or Brexit Party begin? ... The mainstreaming of the far right – in terms of ideology, politics, and organization – that characterizes the fourth wave [of radical right politics] has made the borders between the racial right and the mainstream right ... more and more difficult to establish. (Mudde, 2019, p. 23)

Mudde's words here were written before Boris Johnson (PM, July 2019–September 2022) and Liz Truss (PM, 6 September–20 October 2022) took the UK Conservative Party on a firmly hard-right, populist swerve. Since then a number of senior members of the Conservative government publicly expressed views that would formerly have been considered unacceptable in mainstream politics. This is an example of the shift of the 'Overton window', an idea coined by the US policy analyst Joseph Overton to describe the ways that a society's acceptance of certain ideas may shift over time.[8] The 'window' reflects which elements of public policy are imaginable, possible, desirable and accepted; elements that lie outside the window are unthinkable and unacceptable.[9]

Recent examples of the shift of the Overton window in the UK include, but are not limited to: Boris Johnson's description of women wearing hijabs as 'letterboxes', and Suella Braverman's use of language typical of antisemitic conspiracy theories.[10] Such speech appeals to the more extreme individuals in or beyond the Conservative Party, yet also carries plausible deniability if an accusation of racism is made. This type of 'softer' presentation of hard-right politics is described in a briefing paper presented to the UK government by the research and campaign group Hope Not Hate:

> When talking about the mainstreaming of the far right it is less a matter of traditional far-right politics, namely crude racism, anti-immigrant racism, antisemitism and vitriolic homophobia having become acceptable in British society; in fact, while there are still problems with these issues, they remain, for the most part, beyond the pale for the majority of people. The more extreme elements of the British far right that still campaign around these issues have no electoral success at all and attract tiny numbers. The elements of the far right currently growing

and attracting supporters are those individuals and groups ... that consciously eschew this sort of extremism and even claim to oppose it. Those who publicly limit their racism to Muslims, bemoan the supposed suppression of their rights and freedoms and claim to represent the oppressed 'people' versus a corrupt 'elite' echo the views of much larger sections of the British public and thus have found success in attracting larger numbers than at any time since the 1930s. (Mulhall, 2019)

Mudde's classification above was based upon the extent to which each movement is a threat to democracy, which is related to but not coterminous with the content of its ideology. It is helpful to hold alongside this a definition more focused upon that content. Here I quote from James Crossley's Chapter 7 in this volume:

I define 'far right' in general, popularly understood terms to cover known nationalist, anti-leftist, and anti-liberal movements ranging from those whose object of hate is typically Muslims and Islam (e.g. English Defence League, Tommy Robinson, For Britain) to those who are more fascistic and overtly racist (e.g. Patriotic Alternative, National Action, British National Party).

It will be clear by now that people with hard-right opinions are far from homogeneous. (And we have not even begun to tease out the demographic differences that they demonstrate. This is discussed further in my Conclusion to this book.) Additionally, the precise mix of views that they espouse will vary, and sometimes be entirely contradictory – particularly around the question of antisemitism.[11] Categorizing the distinctives of far-right ideology is therefore a complex and imprecise science, but I offer the following heuristic list, derived from a variety of sources (Mudde, 2019, pp. 24–48; Gushee, 2023, pp. 42–59; Whitehead and Perry, 2020, pp. xix–xx):

Elitism: some groups are superior to others. Difference is often constructed along racial or ethnic lines, but may alternatively reflect (or be expressed as) religious differences.

Nativism: citizenship of particular countries should be restricted to those who are of its 'native' ethnicity. This may be expressed as ethnopluralism: the ideology that people of different ethnicities should live separately.

Authoritarianism: the weakening or loss of democratic norms such as civil liberties, free and fair elections; and the harsh punishment of infringement against authority.

Anti-corruption: a stance against financial corruption or moral degeneracy (often focused on traditional family and gender values).

Christian Nationalism. This category is not independent of the ones above, as it may contain elements of them all, but it is significant enough to merit its own mention. Writing in the American context (although the phenomenon is far from confined to the USA), Andrew Whitehead and Samuel Perry describe it as follows:

> An ideology that idealizes and advocates a fusion of American civic life with a particular type of Christian identity and culture ... [T]he explicit ideological content of *Christian* nationalism comprises beliefs about historical identity, cultural preeminence, and political influence. (Whitehead and Perry, 2020, pp. xix–xx)

It may already be apparent that there are elements from this list that would find ready approval in certain Christian circles. The idea of 'cleaning up' the morality of society; the restoration of 'family values'; the recovery of a 'Christian' past in the face of the 'threat' posed by Muslim immigrants; the re-establishment of 'law and order' may all trigger positive associations and open up pleasing possibilities.

During the final stages of preparation of this edited collection for publication, David Gushee's book *Defending Democracy from Its Christian Enemies* was published. Although Gushee does not deal explicitly with the UK (his examples are drawn from the Americas and Europe), his analysis of why hard-right policies can be so appealing to Christians is compelling.

Gushee prefers the term 'Authoritarian Reactionary Christianity' to 'Christian Nationalism', as he considers it to have better explanatory power (pp. 60–1). He argues that authoritarianism, defined above, finds a positive reception in the minds of many Christians because they are steeped in the pre-modern worldview within which the Bible was written. It is easy to see how this could take place if texts such as Hebrews 13.17 ('Have confidence in your leaders and submit to their authority, because they keep watch over you as those who must give an account') are dragged-and-dropped into the contemporary world without the hard-work of exegesis and hermeneutics. Further, Christian tradition has often leaned heavily into authoritarian systems and structures. Consider the top-down hierarchy of the Catholic or Anglican Churches, or the positioning of pulpits 'six feet above contradiction' in many churches of the Reformed tradition. Gushee summarizes it thus:

> The claim here is that Christianity, with its ancient roots, carried forward many authoritarian, pre-democratic, and even antidemocratic tendencies into the modern world – centuries after politics in many historically Christian lands embraced democratic norms. (p. 64)

The 'reactionary' element of Gushee's preferred terminology derives from the historically recurrent tendency of Christians to react against cultural moves that they perceive as threatening to their influence or the moral climate (p. 68). Gushee identifies a number of key moments when such reactionary instincts have been aroused.

> The rise of reason and science and weakening of religious authority, the rise of democracy and weakening of monarchy, the rise of worldview pluralism and weakening of the hegemony of Christian ways of organizing reality, the enfranchisement of non-majority religious believers and non-Christians and end of majoritarian Christian power, the rise of secular institutions and weakening of the (dominant) church – all have routinely evoked strong Christian opposition. (p. 67)

In our current climate, there is ample empirical evidence that the rise of various feminisms; the Black Lives Matter movement (along with its more controversial academic counterpart Critical Race Theory); the legal shifts around human sexuality and abortion; and the rise in immigration, especially from Muslim-majority nations, have and will continue to provoke a strong reaction among some Christians. If the reader turns back to the handful of examples with which this chapter began, it will be apparent that such factors are in play.

The Claim to Christianity

In their book *The Claim to Christianity* (2020), Hannah Strømmen and Ulrich Schmiedel examine three far-right movements in Europe, with particular attention to the theological claims that they are making. In contrast to standard explanations that such groups simply instrumentalize Christian images and language, without having any genuine claim upon it, Strømmen and Schmiedel argue that these groups do indeed have a theology, one that the Church must respond to. In the light of their findings, they throw out a strong and, to some, controversial challenge to the European churches.

First, many churches choose to try to bolster democracy by bringing people together for contestation or consensus. Such churches seek to be neutral spaces, so-called 'intermediate institutions' (Church of England, 2015, p. 36), where people from the right and left of the political spectrum can meet for contest or to seek consensus. A better approach, Strømmen and Schmiedel suggest in *The Claim to Christianity* (p. 140), is for churches to move from neutrality to positive and vigorous advocacy for the most marginalized in society, which often includes the racial and religious outsider.

Their second challenge concerns the essentialization of Christianity. A common response by the Church to so-called 'Christian' terrorism or hate speech is to dissociate from it; to deny that these protagonists have anything in common with 'true Christianity'. This manoeuvre can allow churches to feel that they are 'off the hook', rather than appreciating the need to engage with, and take responsibility for, the real and disturbing rhetoric and praxis being proffered in their name. Strømmen and Schmiedel urge a more responsible approach which acknowledges rather than dismisses the issue:

> Trained theologians might not like political readings of the Bible. Biblical scholars might say that they are historically implausible, that they are hermeneutically incorrect, or that they are wilfully wrong. But these readings are still there. The theologies that run through the far right didn't appear out of nowhere. (Strømmen and Schmiedel, 2020, p. 8)

Strømmen and Schmiedel challenge Christians not to retreat into trenchant denialism, but to understand their faith as a lived religion that nobody owns; a project rather than a possession.

This leads us to their third challenge: churches need to allow the spotlight to be turned upon their own historical Islamophobia, and the tacit theologies that have fostered extremism. And, in the present day, they need to promote positive contact between Muslims and Christians in order to foster understanding and mutual respect (pp. 130–42).

The Claim to Christianity has been acclaimed as an important piece of public theology. 'Overall, this book is an excellent contribution to the field of Muslim-Christian relations in the context of the far right,' said a review in the Centre for Muslim-Christian Studies (Jones, 2021). Another reviewer described it as 'impressive', an 'exemplary work of public theology' (Roberts, 2021). 'The larger question, of which the authors are certainly aware, is what kind of theology would be equal to the task of resistance,' mused Peter Selby in the *Church Times* (Selby, 2020).

The Hard-Right Colloquium Project

When I read *The Claim to Christianity* in early 2021, I was personally struck by the significance of the challenge that it throws out. It was clear that it would not receive approval in every quarter, and I myself had some disagreements with parts of it.[12] None the less, I felt that it was a challenge that should not be ignored. The potential cost is too high. But as I looked around the British denominations, at their official publications, their blogs, their social media engagement, and their podcast activity, I could not detect that the provocation that Strømmen and Schmiedel had thrown out was under serious discussion.

Therefore, along with my colleague[13] Maria Power, and in collaboration with the book's authors, I put in a grant application to the British Academy in the spring of 2022, aiming to organize and run a colloquium on the topic. We were delighted that our application was successful, and wish to express our gratitude to the British Academy for making possible the work upon which this book is based.

In May of 2023 we gathered a group of 14 invited participants for a 24-hour consultation (Nick Spencer was unavoidably prevented from attending but has contributed to the project with a chapter in this volume (Chapter 10)). The participants came from a range of faith backgrounds, scholarly disciplines or coal-face experience, and exhibited a diversity of perspectives towards the question in hand, which was:

> How should the UK Church respond to the rise of the radical right, especially in view of the theological rhetoric made by some far-right groups, and with particular attention to the challenges raised in the book *The Claim to Christianity*?

We are grateful to all who generously gave of their time in the preparation of their papers, the participation in the discussion, and the subsequent chapters in this volume.[14] The participants and book contributors are listed below in alphabetical order.[15] The contributors' biographies are provided at the front of this book, but their nationality and religious or denominational affiliations are listed here:

Martin Accad: Lebanese Non-Denominational Christian.
William Allchorn: British Baptist.
Shenaz Bunglawala: British Muslim.
James Crossley: no religious affiliation; British.
Bonnie Evans-Hills (*paper not represented in this book*): British (Scottish) Anglican.
Henrik Frykberg: Swedish Lutheran.
Steinar Ims: Norwegian Lutheran.
Deborah Kahn-Harris (*paper not represented in this book*): American/British Jew.
Helen Paynter: British Baptist.
Maria Power: London Irish Catholic.
Ulrich Schmiedel: German Lutheran.
Nick Spencer (*absent*): British Anglican.
Hannah Strømmen: British/Norwegian Anglican.
Steve Tinning (*paper not represented in this book*): British Baptist.
Chris Wilson: British (N.I.) Evangelical/ Anglican.

Most of our participants have been able to offer a chapter in this book. The preliminary papers, written before our discussion, were revised in the light of our conversations, before submission for the volume. This book therefore attempts to represent something of the richness of the conversation and our emerging points of agreement and disagreement, before offering some practical recommendations. The chapters have been grouped into sections (Parts 1, 2, 3 and 4) in order to bring together contributions that particularly relate to one another. We hope that this will allow evaluation and comparison. Each part concludes with a response from Hannah and Ulrich.

First, in Part 1, we have contributions from Henrik Frykberg and Steinar Ims (Chapters 1 and 2), both Lutheran priests in Scandinavia. Henrik and Steinar have both been involved at the 'coal-face' of this issue. Readers may recall the dreadful atrocity perpetrated by an extreme-right terrorist on the Norwegian island of Utøya on 22 July 2011. Steinar brings a reflection on the Norwegian Church's response to that event. Sweden, too, has its share of challenges from the hard right, as Henrik outlines.

We then bring an interfaith perspective (Part 2), with contributions from a Christian interfaith expert and a leading British Muslim. Martin Accad (Chapter 4) brings lessons from Lebanon, where he works with and learns from Muslim partners. Shenaz Bunglawala (Chapter 5), who is interim director of the Christian Muslim Forum, engages with Strømmen and Schmiedel's book from a Muslim perspective, generously engaging with the ways in which Muslims and Christians might be allies in the cause against the hard right.

Part 3 draws on the expertise of two political specialists. James Crossley (Chapter 7) is a political scientist with a particular interest in the role of religion in the political space. His contribution is paired with William Allchorn's chapter (Chapter 8); William is a specialist in the radical right in the UK and beyond.

Finally, in Part 4, we turn to hear from two Christian theologians: Nick Spencer (Chapter 10) and Chris Wilson (Chapter 11). In a work that has intentionally listened to the voices of experts from a range of specialisms, it is particularly helpful to allow explicitly Christian theological reflection to have (almost) the last voice.

Finally, in the Conclusion, I attempt to distil our learning and draw out some practical recommendations for the UK Church. This is followed by an Afterword from Strømmen and Schmiedel.

Our hope is that this book will provoke a response: that it will inform, challenge and inspire. Ultimately, our hope is that it will help the UK Church to be more resistant to, and responsive to, the hard-right movements with their theological claims.

Notes

1 https://www.theguardian.com/world/2014/may/13/police-far-right-invasions-bradford-glasgow-mosques-britain-first (accessed 5.4.24).

2 https://www.theguardian.com/world/2020/aug/28/far-right-activists-filmed-hassling-asylum-seekers-in-hotels (accessed 5.4.24).

3 https://commonslibrary.parliament.uk/research-briefings/cbp-8537/ (accessed 5.4.24).

4 https://www.churchofengland.org/news-and-media/news-and-statements/bnp-and-national-front-incompatibleteaching-church (accessed 5.4.24).

5 https://www.theguardian.com/world/2023/nov/24/geert-wilders-victory-confirms-upward-trajectory-of-far-right-in-europe (accessed 5.4.24).

6 Viktor Orbán, speech commemorating the 170th anniversary of the 1848 revolution, 15 March 2018, quoted in https://freedomhouse.org/article/his-own-words-preoccupations-hungarys-viktor-orban (accessed 5.4.24).

7 Viktor Orbán, interview with Pannon RTV in Subotica, Serbia, 27 March 2018, quoted in https://freedomhouse.org/article/his-own-words-preoccupations-hungarys-viktor-orban (accessed 5.4.24).

8 It has proved impossible to identify the original work by Joseph Overton upon which the now-popular theory is based. A helpful explanation can be found here: https://www.mackinac.org/about/authors/12 (accessed 5.4.24).

9 For a popular-level demonstration of the shifting of the Overton Window in the USA during the early months of the Trump administration, see https://youtu.be/_v-hzc6blGI (accessed 5.4.24).

10 On Johnson's reference to 'letterboxes', see https://www.bbc.co.uk/news/uk-politics-45083275 (accessed 5.4.24). Suella Braverman's use of the term 'cultural Marxism' is discussed here: https://www.theguardian.com/news/2019/mar/26/tory-mp-criticised-for-using-antisemitic-term-cultural-marxism (accessed 5.4.24).

11 While hard-right ideology has traditionally been antisemitic, this is, in some contexts, now being replaced by a pro-Israel stance with respect to the Israel–Hamas conflict current at the time of writing. See, for example, https://www.theguardian.com/commentisfree/2023/nov/27/jewish-antisemitism-support-israel-gaza-zionism (accessed 5.4.24).

12 These are discussed more in my concluding chapter.

13 In addition to her other roles, Maria Power is a Research Associate at the Centre for the Study of Bible and Violence, of which I (Helen Paynter) am Executive Director.

14 We are also grateful to Abi Reid who managed the event administration so ably, and to Victoria Paynter, who scribed for us.

15 It is to our lasting regret that we do not have any Black contributors to this project. Circumstances out of everyone's control prevented the scholars we had lined up from participating, either in the colloquium, or by submitting a paper for discussion at the event. We considered inviting contributions after the event, but this felt too much like tokenism. The main purpose of the colloquium was to reflect *together*, and the chapters offered here have been reworked in the light of that consultation.

References

Church of England, 2015, *Who is My Neighbour? A Letter from the House of Bishops to the People and Parishes of the Church of England for the General Election,* https://www.churchofengland.org/sites/default/files/2017-11/whoismyneighbour-pages.pdf (accessed 5.4.24).

Gorski, P. S. and S. L. Perry, 2022, *The Flag and the Cross: White Christian Nationalism and the Threat to American Democracy*, Oxford: Oxford University Press.

Gushee, David P., 2023, *Defending Democracy from Its Christian Enemies*, Grand Rapids: Eerdmans.

Hope Not Hate, 2021, *State of Hate Report 2021*, https://hopenothate.org.uk/2021/02/20/state-of-hate-2021-backlash-conspiracies-and-confrontation/ (accessed 5.4.24).

Hope Not Hate, 2023, *State of Hate Report 2023*, https://hopenothate.org.uk/2023/02/26/state-of-hate-2023-rhetoric-racism-and-resentment/ (accessed 5.4.24).

Jones, Simon, 2021, 'Hannah Strømmen & Ulrich Schmiedel, 2020, "The Claim to Christianity: Responding to the Far Right"', Centre for Muslim-Christian Studies https://www.cmcsoxford.org.uk/resources/bookreviews/claim-to-christianity (accessed 5.4.24).

Mudde, C., 2019, *The Far Right Today*, Cambridge: Polity Press.

Mulhall, Joe, 2019, *Modernising and Mainstreaming: The Contemporary British Far Right*, Hope Not Hate, https://assets.publishing.service.gov.uk/media/

5d8b882740f0b6098d33fefa/Joe_Mulhall_-_Modernising_and_Mainstreaming_The_Contemporary_British_Far_Right.pdf (accessed 5.4.24).

Peace, Timothy, 2016, 'Religion and Populism in Britain', in Nadia Marzouki, Duncan McDonnell and Olivier Roy (eds), *Saving the People: How Populists Hijack Religion*, London: Hurst & Co., pp. 185–201.

Roberts, Stephen, 2021, 'The Claim to Christianity: Responding to the Far Right, written by Hannah Strømmen and Ulrich Schmiedel', *International Journal of Public Theology* 15(2), pp. 293–5.

Selby, Peter, 2020, 'The Claim to Christianity: Responding to the Far Right, by Hannah Strømmen and Ulrich Schmiedel', *Church Times*, 6 November, https://www.churchtimes.co.uk/articles/2020/6-november/books-arts/book-reviews/the-claim-to-christianity-responding-to-the-far-right-by-hannah-stroemmen-and-ulrich-schmiedel (accessed 5.4.24).

Strømmen, Hannah and Ulrich Schmiedel, 2020, *The Claim to Christianity: Responding to the Far Right*, London: SCM Press.

Vegter, A. and M. Kelley, 2020, 'The Protestant Ethic and the Spirit of Gun Ownership', *Journal for the Scientific Study of Religion* 59(3), pp. 526–40.

Whitehead, A. L. and S. L. Perry, 2020, *Taking America Back for God: Christian Nationalism in the United States*, Oxford: Oxford University Press.

PART I

From the Coal-face

I

A Norwegian Perspective

STEINAR IMS

Introduction

In Strømmen and Schmiedel's *The Claim to Christianity* the Norwegian context is described in Chapter 3, 'The Terrorist Right', which deals with responses from the Church of Norway to the terror carried out by Anders Behring Breivik on 22 July 2011. Even if Breivik was acting alone, inspired by global online forums and milieux, there are of course populist and far-right environments in Norway, and strong xenophobic and racist perceptions of 'the other'. Both Breivik's extreme ideas and this more 'everyday' type of racism needs to be addressed by the Church of Norway and in the theology the Church stands for.

Strømmen and Schmiedel state that their analysis shows that ' ... the Church [of Norway] proclaims a Christianity that challenges Breivik's claims head-on. The Church posits a more critical and self-critical Christianity that doesn't need to be fixed in a monolithic identity that counters others' (2020, p. 40). If this analysis is right, how did the majority Church in Norway manage to do this? The Church of Norway has been a strong, majority *'folkekirke'* (Church of the people) with strong ties to the state as a former 'state-Church'.[1] It has been part of a hegemonic culture that has itself at times, as we shall see, contributed to oppression of minorities as 'the others', and/or included them involuntarily in 'the sameness' that fits in with the majority ideal. My claim is that in so far as the Church of Norway is able to do what Strømmen and Schmiedel suggest, it is the result of a self-critical process within the Church; a process that it has had to go through in response to, and together with, other faith and life-stance partners.[2]

I will in the following give a Norwegian contribution to the response to the far right; first, by describing the 'absence' of the far right in a Norwegian context; second, by examining the difference between religions and life-stances in the 'neutral public space' versus the 'open public space' in the Norwegian discourse; third, by looking at examples of how faith and life-stance dialogue is understood in a Norwegian context. Here I will include an important contribution from a Sámi position, one of the fundamental challenges the Church faces from within. I will conclude with some reflections on polyphony, 'communities of disagreement' and 'brave spaces'.[3]

The Absence of the Far Right in Face-to-face Encounters

Part of the problem is the apparent absence of far-right interpretations of religion (and in general all extremist interpretations) in arenas of dialogue where the Church can confront them. This is not to say that they do not exist. But even 'moderate' xenophobic views seldom come into the everyday conversations in the Church. This might be a good sign. At least people *know* that the Church does not approve of these attitudes. But is it then possible for us to meet representatives of these ideas for conversation and dialogue? Are they present? I strongly believe in the positive and nuancing potential for each individual that participates in face-to-face encounters. This is what we find examples of in the contact hypotheses described in *The Claim to Christianity* through the work of Gordon W. Allport, and which have also largely influenced practical dialogue work today. But the problem is when some are completely absent from places of interaction. Personally, I have very few such experiences of knowingly encountering people from far-right circles, even after many years involved in dialogues.[4]

At the same time, I don't always know what people 'really' mean when we meet in dialogues. This is also one of the classical accusations made by those sceptical to interfaith dialogue with the 'naïve' partner (the Christian partner in interfaith dialogue with Muslims). Agendas may be hidden, and dialogue is only used to cloak the 'real' purpose, whatever that is. This accusation might be true to an extent, but what is the alternative? Perhaps the unspoken, whether this be conscious or unconscious, also contains some quite extreme opinions? The hope is that perhaps these opinions are corrected in ways that we do not see or notice as part of the dialogue. In *The Claim to Christianity*, Gordon Allport's contact hypothesis is extensively discussed as one of several methodologies to solve the 'problem' of far-right Christianity. But what if the people we try to confront, some of the most important interlocutors, are absent? This is not the same as methods of confronting or avoiding confrontation in the public space, as Henrik Frykberg discusses in connection with the

Qur'an burnings in Sweden.⁵ As mentioned above, maybe they are present in some way or other that might not be 'visible' at first sight. The semantic struggle for Christianity cuts to the core of theology (Strømmen and Schmiedel, 2020, pp. 155–6), but it might be fought in places that are not obvious.

'Neutral' Versus 'Open' – a Norwegian Discourse

In *The Claim to Christianity* the Church of Norway resource material 'Sier vi' is described as an example of how the Church responds to the far right (pp. 55–9). This material was first published in 2013, the same year as the government white paper on faith and life-stance policies in Norway was published.⁶ The white paper introduces the term 'life-stance open society' as a basis for Norwegian policy that contrasts with other secular ideas about religion and 'neutrality'. Both publications are highly influenced by a long discourse in Norwegian society about the term 'neutrality' used about religious and life-stance belonging and its place in the public sphere. The white paper addresses eight principles for a holistic policy, with a final principle that is introduced in the report: 'Everyone should accept being exposed to other people's religious and life-stance practices in the public space' (NOU, 2013, pp. 17–18, author's trans.). This is the key principle that underpins the idea of a life-stance open society. It is now the main term used in public discourse, even if it is still contested. This did not come about by chance. Several of the members in the white paper committee had a background from dialogue-work in Norway.

Definitions of Dialogue

Within the Church of Norway, the work and theological reflections on dialogue conducted at the Dialogue Centre Emmaus⁷ have been highly influential. At the Centre, the following definition of dialogue was adopted: '[Dialogue is a ...] mutual encounter between equal parties, without hidden agendas, not aiming at transforming the other but at taking part in a mutual transformation that may happen through the encounter.'⁸ This definition has been held up as the most used example of ideal dialogue in the Church of Norway as a whole. It has never been interpreted in dogmatic ways, but is viewed as a working tool.

A small, practical digression is necessary here. In the dialogue work

I have personally been involved in and know of, it has become usual to start any dialogue-related activity (courses on dialogue, gatherings for students on dialogue or in interfaith dialogue groups) by defining the term 'dialogue' through building upon the experiences of the people who are present. The term is thereby personalized for all in the group, and in this way also 'owned' by the group. The relevance of this will become clear shortly.

The Dialogue Pilots and Faith-based Method of Dialogue

In 2013–14 the Church Dialogue Centre in Oslo started to explore the possibility of creating an academic course in dialogue. This was done in collaboration with three Muslim communities and the Oslo branch of the Norwegian Humanist Association. The idea was to combine training in practical dialogue techniques with a theoretical dialogue-education at university level. Facilitation of workshops has always been primarily in high schools, where the age difference between pupils and students is not too big. By making it a university course, with 20 credits, it was possible to ensure students' attendance, and the quality and status of the course. In addition, each student applying for the course has to go through an interview to be accepted, an examination of their motivation and willingness to share personal life stories about faith or life-stance conviction. After completing their education, the students could be certified to continue working as 'Dialogue Pilots' in schools for example. The prerequisite, as during the study's practical education course, was that at least two or three Pilots should carry out workshops or courses, and that these two or three never had the same background in terms of their religious or life-stance communities. The first group graduated in 2016 and to date over 80 Dialogue Pilots have graduated.

Experience with the 'Subjective' Versus the 'Objective' Dialogue

At the start of the Dialogue Pilots programme, the board wanted to use professionals from the renowned Nansen Center for Peace and Dialogue, which is part of the Nansen Humanistic Academy, for the practical dialogue training. This is the part of the study for which the programme owners are responsible, whereas the more theoretical part is the responsibility of the Faculty of Theology, University of Oslo. Since its inception in 1938 the Nansen Academy has provided humanistic ideals in Norway and has popularized humanism as a philosophy in Norway. The Nansen Center's peace-work, not least through the Center's emphasis on dialogue, has also had a great ideological influence, particularly in Norwegian foreign policy. Among other things, the Center has worked, through the 'Nansen Dialogue', with conflict management mainly in the Balkans, but also in other parts of the world.

What became clear during the first year of studies was a huge difference in the understanding of dialogue facilitation, to the extent that it made training for the students difficult and at times confusing.[9] In the humanistic tradition of the Nansen Center, the role of the dialogue's facilitators was clearly neutral. In the faith-based tradition, the role was initially rooted in the facilitator's own faith or outlook on life, and their stories. The Dialogue Pilots' background from the dialogue environment in Oslo placed an emphasis on the attempt to distance themselves from the 'representative' in the dialogue, and was oriented towards the participant's 'personal' anchoring. To put it bluntly, in dialogue the participants are not very interested in listening to introductions about the Christian Trinity or the Five Pillars of Islam. They are more concerned with what the individual's faith- and life-stance means for them in everyday life and in important life events. This was especially true in the Dialogue Pilots' work and meetings with students in schools, where 'de-mystifying' the rituals and praxis connected to faith and conviction is extremely important. Through life stories and dialogue the pupils are challenged to nuance their ideas of what a 'devotee' or 'believer' is, by showing the diversity within the different traditions. Where the Nansen Center had facilitated dialogue between warring parties from the Balkans and assumed a neutral role in order to be able to do this in a way that built trust and credibility, the dialogue among faith and life-stance actors in Norway started out by clarifying what tradition each one belonged to in order to do the same. In line with this, the Dialogue Pilots always make explicit their own background and beliefs or outlook on life (or, for some, their ambiguous relationship with this) at the start of workshops and courses. Although the Muslim, Christian and Humanist Dialogue Pilots go from this position to the position of an 'inclusive' facilitator, they still might have an exemplary function to the high-school pupils, even to the extent that they represent something 'different' from what the Muslim, Christian and Humanist pupils identify as their own tradition.

As a result of these differences, the cooperation between the Dialogue Pilots and the Nansen Center on the practical dialogue training ended after one year. It has since been run by the Dialogue Pilots' own professionals through the collaborating institutions.

Opposition Within, the Church and the Sámi People

This 'polyphony' of voices, even to the extent of confrontation, has resonance also within the Church of Norway. I would argue that the way the Church handles theological challenges from within can help broaden the theological response to the far right. Here I offer an example where the challenge arose from a Sámi perspective. The Sámi are the recognized indigenous people of Norway. For the last 30 years, the Church has gone through a (partial) process of apology and restitution for historical transgressions against the Sámi. But theological reflections on the Lutheran tradition and Sámi practice, spirituality and cosmology from Sámi theologians is a new contribution to the Church.

In 2020 the theologian and Sámi scholar Tore Johnsen finished his PhD, 'The Contribution of North Sámi Everyday Christianity to a Cosmologically Oriented Christian Theology'.[10] This was the first academic North-Sámi theological contribution to Norwegian Lutheranism. It fits in with the development of Sámi self-awareness and insistence of being heard in the majority population and the majority Church where most are members.[11] Johnsen's research takes its starting point in the Sámi everyday spirituality and sets this up against the prevailing Western cosmology as expressed in the dominant Norwegian Lutheranism. The study is based on a qualitative study in which 28 Sámi from four inland municipalities were interviewed about spiritual traditions associated with Sámi religious practice in everyday life as they experienced it growing up, and how they practise it today.

An anecdote at the beginning of the study illustrates one of Johnsen's main concerns. One of Johnsen's informants was a woman in her sixties. She tells of when she cut 'shoe grass', for insulation in shoes. On arrival in the wetlands where the grass grows, she would speak to the place. Then she would say a prayer in the name of the Father, the Son and the Holy Spirit before she cut some grass, collected it in a bundle, and said: 'Please don't cut my hands' (the grass is coarse when it is cut). Only then could she start the work of harvesting the grass. At a seminar she described this practice and the words that she used. One of the people present was a Norwegian Lutheran priest who responded by saying that this was worship of the creation instead of the Creator. The woman found this offensive, and said at a later stage that this is what happens when you are not careful about what you share about Sámi traditions (Johnsen, 2023, pp. 2–3). According to Johnsen, the woman's practice in Sámi tradition expresses a holistic and cross-relational cosmology, while it appears for the priest as an expression of spiritual and theological chaos that breaks with the hierarchical cosmology within the Lutheran, traditional teaching that goes in line from top to bottom or vice versa.

This anecdote provides an insight into the historical relationship between Sámi and Norwegian (Western) understandings of reality, theology, anthropology and politics. In short, it shows how the Sámi faith, culture and traditions have been defined in the worldview of those in power. It has been discredited as representing something that is without 'logic bounds' and ultimately chaotic.

Johnsen's reflections on Sámi spirituality and cosmology are fundamental challenges to the Church of Norway as well as to the Western way of thinking. It goes to the core of our perspectives and tendencies in theology to think in terms of hierarchies and bilateral/binary relations. One of the obvious challenges that Johnsen's writing poses is to some of the ideas that are described in Chapters 4 and 5 of *The Claim to Christianity*, which offer a description of how 'democracy' is linked to Christianity, and to Christian values such as compassion, community and citizenship. It plays out to the far right's worldview where everything is understood in simple dichotomies: good and bad, right and wrong, etc. (See examples of this in Strømmen and Schmiedel, 2020, pp. 83, 103 and 110.)

So even if Islam and Muslims are to be respected in a plural society, the worldview of Christianity is the foundation for this possibility of an open and welcoming society (in 'contrast' to Islam). Such a strategy plays indirectly into the far right's 'theological trap', according to Strømmen and Schmiedel. Johnsen's argument is that both Church and society must go beyond what we perceive as the given cosmology. This should affect our way of thinking theologically, as well as in any other aspect of life and society. The binary world we have constructed is not an adequate frame of reference. Multilateral understandings of relations, such as those found in Sámi cosmology, can contribute to a more robust and flexible interpretation and theology. Here we are faced with a challenge that addresses fundamental understandings of (the churches') theologies. But it also goes to the core of the worldview of the populist far right where simple dichotomies are essential to the way of thinking, as Strømmen and Schmiedel have shown.

If the Church were able to constructively meet, discuss and be corrected by such a fundamental challenge to classical, Lutheran theology, we would have a totally different situation. But how to do this? I would argue that there are possibilities to develop theological strategies for either incorporating or adding this perspective to the *theologies* of the Church. Johan Goud argues that a monotheist tradition has this ability provided three factors are acknowledged: the revolutionary potential within radical monotheism; the essential importance of interpretation within the monotheist traditions (having to relate to the texts of Holy Scriptures); and, as a result of these, the ability and duty of putting one's own tradition into perspective. This requires the acknowledgement that evil comes from within, not externally, and this also applies to our religious communities (Goud, 2020, pp. 93–6).

'Communities of Disagreement'

The challenge of facing internal diversity and disagreement has been described. But how then does one face what could be understood as 'external challenges' for the Church, central to far-right rhetoric: the plural society that also includes Muslims and other immigrant religions and cultures?

One of the most prolific faith and life-stance institutions in Norway, with a strong political voice, is the Council for Religious and Life Stance Communities in Norway (STL).[12] The STL has adopted a term for this developed by the sociologist Lars Laird Iversen: 'Uenighetsfellesskapet'. The term is difficult to translate to cover the nuances: 'Community of disagreement'. By using Iversen's term, 'Community of disagreement', the STL points to the fact that we are de facto a (faith and life-stance) community, but we don't need to share (all) values. A minimum is to share rules of engagement and rules of coexistence. This is the platform on which we can discuss values. And as long as the rules are clear we should not be afraid of the discussions and the disagreements between us.

Polyphony and Self-criticism

Where do these examples from the Norwegian context leave us in responding to the far right? One of the problems with the far right and new racism is the lack of places to discuss and to counter, face to face, the understanding of Christendom that the far right in some way or another promotes. The majority of expressions of the far right are hidden within social media forums and are not visible in the streets. They are present in politics and society, but not as expressions of direct violence or direct instigations to violence. Racism is, as it is in most places, within the (often inherited and unexamined) attitudes and perceptions of 'everyman'.

In *The Claim to Christianity* the church responses outlined in the book are categorized as 'the consolidating church' and 'the challenging church'. I agree with the use of these terms in the broader sense, but I think there are two areas that are not completely covered in this description.

The first is in reference to the 'polyphony' within the different traditions that needs to be understood and addressed. For the Church of Norway this also comes from the Sámi contribution described above. It is not enough to be self-critical. The Church needs to listen to the voice of criticism from within *and* absorb, or perhaps add, theological contributions from the Sámi into the theological thinking of the Church as such. In the words of Sven Thore Kloster:

> a theology that seeks to accommodate plurality and interpretive conflicts should encourage articulation of multiple weak hegemonic interpretations in order to expand the interpretive space, to help clarify theological differences, and to mobilize people in theological meaning-making and involve larger parts of human life in theological work. (Kloster, 2019, p. 251)

The second is covered through the description of the Dialogue Pilots' 'subjective' mediated dialogue, where the mediators are open about their faith or life-stance affiliation, and space is opened for trustful exchange about faith and life-stance with the 'de-mystifying' ('normalizing') of faith or conviction in the public sphere. At the same time, the ideal dialogue definition has its weaknesses. There is of course never a room of 'equal parties' with no 'hidden agendas'. But this becomes a more urgent issue when considering the history of the Sámi in Norway. With a long history of oppression, the ideal of 'equal parties' with no 'hidden agendas' could sound hollow coming from the oppressor. The Sámi could argue for special considerations well beyond what is secured through the human rights and the convention of indigenous people. The decolonizing project that Johnsen has started within theology should involve more than dialogue and meetings. It should entail a cost for the historic oppressor, in terms of symbolic actions as well as through allocation of money and resources.[13]

What the Dialogue Pilots do is acknowledge the need to listen to different stories, acknowledging that *my* truth is not necessarily *your* truth, but it is still *a truth*. There is a polyphony of truths that might even be able to define the rules of the space where these truths are shared. This also resonates with the 'new' description of the Norwegian society as a 'faith and life-stance open society' in contrast to a 'faith and life-stance neutral society'. In a lecture he gave for the Dialogue Pilots in January 2023, Lars

Laird Iversen referred to the need for 'brave' spaces as an extension to the 'open' spaces. I believe there is truth in that.

Where Does the Far Right Come in?

I started out by pointing to the difficulty of engaging in face-to-face meeting and dialogue (or, at least, meaningful exchange) with the far right as well as with people who hold 'moderate' xenophobic or even racist opinions. In a Norwegian context I would argue along two lines to be able to counter the apparently theological logic of the far right:

1. If we open for a dialogue-oriented plurality of voices, we cannot silence the voices of the far right, even within the field of theology and Christian interpretation. We need to find ways to invite these far-right voices, open or more subtle or even 'hidden', into the churches for discussion and confrontation. We need to listen to their stories (whoever 'they' are) and confront their interpretations, tell our stories and challenge xenophobic and racist opinions, through a conversation about theology. We need to call them out if they do not accept the invitation or are not willing to agree to the rules of encounter.
2. Through a radical openness, a self-critical approach and willingness to be changed, I think that the Church and our theology can become more robust in meeting the challenge of the far right. This kind of theology is the most relevant theology we can explore. Context will contribute to the 'theological borderland', an area with blurred borders where sensitivity and awareness of history meets current challenges. We are all contributors to theological thinking, development and renewal within our own (Christian) traditions. According to Kathryn Tanner, 'the distinctiveness of a Christian way of life is not so much formed by the boundary as at it; Christian distinctiveness is something that emerges in the very cultural processes occurring at the boundary' (Tanner, 1997, p. 115).

Johan Goud points to the importance of this self-criticism; it has become '... a stylistic quality of modern theology' (Goud, 2020, p. 100). It is a means, in the tradition of liberal democracies, of considering our belief or conviction as both truth and opinion. If we manage to distinguish between truth and opinion according to context and to whom we interact with, we can also see our own interpretations ('truths') as limited and not necessarily the representation of God. That allows us to be self-critical, perhaps even able to laugh at our own expense and at the expense of human interpretations in general. There is strength in such an ability.[14]

Notes

1 The Church of Norway was the state-church until 1 January 2017. It still has a position in Norway where it can be argued that the full separation between state and Church is incomplete.

2 The Norwegian term 'livssyn' has been translated into the English 'life-stance' and refers to non-religious communities ('convictions') in the Norwegian law system that are treated equally with the faith communities.

3 Iversen, Uenighetsfellesskapet.

4 One experience comes to mind: the group 'Stop islamiseringen av Norge', SIAN ('Stop Islamization of Norway'), which is responsible for most Qur'an burnings in Norway, was present in a dialogue-meeting in Drammen Library on 11 November 2021 with the theme 'Prayer Calls and the Use of Church-bells – Can We Talk about it?' It was interesting how the conversation after the introductions, sitting in a circle, was almost torpedoed by the four SIAN-members present through interruptions. Through a collective 'mini-workshop' from the others present, including some high-school pupils who happened to be there, the ground rules of dialogue were laid out for the four SIAN-members to agree upon, or to leave. They agreed, and the conversations could continue, including for the SIAN-members to come with their Islamophobic opinions.

5 The group 'Stop Islamization of Norway' (SIAN) has burnt Qur'ans in Norway on a regular basis. For further reading about the situation in Norway, see Bangstad, Sindre and Marius Linge, 2023, *Qur'an Burning in Norway: Stop the Islamisation of Norway (SIAN) and Far-right Capture of Free Speech in a Scandinavian Context*, Ethnic and Racial Studies, doi: 10.1080/01419870.2023.2268168 (accessed 5.4.24).

6 'The Life-stance Open Society – A Holistic Policy on Faith and Life-stances (my translation), NOU 2013: 1 Det livssynsåpne samfunn.

7 This name was used between 1991 and 2009. Now the Centre is called the Church Dialogue Centre in Oslo.

8 Grung, Anne Hege, 2016, *Gender Justice in Muslim Christian Readings. Christian and Muslim Women in Norway Making Meaning of Texts from the Bible, the Quran and the Hadith*, Boston: Brill, p. 68.

9 The following description is based on conversations with the heads of the study programme: Iselin Jørgensen, Tonje Kristoffersen and Hanna Barth Hake. All of them are presently or previously affiliated to the Church Dialogue Centre in Oslo.

10 Johnsen is the former General Secretary of the Sámi Church Council within the Church of Norway. He is now assistant professor at VID Specialized University, Tromsø.

11 '– Vi må begynne å fortelle en sannere historie', interview with Tore Johnsen in the newspaper *Vårt Land*, 2 December 2022.

12 The Council has 15 member organizations and represents approximately 80 per cent of the Norwegian population.

13 Acknowledgement to Gyrid Gunnes's lecture in Erkebispegården in Trondheim, 13 March 2023.

14 Another issue for debate is whether humour and implicitly self-criticism is at all present in the theology and mindset of the far right.

References

Bangstad, Sindre and Marius Linge, 2023, 'Qur'an Burning in Norway: Stop the Islamisation of Norway (SIAN) and Far-right Capture of Free Speech in a Scandinavian Context', *Ethnic and Racial Studies* 47(5), pp. 1–22.

Goud, Johan, 2020, 'The Value of Self-Criticism (Theology versus Violence)', in Moha Ennaji (ed.), *Managing Cultural Diversity in the Mediterranean Region*, Newcastle upon Tyne: Cambridge Scholars Publishing.

Iversen, Lars Laird, 2014, *Uenighetsfellesskapet. Blikk på demokratisk samhandling*, Oslo: Universitetsforlaget.

Johnsen, Tore, 2020, 'The Contribution of North Sámi Everyday Christianity to a Cosmologically Oriented Christian Theology', PhD submission, Edinburgh: University of Edinburgh publication.

Johnsen, Tore, 2023, 'Luthersk teologi, kolonial makt og Sámisk tradisjon – utkast til en dekolonial teologi', *Kirke og kultur* 1.

Kloster, Sven Thore, 2019, *Towards an Agonistic Theology: A Political Reading of the Concepts of Tradition in the Christian Theologies of Gerhard Ebeling and Kathryn Tanner*, Oslo: Acta Theologica No. 76, Faculty of Theology, University of Oslo.

NOU (Norges offentlige utredninger), 2013, *Det livssynsåpne samfunn – En helhetlig tros – og livssynspolitikk*, no. 1, 2013, Oslo: Departementets servicesenter, Informasjonsforvaltning.

Strømmen, Hannah and Ulrich Schmiedel, 2020, *The Claim to Christianity: Responding to the Far Right*, London: SCM Press.

Tanner, Kathryn, 1997, *Theories of Culture: A New Agenda for Theology*, Minneapolis: Fortress Press.

2

From Prejudice to Pride: Towards an Organized Anti-racist Community

HENRIK FRYKBERG

Strømmen and Schmiedel's *The Claim to Christianity* has a good deal to contribute to the struggle against racism. I have, for example, found the different typologies the book offers on forms of right-wing extremism and the churches' responses to it useful. But my own experiences of interfaith relations, especially the last couple of years' work with Muslims, points in another direction than the book's emphases on right-wing movements, the semantic struggle and the use of the contact hypothesis.

Right-wing extremist movements and activists are only the tip of the iceberg of racism, and too much focus on the tip might cause one to miss how dangerous and crucial is that which lies beneath the surface. Too strong a focus on the semantic struggle might become elitist, where an ordinary Christian doesn't feel invited or hasn't the knowledge to be able to contribute. This struggle is of course important, and is already fought, and the discussion in *The Claim to Christianity* is of great help. Similarly, the book's use of the contact hypothesis could also prove unhelpful with its focus on the prejudices of individuals, thereby missing what lies below the tip of the iceberg: structural racism.

At the same time there is, especially in the last chapter of the book, a recognition of the practices of 'congregations and communities away from the public eye, sometimes with and sometimes without church leadership involvement' (Strømmen and Schmiedel, 2020, p. 159). However, the book does not develop this theme. It is in this area that I would like to focus on in my chapter by giving a response from Sweden on the question of how churches can fight racism and serve society to promote cohesion and reduce polarization.

During Holy Week 2022, Swedish society was tested by an election tour of the Danish-Swedish right-wing extremist Rasmus Paludan, for the party Stram Kurs (trans. Hard Line). This tour involved burning the

Qur'an in the suburbs of several Swedish cities. In some places, but by no means all, riots broke out, described in the media as the 'Easter Riots'. Religious communities were involved in responding to these acts of hate. They either encouraged their communities and members of the public not to attend in order not to be threatened or provoked; or they chose to attend in order to calm the agitated or to conduct activities to detract focus from the Qur'an burning.

The questions I would like to investigate are whether the local organizing of religious congregations and other parts of civil society can be perceived as:

1 a resistance to Paludan's limited actions
2 a resistance to racism in a broader sense
3 a concrete fulfilment of the anti-racist society we want.

The structure of this chapter follows a theory of three factors that are crucial for riots to occur (Bergqvist et al., 2022, p. 3). I first describe the *structural* factors: the racism, Islamophobia and socioeconomic vulnerability that particularly affect Sweden's suburbs. These structural factors will then serve as a background to a brief description of the *destabilizing* factors: Paludan's actions and, in some cases, the actions of the police.

The main part of this chapter consists of a description and analysis of how religious communities and other organizations of civil society managed to contribute constructively to counteract the third factor: the *legitimization* of initiating or participating in riots. What distinguished the work they did, and what characterized the organizing, which seems to be one of the success factors in this work? I conclude with a discussion of what answers the results can be said to give to my three questions.

Ten semi-structured interviews, together with literature, constitute the sources for this chapter. The interviews were between 30 to 60 minutes long, conducted via video call during November and December 2022. One person from the Church of Sweden and one member of a Muslim congregation in each of five different suburbs were interviewed about their experience. Listed in order of the discussion below, the locations were Råslätt, Jönköping; Skäggetorp, Linköping; Vivalla, Örebro; Kronoparken, Karlstad; and Angered, Gothenburg.

The Suburbs

Paludan was aiming to use the socioeconomic and racist segregation to which Muslims are exposed in Sweden's most vulnerable suburbs to trigger riots, and thus obtain evidence that Muslims are violent. The Qur'an burnings are thus not isolated events, but should be seen as part of a larger context. For many Muslims, the Qur'an burning can go almost unnoticed or is at least an isolated event, while structural racism affects them every day. As Imam Salahuddin Barakat says: 'The most dangerous thing is not the Qur'an burnings themselves but the context in which they take place – structural Islamophobia' (DN; 23-02-03, see also Poljarevic, 2022). The structural factor is described in this way:

> Riots are more likely to occur at times and places where parts of the population have relatively poorer living conditions, where residents feel that they themselves and their neighbourhood are discriminated against by the state, and where trust in the police is lower. (Bergqvist et al., 2022, p. 3, my trans.)

Between 1965 and 1975, one million flats were built in the newly created suburbs of Swedish cities, often referred to as the 'Million Programme', in order to address housing shortages, reduce overcrowding and raise housing standards. However, the neighbourhoods quickly gained a bad reputation and many who could afford to moved away, while people with fewer financial resources remained. Today, average income and life expectancy are considerably lower and unemployment higher in these suburbs than in more affluent parts of the cities.

Irene Molina, Professor of Human Geography at Uppsala University, has shown that segregation is also racialized:

> In Sweden, residential segregation has very rapidly reached extreme levels of spatial separation along racial markers. A complex set of discursive, political (read housing policy, immigration policy, urban planning policy, etc.), as well as everyday life and institutionalized practices have interacted in the racial formation of Swedish housing. (Molina, 2005, p. 106, my trans.)

In the various suburbs of the Million Programme, up to 90 per cent of the population may have a foreign background, compared to 20 per cent of Sweden's population.

A report from the Swedish Agency for Support to Faith Communities, with statistical material from 2019, shows that among those who identify themselves as religious, Muslims have the highest proportion of parents with a foreign background (90 per cent). Muslims also have the lowest average income and the highest proportion of unemployed (Willander and Stockman, 2020). Muslims constitute a significant part of the population in the Million Programme suburbs. A report by the Equality Ombudsman states that 'discrimination related to religion or other beliefs is a widespread societal problem that occurs in all areas of society and affects individuals of different religions and beliefs' and that 'discrimination against Muslims is widespread' (Diskrimineringsombudsmannen, 2022, my trans.).

In social policy debate and practice, the suburbs of the Million Programme are subjected to control and security measures where the residents become passive objects: problems to be solved. 'Stereotypes of criminality, "race", culture and religion have produced a moral panic that not only helps legitimize the division into "us and them", but also reinforces the sense of exclusion for people living in these areas' (Sernhede, 2006b, p. 278, my trans.). An interviewee says:

> Well, you know, it's the classic case that if you have the wrong name, if you have the wrong skin colour, if it's apparent that you belong to another religious group that people are suspicious of, it's a lot, doors are closed to you in society (my trans.).

Paludan and the Police

During the spring and up to the elections in September 2022, Paludan organized 74 demonstrations. In around 19 of these, at least one Qur'an was burned (Civil Rights Defenders, 2022; Expo, 2023). Qur'an burnings have occurred in Sweden before and this has sometimes resulted in riots, but not with the same severe consequences for the police (183 injured) and those sentenced to relatively long prison terms for these acts.[1] Paludan seeks permission to carry out his hate actions in the very places, the suburbs of the Million Programme, where Islamophobia and socioeconomic vulnerability affect people the most. Burning the Qur'an here is an example of a *destabilizing factor*.

In some places, riots occurred even before Paludan arrived. There, the police's protection of Paludan is perceived as the destabilizing factor and it is the police, not Paludan, that people are acting against. A couple of the interviews describe young people's frustration with the way the police act daily, where young people are suspected and risk being stopped based on what they perceive as racial profiling (Schclarek Mulinari, 2017; Sverige, 2006; Sernhede, 2006b). The perceived legitimization and defence of Paludan's actions in burning the Qur'an by the police, who give him 'his right to do what is so offensive to us', as one informant describes it, is the last straw, a clear signal that the police and most of the society are not on the side of Muslims (Holgersson, Bünzli and Shamhi, 2023).

Civil Society Organizing

For a riot to occur, a *legitimizing* factor is also needed, 'a context for the individual to justify and legitimize their participation in the riot' (Bergqvist et al., 2022, p. 4, my trans.). This factor is more elusive than the other two and is not under Paludan's control, which may explain the very different outcomes of his initiatives, with violent riots in one place and calm in another. Here both civil society and the police may have engaged in actions that discouraged individuals from initiating or participating in the riots. The following, based on the interview material, describes how the religious communities and civil society in each location were organized, what the relationships with the police – and, in some cases, the municipality – looked like, and how the religious communities and civil society acted.

Råslätt

In Råslätt, Jönköping, local relations in the suburb are described in terms of a culture of organizing. There is an active civil society, with good contacts with local enterprises, as well as the neighbourhood police and the municipality. There are several leaders who are trusted among the residents; people who have been in the area for a long time. People take responsibility for one another, for democracy and their neighbourhood, which they protect and are proud of.

The police invited a few local organizations to a dialogue meeting in Råslätt on the evening before Paludan was due to arrive. There they informed them of the existing law and its limitations, and that they could not refuse a demonstration permit. In this situation, the police did not seem interested in dialogue, and one of the informants perceived them as treating the religious communities paternalistically. The meeting was broken up by the representatives from civil society when they stood up and left the room as a result of this:

All in all, there was quite a bad atmosphere at that meeting, and it was probably me who first lost patience and said this is not a dialogue meeting and left, and after that it broke up and some of us civil society representatives gathered without the municipality and police in a meeting immediately afterwards (my trans.).

The congregations also found it difficult to communicate with the police outside the dialogue meeting; they were sent from one person to the next and could not get in touch with people at the right level. An appeal about Paludan's demonstration permit sent by a Muslim congregation was not processed because it was allegedly sent to the wrong address, even though it was sent to the address given by the police.

Paludan had obtained a permit to operate in the square next to the church. Some had proposed ringing the church bells as had happened on a previous occasion. When Paludan was about to start speaking, the priest started the bells, and the sound drowned him out. Other members of civil society, including people from youth clubs and religious communities, were present in the square to try to calm those who felt threatened. The police knocked on the church door to stop the priest, who was questioned and reported by the police for disturbance of public peace. Once the church bells fell silent, five Muslim men prayed in the square in front of Paludan. Only the bell ringing had been discussed beforehand, the other actions were spontaneous:

After everything had settled down on Maundy Thursday, there were several individual police officers who came up to several of us civil society representatives, because, as I said, we were all there, even the mosques were represented, and the Hindu temple as well, and the tenants' association, and the Social Democrats and all sorts of people, and the police said 'today it was you who protected us, not us you' (my trans.).

Skäggetorp

In Skäggetorp, Linköping, a town to the north-east of Råslätt, the residents had tried to organize after a Qur'an burning incident in 2020, but as a result of the coronavirus pandemic and for other reasons were not successful. On this occasion they were only informed about Paludan coming the day before he was due to arrive. In the meeting with the police, residents objected to the short notice, which made it difficult to inform the public; the timing of the event, which coincided with both Easter and

Ramadan; and the intended location, in the centre of town. However, the police were perceived as only wanting to inform the public about the decisions made and what would happen. The Church of Sweden and the Muslim congregations urged people not to attend the event, but otherwise did not do much either individually or together. Before Paludan arrived, a violent riot broke out, where many police officers were injured.

The interviews testify that following this the police demonstrated a change in attitude, along with an increased degree of organization by the religious congregations in Skäggetorp. On the initiative of a member of the Church of Sweden, people are meeting in networks in a way that has not occurred in recent years:

> but also, that the police think it is so important. Because I'm not sure they get anything out of it every time they sit there, but they think it's so important to have two different ones, an area police and a municipal police. I also asked them if they saw us as an asset in their work ... and they saw it as absolutely an asset and a ... well, maybe a ... necessity, to have this relationship, because they also learn, and they listen much more than they themselves talk. So yes, if you want to say something positive about this whole mess, the dialogue has taken off in a good way, I think (my trans.).

Vivalla

Farther north, in Vivalla, Örebro, interfaith relations are described as both structured and cultural, which new church employees and new church congregants can easily join. Here the municipality stands behind an interfaith council, where congregations and the public sector meet. There is also an interfaith network called 'Faith meets Faith', with a youth section: 'Faith meets Faith Young'. In Vivalla, there is an active civil society with friendly ties between those active in the area, and also from the municipality and with the neighbourhood police officers.

On Good Friday, Paludan was due to come to Vivalla. The police and the public had received reports of riots in Linköping and Norrköping the day before, and that same day at lunchtime there were also riots in Rinkeby, Stockholm. Already the day before, the police had advised civil society not to attend Paludan's provocation. The vicar also advised against being present, after discussions with the police.

The youth organization For the People had initiated an action to 'surround and shower' Paludan with flowers. However, when the police advised against it, the action was changed to a meeting in the centre of Vivalla, where they gave the flowers to the mosque. The location of Paludan's provocation was also moved, from the suburb of Vivalla to a park in the centre of nearby Örebro. Despite this, there was a violent riot.

This created frustration among the congregations, who were unable to be there to try to calm things down. However, after the riot, young people from Vivalla cleaned the park and were praised in the media for doing so (SVT-nyheter, 2022). When Paludan later reapplied for a permit, the police had changed their position and wanted civil society on site. After meeting with the police and receiving good advice from Flamman (an organization with experience in dealing with similar events), the congregations were present and contributed to a calm atmosphere at Paludan's next demonstration. The mosque also organized activities that brought together 150–200 young people, with the presence of church staff.

Kronoparken

In Kronoparken, Karlstad, to the west of Vivalla, there were 'security meetings' at the initiative of the municipality, and a few interfaith initiatives, but the mosque association none the less stood comparatively alone when Paludan came. Immediately after the Easter events in other cities, organizations affiliated with the mosque had begun planning a barbecue in case Paludan were to appear in Karlstad. In July the mosque was informed by the police only shortly before Paludan was due to arrive, but was thus well prepared. The barbecue was organized at a different location from Paludan's hate act, but at the same time.

At meetings with the police and the municipality, the congregation criticized the fact that they had been given such short notice. They also demanded protection of their barbecue, as they felt there was a risk that Paludan's local supporters could cause trouble. The police finally agreed to assign a minivan with two police officers to guard the barbecue.

The mosque association asked for food donations from local businesses for the party. The barbecue attracted so many people that Paludan received very little attention. 'Young angry men can destroy a lot, but there is no limit to what young happy men can accomplish,' a local newspaper editorial wrote appreciatively afterwards (Jalalian, 2022, my trans.). The following week the police and the fire brigade came to thank the congregation for the good work they had done.

Angered

We turn finally to Angered, which is south of Karlstad and west of Råslätt. The story here is different. Angered has had an interfaith council since 2017. This includes civil servants and politicians from the city district, in addition to representatives of the religious communities, and a co-opted local police officer. Prior to a visit by Paludan in 2020, Muslim congregations in Gothenburg also organized themselves into a Muslim network, the Muslim Cooperation Group (Muslimska samverkansgruppen). These two networks have been active in various social issues and the relationship with district politicians and officials, as well as with the police, is described as trusting and good. There is a shared and distributed leadership in the networks, where people share knowledge with one another.

In Angered, the networks were given information by the police well beforehand and had several dialogue meetings with them and city officials, before the police had even decided on a permit for Paludan. The police did not provide ready-made answers but were perceived to understand the necessity of contact and meetings with, especially, the Muslim congregations. They trusted, respected and listened to one another, and the police expressed a 'desire for this not to hit Muslims so hard'.

Here, too, the religious communities worked primarily to inform people about the event and give the police legitimacy by talking about how willing they were to listen to the congregations. The police's efforts, including having a large force on site and moving Paludan to a less sensitive area, contributed greatly to the fact that no riots broke out.

Conclusions on Civil Society's Ability to Contribute

In all five locations, relationships and organizing between congregations and with other organizations in civil society as well as the police and municipality existed even before Easter. Structured interfaith councils with members from the municipality existed in a couple of cases; in the same places there were also structured multilateral and bilateral inter- and intra-faith networks without the participation of the municipality. In one place, there was an emerging interfaith network without the participation of the municipality. In the interviews, Råslätt appears to have the strongest organizing of congregations and other civil society, but without a formal interfaith network.

The police's short notice, and their attitude at the meetings that they initiated, indicate that in some cases the police did not see the congregations as genuine partners with their own ability to make a serious contribution. On the contrary, the religious communities seem to have been perceived more as passive objects of information. One informant suspects that the police may have waited to provide information out of fear that the congregations would contribute to increased unrest if they were given more notice. In another place, the municipality invited civil society but not the Muslim congregations to a meeting, which of course created suspicions of discrimination. The exception was the police in Angered. They initiated dialogue at an early stage with a willingness to listen and learn from the congregations in the interfaith council and the Muslim cooperation group.

These three factors – the organizing of civil society, the amount of notice given, and the strength of relationship with the police – both individually and together enabled congregations and other civil society organizations to offer resistance. The interviews show how a strong civil society, even with short notice and relatively poor contacts with the police at the time, still managed to contribute constructively. Good relations with the police must build upon a civil society that is well organized. This seems to enable civil society to plan ahead but is not essential for this.

Organizing thus appears to be a key factor in the ability of religious communities and civil society to contribute. What characterizes this organizing; what makes it strong? First, *time* (again) and *place* are important. This is about relationships that have been built locally over many years, attending meetings together, celebrating holidays and sharing one another's grief. 'One knows a lot of people from different cultures spend time together and visit one another in moments of grief, it's a long-standing tradition.' One of the informants emphasized the importance of providing time for informal networking to better understand the role of one's own organization:

> Networking is really … yes, you can be there for an hour and talk and plan a peace walk, but if you sit for two and a half hours, you will learn much more. It's to be effective … to sit for another hour and not have an agenda yourself, but to see: What is the agenda here … in an area where I'm not completely at home. Networking is an underdeveloped, educational model (my trans.).

Time together leads to the development of *shared experience and knowledge*, another characteristic of organizational strength. It seems, for example, that the local Church of Sweden parish and other non-Muslim civil society organizations understand what Paludan's hate actions mean for the Muslim community, in a different way than, for example, the police. There is also a shared knowledge of local conditions, both the physical environment, such as safe and unsafe places, and knowledge of relationships, conflicts and everyday lives, and challenges of the various minorities, especially for the young people.

The deep relationships and the shared knowledge and experience contribute to a third characteristic, *pride* in one's neighbourhood and the knowledge one has about it. This also emerges from the interviews: having something to contribute, not only to the local neighbourhood, but having the understanding that the common local knowledge one has developed is important to the entire city and country (Sernhede, 2006a, p. 117). This often becomes a counter-narrative to the story about the neighbourhood that is seen in the media and the public debate:

> Many people said that we are still a healthy neighbourhood, a neighbourhood that is doing well ... Many people have the feeling that ... People talk about us being the best and so on. The Minister of Justice was here last spring and praised Råslätt ... He visited the church ... Many feel proud (my trans.)
>
> Skäggetorp needs people, not just politicians, to dare to come here and see how fantastic the neighbourhood is. There are many good forces to utilize in the neighbourhood. I have learned that you can always count on the people of Skäggetorp. I am saddened by the fact that so many want to impose a stereotypical self-image on the people of Skäggetorp, it gets difficult to resist. Skäggetorp needs to be listened to by society, by all people. (Katja, 2022, my trans.)

A fourth and fifth characteristic of organizing is that, based on experience, knowledge and pride, groups are prepared to *cooperate* with the rest of society and to *resist* if one is not taken seriously. They stand up for their understanding and knowledge of, for example, the felt significance of the Qur'an being burned at the heart of where they live and usually feel safe. If necessary, they will organize independently of – and sometimes in conflict with – the efforts of the rest of society, such as the bell ringing in Råslätt, or the barbecue in Kronoparken.

But such acts of disobedience do not imply a general rejection of, or conflict with, for example, the police. On the contrary, informants speak appreciatively of good relations with known neighbourhood police officers, and of cross-sector collaboration for the common good, if the knowledge and pride they carry is taken seriously.

The Church and Racism

The three questions I posed in the introduction to this chapter were, first, whether one can perceive the local organizing of religious congregations and other civil society as a resistance to Paludan's actions? Second, can we also see this as a resistance to racism in a broader sense and even, third, a concrete fulfilment of the anti-racist society we want?

The results of the interviews indicate that religious congregations and organizations in civil society managed to resist the visible racism in Paludan's actions. In all locations, Paludan's actions seem to have further strengthened the organizing and increased the understanding of its importance.

Is it possible to see whether the organizing also resisted racism in a broader sense? By a broader sense, I mean the hidden structural racism I have described as the basic conditions for Paludan's ability to 'succeed' in his endeavour, to provoke riots and thereby obtain evidence that Muslims are violent (Grolopo, 2017, p. 227). Different forms of racism relate to and can reinforce one another. Conversely, fighting structural racism can also make it more difficult for Paludan's limited actions to 'succeed'.

In a research study aimed at developing methods to measure the impact of racism on people's living conditions, Mattias Gardell, scientific director of the Centre for Multidisciplinary Studies on Racism and holder of the Nathan Söderblom Chair of Comparative Religion at Uppsala University, writes critically about three commonly held assumptions about racism in Sweden:

> That racism is rooted in intolerance; that racism is reproduced by racists; and that racism is based on the notion that humanity can be divided into a certain number of biological races. All three assumptions localize the problem of racism in the defects of individuals and their (lack of) personal ethics, (malicious) intentions and (erroneous) beliefs. (Gardell, 2022, p. 20, my trans.)

Through such perceptions, Gardell argues, racism will not be perceived as a political problem for society, but will be about individuals' ability to be tolerant of other individuals. Racism could then be curbed through therapeutic and awareness-raising efforts where civil society can be useful in projects with dialogue groups, multicultural meeting places and information campaigns.

Much of the development of Gordon Allport's contact hypothesis (Strømmen and Schmiedel, 2020, pp. 130ff.) has gone in this direction, as

Kevin Durrheim, Distinguished Professor in Psychology at the University of Johannesburg, and John Dixon, Professor of Public Administration at the Middle East Technical University, Ankara, write in an article about the hypothesis. Writing in the context of the Civil Rights Movement, Allport's 'theory of social change did not rest on the idea that prejudice was primary and that social change could be implemented by prejudice reduction', Durrheim and Dixon write. But researchers in the development of the hypothesis 'increasingly sought to specify the ideal conditions under which contact reduces negative attitudes and stereotypes – not as part of a broader process of social and political change rooted in institutional settings but as a valuable end in itself' (Durrheim and Dixon, 2018).

But if racism is not only about the opinions and attitudes of individuals, but also about racist structures in society, then 'the solution must be sought politically and involve ways of creating an equal and solidary society with social justice and equal conditions for all' (Gardell, 2022, p. 20, my trans.; see also Molina, 2005, pp. 101f.; Durrheim and Dixon, 2018). In such work, the primary purpose of bringing people and groups together is not to remove the prejudice of individuals and groups, but to organize themselves to change racist political structures.

The broader definition of racism also includes not being taken seriously, not being listened to, being questioned and suspected, defined by others, and being treated as an object because of the possession of a 'foreign' name. In the interview material, the unwillingness and inability of the police and municipality to listen to the knowledge developed in the community and their paternalistic treatment of the faith communities in some places can be seen as an example of this.

Postcolonial theory works with this silencing of experience and knowledge. Maimuna Abdullahi, Adrian Grolopo, Lena Sawyer and Hanna Wikström write about Walter Mignolo's concept of epistemic murder, which refers to how colonial domination processes have erased 'a diversity of knowledge forms and understandings originating from the colonized parts of the world' (Abdullahi et al., 2021, pp. 267f., my trans.; see also Mulinari, 2020; and Naussner, 2019). These processes are ongoing, as we have seen. Wikström states that strategies to resist this erasure 'can focus on flat organizing, collective work across borders where different groups come together in solidarity and with common goals, or on broadening the canon of voices with the power to define' (Abdullahi et al., 2021, p. 274, my trans.).

The Church of Sweden has a large potential to fight not only visible racism but to organize with others at the local level to tackle structural racism. Concrete expressions of this way of working and organizing have emerged in the interview material. We have received examples of listening and letting other voices and other stories emerge in addition to the majority society. Voices and stories that both make life more complex and are needed to find solutions to the challenges we face.

This is not a question of fusion but of continued respect for diversity and difference. What can unite, then, is not culture, religion or ethnicity, but the choice to work for the common good. Sernhede writes about how the suburbs are characterized by volatility, fragile communities and extreme ethnic heterogeneity where the neighbourhood itself does not become a starting point for community building. Instead, for adults, more limited entities such as the family, the ethnic group or religion provide stability and security (Sernhede, 2006b, p. 279).[2] Feminist urban planner Leoni Sandercock recognizes these limited and restrictive communities yet writes hopefully that a shared sense of belonging can be found in a shared political endeavour. 'A sense of belonging, which is important in any society, cannot be ethnic or based on shared cultural, ethnic or other characteristics. A multicultural society is too diverse for that. A sense of belonging must ultimately be political, based on shared commitment to a political community' (Sandercock, 2003, p. 104; see also Ritchie, 2019, p. 79).

According to Luke Bretherton, Professor of Moral and Political Theology at Duke University, USA, *listening, commitment to place* and *building strong institutions* are three civic practices for interfaith organizing to strengthen the common good through joint action. We recognize all three practices in the interview material. If we share a place with other people, there is an interest in maintaining good relations with them. From a commitment to the place and the people there, a common narrative and a shared social and political life can grow. By *strong institutions*, Bretherton refers to the need for institutions such as churches and mosques that have been – and will be – in place for longer than individuals who are often mobile and insecure. Individuals might move for better housing, jobs or back home while the churches and mosques stay where they are. These non-pecuniary institutions where people 'do not come together for either commercial or state-directed transactions, but who instead come together to worship and care for each other; serve as spaces where it is possible to sit down and listen to each other and develop mutual trust' (Bretherton, 2011, p. 372; see also Sandercock, 2003).

In this chapter, we have seen examples of how the religious communities and civil society's work before, during and after Paludan's actions can exemplify Bretherton's three features, which can be seen as a concrete manifestation of a democratic and anti-racist society, with the voices and rights of every person and group listened to and taken seriously.

Notes

1 The Institute for Research on Multi-religiosity and Secularism (IMS) wrote a report on the relationship between religious communities and the police during the burning of the Qur'an in 2020, and an external evaluation of the events of Easter 2022 includes a critical assessment of how the police acted (Sorgenfrei et al., 2022; Holgersson, Bünzli and Shamhi, 2023).

2 Sernhede says that, on the other hand, children and young people find it easier to connect with one another and build common stories through common meeting places in, for example, schools and leisure centres.

References

Abdullahi M. et al., 2021, *Kolonialitet, dekolonialt tänkande och socialt arbete*, in M. Dahlstedt et al. (eds), *Socialt arbete: rörelse, motstånd och förändring*, 1st edn, Lund: Studentlitteratur.

Bergqvist, M. et al., 2022, '*Demonstrationer och våldsamma upplopp: En kunskapssammanställning*', https://lnu.se/contentassets/bffd9a5c8a2c41089ab14191988 1313a/lnu_cpu_rapport_221206.pdf (accessed 5.4.24).

Bretherton, L., 2011, 'A Postsecular Politics? Inter-faith Relations as Civic Practice', *Journal of the American Academy of Religion* 79(2), https://academic.oup.com/jaar/issue/79/2 (accessed 5.4.24).

Civil Rights Defender, 2022, Polisanmälan Frölunda 220629, https://crd.org/wp-content/uploads/2022/06/Polisanmalan-HMF-Frolunda-torg-Med-kallhan visningar-pdf.pdf (accessed 5.4.24).

Diskrimineringsombudsmannen, 2022, *Redovisning av uppdrag att utveckla kunskap om diskriminering som har samband med religion eller annan trosuppfattning*, https://www.do.se/download/18.71c46fcf184c78ffadd7b/1669877965291/ regeringuppdrag-slutredovisning-diskriminering-religion-LED-2021-510.pdf (accessed 5.4.24).

Durrheim, K. and J. Dixon, 2018, 'Intergroup Contact and the Struggle for Social Justice', in Phillip L. Hammack (ed.), *The Oxford Handbook of Social Psychology and Social Justice*, New York: Oxford University Press.

Gardell, M., 2022, 'Vad är rasism? Rasism som teknologi', in Edda Manga, Mattias Gardell, A. Behtoui, R. León Rosales and A. Ekelund (eds), *Att mäta rasism*, Norsborg: Mångkulturellt centrum, http://uu.diva-portal.org/smash/get/ diva2:1708376/FULLTEXT01.pdf (accessed 5.4.24).

Grolopo, A., 2017, *Antirasistisk ordbok, Antirasistiska akademin, Printon*, http:// www.antirasistiskaakademin.se/wp-content/uploads/2017/06/Antirasistisk-ord bok.pdf (accessed 5.4.24).

Holgersson, S., L. Bünzli and H. Shamhi, 2023, *En EXTERN utvärdering av påsk uppploppen och dess efterspel*, Institutet för polisforskning, https://liu.diva-portal. org/smash/get/diva2:1726540/FULLTEXT01.pdf (accessed 5.4.24).

Jalalian, H., 2022, *Unga glada män såg till att Karlstad besegrade Paludan*, Värmlands Folkblad 2022.07.22, https://www.vf.se/2022/07/22/ledare-unga-glada-man-sag-till-att-karlstad-besegrade-paludan-a046e/ (accessed 5.4.24).

Katja, Svenska kyrkan i Linköping, 2022.04.07, Facebook, https://www.facebook. com/profile/100064302115221/search/?q=katja (accessed 5.4.24).

Larsson, G., 2022, *Koranbränningar och påskkravallerna*, IMS rapport nr 5, IMS Institutet för forskning om mångreligiositet och sekularitet, https://www.sh.se/download/18.6e391b90182e95cdd752836d/1662450988097/Rapport%205_220905%5B3291%5D.pdf (accessed 5.4.24).

Molina, I., 2005, 'Rasifiering', in P. Sverige de los Reyes and M. Kamali (eds), *Bortom vi och dom: teoretiska reflektioner om makt, integration och strukturell diskriminering*, report in the governmental investigation on power, integration and structural discrimination, Stockholm: Fritzes offentliga publikationer, https://www.regeringen.se/contentassets/10ca6c4d2daf4916a6fcf7e91bdee5b8/bortom-vi-och-dom---teoretiska-reflektioner-om-makt-integration-och-strukturell-diskriminering-del-1/ (accessed 5.4.24).

Mulinari, P., N. Tahvilzadeh and L. Kings, 2020, *Dekolonialt socialt arbete om relationen mellan gräsrotsrörelser och kritiskt socialt arbete i den urbana periferin*, Socialvetenskaplig tidskrift, http://urn.kb.se/resolve?urn=urn:nbn:se:mau:diva-40367 (accessed 5.4.24).

Nausner, M., 2019, 'Gräns och delaktighet i migrationens tid – kulturteoretiska och teologiska perspektiv', in J. Ehnberg and C. Nahnfeldt (eds), *Samhällsteologi: forskning i skärningspunkten mellan akademi, samhälle och kyrka*, Stockholm: Verbum.

Pohl, D. (ed.), 2022, *Svensk rasideologisk miljö 2022*, https://expo.se/tidskriften/svensk-rasideologisk-milj%C3%B6-2022 (accessed 5.4.24).

Poljarevic, E., 2022, 'The Islamophobic Context and Significance of Qur'an Burnings', *Islamic Horizons*, September/October 2022.

Ritchie, A., 2019, *Inclusive Populism*, Notre Dame: University of Notre Dame Press.

Sandercock, L., 2003, *Cosmopolis II: Mongrel Cities in the 21st Century*, 2nd edn, London: Continuum.

Sarnecki, J. (ed.), 2006, *Är rättvisan rättvis?: tio perspektiv på diskriminering av etniska och religiösa minoriteter inom rättssystemet*, report in the governmental investigation on power, integration and structrural discrimination, Stockholm: Fritzes offentliga publikationer, https://www.regeringen.se/contentassets/106cc584ae1a489db46fde9bbbc090ab/ar-rattvisan-rattvis-tio-perspektiv-pa-diskriminering-av-etniska-och-religiosa-minoriteter-inom-rattssystemet-sou-200630/ (accessed 5.4.24).

Schclarek Mulinari, L., 2017, *Slumpvis utvald ras-/etnisk profilering i Sverige*, Stockholm: Civil Right Defenders, https://crd.org/wp-content/uploads/2018/03/CRD-5600-Rapport_Slumpvis-utvald_final.pdf (accessed 5.4.24).

Sernhede, O., 2006a, 'Förortens "hotfulla" unga män i: Sverige. Utredningen om makt, integration och strukturell diskriminering', in M. Kamali, *Den segregerande integrationen: om social sammanhållning och dess hinder*, Report in the Governmental Investigation on Power, Integration and Structrural Discrimination, Stockholm: Fritzes offentliga publikationer, https://www.regeringen.se/contentassets/8abbae5ea9c540f4b8a34bc905bb8752/den-segregerande-integrationen-sou-200673/ (accessed 5.4.24).

Sernhede, O., 2006b, 'Los Angered – stadsdelsnationalism och global stamgemenskap, Om hip hop, utanförskap och platsens betydelse', in O. Sernhede and T. Johansson (eds), *Storstadens omvandlingar: Postindustrialism, Globalisation and Migration*, Göteborg and Malmö: Daidalos.

Sorgenfrei, S. et al., 2022, '*Koranbränningar i Malmö och Stockholm' En rapport om polisens arbete med fokus på samverkan med muslimska trossamfund*, Huddinge: Södertörns Högskola, http://www.diva-portal.org/smash/get/diva2:1648043/FULLTEXT01.pdf (accessed 5.4.24).

Strømmen, H. M. and U. Schmiedel, 2020, *The Claim to Christianity: Responding to the Far Right*, London: SCM Press.

SVT-nyheter, 2022, *Ungdomar städade Sveaparken i Örebro efter upploppen: vi ville visa kärlek*, 2022.04.17, Ungdomar städade Sveaparken i Örebro efter upploppet: 'Vi ville visa kärlek', https://www.svt.se/nyheter/lokalt/orebro/ungdomar-stadade-sveaparken-i-orebro-efter-upploppen (accessed 15.5.24).

Willander, E. and M. Stockman, 2020, *A Ett mångreligiöst Sverige i förändring*, Bromma: Myndigheten för stöd till trossamfund.

3

Putting the Semantic Struggle into Practice: A Response to Steinar Ims and Henrik Frykberg

HANNAH STRØMMEN AND ULRICH SCHMIEDEL

How can Christian communities address far-right claims to Christianity when they *don't* encounter them directly? And how can Christian communities address far-right claims to Christianity when they *do* encounter them directly? In their responses to *The Claim to Christianity*, Steinar Ims and Henrik Frykberg (Chapters 1 and 2 in this volume) ask questions from opposite angles. Taken together, these questions cut to the core of the practices of contact that we called for in our book. Since we will delve into ethical, political and theological issues in our conversation with Martin Accad and Shenaz Bunglawala, James Crossley and William Allchorn, as well as Nick Spencer and Chris Williams, we would like to concentrate on practice here. Practices of contact are part of the 'semantic struggle' for Christianity that we write about in *The Claim to Christianity*. Taking up Liane Bednarz's concept (2009, pp. 7–9), we analysed and assessed the theologies of the far right without assuming that there is a clear-cut answer to the question of what counts as Christianity. On the contrary, there is a struggle for the meaning of Christianity in which claims and counter-claims are made. This struggle is on-going. Practices are crucial to it. In streets and squares, practices of contact are sites where Christians and non-Christians are claiming back Christianity from the far right.

Ims argues that churches need to engage with far-right positions, regardless of whether they are explicit or implicit. While he suggests that the fact that these positions are very rarely voiced in churches ought to be welcomed, he stresses that they need to be engaged. It is clear from *The Claim to Christianity* that we agree with his call for engagement. Ims highlights the risks that come with it. On the one hand, there is the danger of overrepresenting the significance of far-right positions, making them relevant even when they aren't. On the other hand, there is the danger of underrepresenting the significance of far-right positions, making them irrelevant even when they aren't. In addition, Ims argues, any dialogue requires those who join it to take the risk of not knowing what the other might be up to, their assumptions, their attitudes and their agendas.

Ims's account of dialogue in the Church of Norway serves as a compelling corrective to attempts at reducing people to their roles as representatives of this or that view. People are more than what they do or don't say about politics. Although Ims doesn't put it quite like this, his analysis of the risks of dialogue stresses the significance of the affects that run through any encounter. Sara Ahmed (2014) has highlighted the importance of affect. According to Ahmed, emotions aren't something an individual simply has. They are relational. They shape our social and cultural practices, including practices of dialogue.

As we argue in *The Claim to Christianity*, we aren't as confident as Ims when it comes to organizing official dialogues with the far right in churches (Strømmen and Schmiedel, 2020, pp. 119–45). Take Frykberg's case of the burnings of the Qur'an in Sweden that are meant to provoke Muslims to riot.[1] Can a church be a place where people discuss whether it's permissible to burn a Qur'an in public? We suspect that such a discussion would lose sight of the agenda behind these burnings, namely to incite a cycle of violence by provoking Muslims so much that they might not see any other way to respond to the provocations than by lashing out. Bringing people from a variety of backgrounds together to react to such burnings in the streets in which they take place seems, as Frykberg argues, more pertinent and more productive. In contrast to a dialogue organized by a church that ought to be conducted eye to eye, people who come together to counter the far right where it is inciting violence can make the differential distribution of power between Muslim minorities and non-Muslim majorities in Europe visible.

Of course, a proper conversation and a practical counter aren't opposites. The issue has to be decided case-by-case. Frykberg makes a compelling argument against concentrating only on the propaganda of the far right. In *The Claim to Christianity*, we draw attention to ethical, political and theological ideas that perpetuate the construct of the clash of civilizations while passing as acceptable (Strømmen and Schmiedel, 2020, pp. 15–36). 'Respectable racism' (Piliawsky, 1984) – a concept that we come back to in our conversation with Bunglawala – *is* racism. Churches are called to counter it.

In *The Claim to Christianity*, we suggest that Gordon Allport's hypothesis that contact corrodes prejudices is crucial to counter the far right

(Allport, 1954; Strømmen and Schmiedel 2020, pp. 130–4). Our respondents have very different takes on Allport's so-called contact hypothesis. Ims points out that it could work in two ways: as a call for contact with those who are targeted by the far right and as a call for contact with the far right. His suggestion that we need to find spaces in which far-right positions that are commonly kept under wraps can be countered is spot-on. Such countering, however, might also work in indirect rather than direct ways – through affects rather than arguments. If affects 'circulate body to body, produced by and producing certain political and cultural phenomena', then we should be attentive to the way practices can be transformative, for better or worse (Black and Koosed, 2019, p. 9).

In contrast to Ims, Frykberg cautions against relying on Allport's contact hypothesis. He suggests that scholarship on Allport contended that changing what is going on in people's heads could put an end to racism. Frykberg is aware that Allport was far less confident that stopping the spread of racism would be so simple. In *The Claim to Christianity*, we go back to Allport rather than the reception of Allport because his seminal study, *The Nature of Prejudice*, helps us to clarify how risky it is to pit racist structures and racist stereotypes against one another. Allport roots his study in the so-called race riots of the 1940s in the USA. Here, he makes a crucial observation: people who had become neighbours didn't riot against one another, while people who hadn't become neighbours did riot against one another (Allport, 1954, pp. 260–2; Strømmen and Schmiedel, 2020, pp. 131–2). The neighbourhood, then, fulfils a vital function in fighting racism. Allport distinguishes between types of contact to show that racism can't be reduced to what is going on in people's heads. As he put it: 'The nub of the matter seems to be that contact must reach below the surface in order to be effective in altering prejudice. Only the type of contact that leads people to do things together is likely to result in changed attitudes' (Allport, 1954, p. 276; Strømmen and Schmiedel, 2020, p. 155).

In *The Claim to Christianity*, we present Allport's proposal to point out that there are conditions for contact to fulfil its function of empowering people to counter racism:

> If people from different backgrounds have contact with each other on a level playing field so that they can discover that they have things in common, they might become less and less prejudiced about each other. Contact can call into question both stereotypes and second-hand stereotypes. (p. 132)

Approached through our interpretation of Allport's analysis, then, the cases that Frykberg presents in his response can be characterized as a confirmation rather than a critique of the significance of contact, particularly where Frykberg writes about the centrality of place. He insists that countering the far right requires 'relationships that have been built ... over many years' so that 'shared experience' runs through the collaboration between people from different and diverse backgrounds (Frykberg, Chapter 2 in this volume). As one of Frykberg's interviewees argues:

> Networking is really ... yes, you can be there for an hour and talk and plan a peace walk, but if you sit for two and a half hours, you will learn much more. It's to be effective ... to sit for another hour and not to have an agenda yourself, but to see: what is the agenda here ... in an area where I'm not completely at home. (Interviewee, cited by Frykberg, Chapter 2 in this volume)

This interviewee comes so close to Allport's account of contact that one could almost put Allport's words into their mouth. All one would need to do is replace 'networking' with 'neighbourhood'.

To be sure, our reading of Frykberg's analysis through the concept of contact isn't about protecting Allport or our analysis of Allport from critique. There are very good reasons to be critical of Allport. There could have been more discussion of these reasons in *The Claim to Christianity*, so we are grateful that Frykberg presents them in his response. He is correct that racist structures inside and outside churches are crucial to making and maintaining racism in society. However, with the help of Allport, we can see that the attitudes of people affect the societies in which they live and that the societies in which they live affect the attitudes of people. There is some sort of dialectics between racist structures and racist stereotypes. This dialectics is precisely the space where the institutions that Frykberg – building on Luke Bretherton (2011) – calls for can have both a personal and a communal impact. Combating racism, then, needs to tackle both of them together: changed structures on the macro-level can change stereotypes on the micro-level and changed stereotypes on the micro-level can change structures on the macro-level. As we wrote in *The Claim to Christianity*, 'Contact is not enough to respond to the rise of the far right, but it is one central component of a challenging and convincing proposal offered by the churches' (Strømmen and Schmiedel, 2020, p. 130).

We agree with Ims's argument – confirmed by Frykberg's cases – that practices of contact need to be rooted in openness. In the discussion of the project of the Dialogue Pilots promoted by the Church of Norway, Ims clarifies the significance of reflecting critically and self-critically on one's own position (Ims, Chapter 1 in this volume). Ims's example of the problems that the Dialogue Pilots were having with training based on a concept of dialogue that requires neutrality illustrates a point that we tried to make in *The Claim to Christianity*: 'Openness ... is not neutrality' (Strømmen and Schmiedel, 2020, p. 140). We wish we had known about this example when we wrote our book because it makes our case in a much more succinct and straightforward way than we did. Ims nuances our ideal types of the 'consolidating church' and the 'challenging church' (Strømmen and Schmiedel, 2020, pp. 92–117). We pointed to the theology of openness, presenting Jewish theologian Ephraim Meir's proposal for openness as a welcoming of the other rooted in the relationality of religion (Meir, 2019). Relationality is – as the Dialogue Pilots aver – *not* neutral. It is about persons with particular positions and particular preferences that play into the practice of contact, whether we do or don't like it.

As scholars of race have been pointing out, being white (and male) has long been a way of passing as the norm, unmarked rather than marked.[2] Christianity emerged from a movement that revolved around a Jew in the Middle East. It is growing outside rather than inside Euramerica. Yet the connection of whiteness to Christianity continues to be assumed. Studies, such as Kelly Brown Douglas's striking *The Black Christ* (2019), continue to call attention to the catastrophic consequences of this assumption inside and outside churches. As she explains in the preface to the anniversary edition of *The Black Christ* that appeared during the presidency of Donald J. Trump:

> Some fifty years after asking my father why white people treated black people so badly, I found myself asking that question again. And once again, it would be images of black children in the street that were haunting me. They were the faces of Trayvon, Jordan, Renisha, and Jonathan. These were young black men and women being murdered at the hands of white people – for no apparent reason other than being black. Worse yet, the white people who killed them were getting away with it. The memory of my father's words, 'Nothing will happen to the white man who did it', was echoing in my mind. History was repeating itself. (Douglas, 2019, p. 14)

Douglas makes it clear that the repetition of history has to do with Christianity supporting white supremacy past and present. Such support is one of the reasons why we are critical of churches that respond to the far right by calling for consolidation. Christian churches posing as neutral protectors who guarantee a corridor in which conversations about controversies can be conducted, thereby assuming that they can speak for both Christian and non-Christian communities, might mean well. Yet they run the risk of reinforcing the construct of the clash of civilizations that they ought to counter.

Commenting on the situation in Germany, theologian Julia Lis (2021) criticizes churches that call for the inclusion rather than the exclusion of political parties on the far right. Ecclesiologically, these arguments assume that the Church is at the 'neutral centre' (Lis, 2021, p. 213, our trans.) of the political spectrum so that it has to allow for all political positions that have won democratic elections. Lis stresses that this assumption merely follows a formal rather than a material understanding of democracy. It also fails to account for the Church as a community that aims to be more than a political club. According to Lis, 'the emergence of solidaric subjectivity is not simply the consequence of pluralist discourses in which the strongest argument prevails. Rather, it arises ... through the struggles of those who have been denied subjectivity' (Lis, 2021, p. 228, our trans.). In these struggles, the Church has to take a stand.

Ims situates his analysis of the Church of Norway's openness to dialogue in a particular external context and in a particular internal one. Externally, the Church of Norway's dialogue is situated in the *livssynsåpne samfunn*, the 'life-stance open society' (Stålsett, 2021). This proposal for government policies that are open to religious and non-religious worldviews comes from the report of a committee that theologian Sturla Stålsett convened. According to Stålsett, the Norwegian neologism 'livssynsåpent' – which means 'open to a variety of live stances' – replaced the traditional term 'livssynsnøtralt' that calls for neutrality (Stålsett, 2018; Stålsett, 2021). As Stålsett argues, 'the word "open" refers to a society that provides plenty of space for the profession of religious and non-religious worldviews, so-called life stances, in all ... visible manifestations' (Stålsett, 2018, p. 116). Countering secularist policies stressing that religion ought to be private rather than public, the *livssynsåpne samfunn* welcomes the contribution that religious and non-religious people can make precisely because they live their lives according to their live stances.

Ims emphasizes that the key principle in the turn towards openness in the *livssynsåpne samfunn* is that everybody needs to accept exposure to life-stances that they might find hard to stomach. He suggests that this principle is also at work in the Church of Norway's material for confirmation classes that we examined in *The Claim to Christianity*. We found this material so compelling because it is intentional about tackling antisemitism, antiziganism and Islamophobia without pretending to be neutral (Kirkelig dialogsenter, 2013; Strømmen and Schmiedel, 2020, pp. 56–9). This leads to a theology that can be both critical and self-critical – and such a theology is 'the most relevant theology we can explore' today (Ims, Chapter 1 in this volume).

Internally, the Church of Norway's dialogue is situated in the challenge that the Sámi have made to theology. Ims's discussion of the indigenous people of Norway, Sweden and Finland captures the way any claim to Christianity is either confirming or countering established power relations, particularly where Christianity has a dominant position. Of course, there are still institutions that decide who gets to sit at the table of theologians who are allowed to talk about Christianity.

Take the example of the North-Sámi Bible, *Biibbal*. On Sunday 25 August 2019, this Bible was processed through a church in Kautokeino/Guovdageaidnu, with church leaders from Norway, Sweden and Finland in attendance.[3] This Bible is the result of over 30 years of work that aimed at addressing the question of who gets to sit at the theological table. In many ways, though, the North-Sámi Bible is the product of a much longer history. While Sámi translators, such as Anders Porsanger and Lars Hætta, were crucial contributors to Sámi versions of biblical texts in the eighteenth and nineteenth centuries, the context of their contribution was one in which the Sámi languages were considered inferior (Henriksen, 2020, pp. 74–8). Particularly during the nineteenth century, there was little interest in supporting Sámi translations of the Bible as a result of policies such as the forced Norweginization of the Sámi (Henriksen, 2020, p. 69). Norway, Sweden and Finland have to grapple with the history and the heritage of this usage of the Bible.

During the tenure of Antje Jackelén as Archbishop of Uppsala, the Church of Sweden and the Sámi Council developed an action plan as part of a reconciliation process (2021).[4] Drawing on the story in which Jesus heals a woman on the Sabbath (Luke 13.10–17), Jackelén apologized for what the Church had done to the Sámi people:

> Today, as Archbishop of the Church of Sweden, I stand before you, the Sámi, and confess that we have *not* engaged with you at eye level. We have been curved inward on ourselves, we have not stood up to racism ... Our backs are bent by the guilt we carry. (Jackelén, 2021)

The reference to 'being curved inward on oneself' takes up Augustine's account of sin as *incurvatio in se ipsum* that Martin Luther adopted and adapted (Batka, 2014). Jackelén stresses that the Church has sinned. It has been turned inwards rather than outwards, revolving only around itself. It has been racist. We will come back to the then Archbishop of Uppsala in our Afterword to this volume. What is crucial here is that Jackelén continues her apology by stating that instead of 'recognizing the image of God in our Sámi sisters and brothers, we tried to remake them in the image of the majority culture' (Jackelén, 2021). She stresses the pain and the shame that the Church engendered, the racism that ran through the colonial projects that the Church has promoted, and the losses – material and immaterial – that the Sámi have suffered (Jackelén, 2021). The action plan connected to the apology has made wide-ranging commitments that are to be fulfilled by 2026.[5] The confession of sins that is captured in the apology, then, is linked to a commitment of sharing political and material resources that undergird power. It contains, as Ims calls for, 'a cost for the historic oppressor' (Ims, Chapter 1 in this volume). Seen in this context, the North-Sámi Bible isn't 'just' a translation. It emphasizes that the sacred scripture of Christianity can be a tool for oppression and a tool for resistance against oppression.

As Helen Paynter argues in *Blessed are the Peacemakers: A Biblical Theology of Human Violence*, it's imperative that we tackle 'the most robust challenges' to the Bible (Paynter, 2023, p. 26). Uncomfortable questions must not be avoided.[6] Musa Dube has cautioned that readings of the Bible are at risk of victimizing and re-victimizing people who have suffered from colonization (Dube, 2000, p. 16).

Ims's reflection on the significance of the internal and the external context, particularly his account of the challenge and the contribution of the Sámi, pushes the theological turn we presented in *The Claim to Christianity* further. Our suggestion was to approach Christianity as a 'project' rather than a 'possession' (Strømmen and Schmiedel, 2020, pp. 135–42). We stressed that Christianity can't be fixed or frozen. Ims also argues that Christianity continues to resist closure and completion, pointing out that speaking as if there was only one way of living a Christian life – as if Christianity could be owned by Christians – is itself a way of exercising power. In the history of Norway, the assumption that Christianity is the possession of the nation has driven state-sponsored Christians to target minorities such as the Sámi for conversion. The challenge today, then, is to continue to ask who is and who isn't considered part of the project of Christianity in a way that is mindful of such histories. The question of 'What can we learn from others?' isn't quite correct then. Such a question would presuppose that there is a clearly circumscribed 'we' that owns Christianity, so it has the power to make room for 'others' who are welcomed or not welcomed to the theological table. Ims's reflections on Tore Johnsen's research on Sámi cosmologies is a powerful way of challenging any such constructions of the 'we' (Johnsen, 2022; Johnsen, 2023). Following Ims, then, 'How do we work together?' might be a better question when thinking through how to counter the far right. The 'we' is – in principle and in practice – open.

Our suggestion that Christians can work with Muslims and that Muslims can work with Christians corresponds to Ims's conclusions. As we will point out in our conversation with Accad and Bunglawala as well as Spencer and Wilson, the point is not to put the burden of figuring out Christianity on to Muslims. It is not a point that can be abstracted from a context in which Christianity continues to be in a privileged and powerful position. On the contrary, it is precisely about addressing the relationship between majority and minority, both inside and outside churches in Europe.

The relationship between majority and minority is also at stake in Frykberg's response. He is correct when he cautions that a focus on the statements of churches runs the risk of elitism. But what impressed us so much about the Church of Norway is that 'what runs through most of the statements in the discussion of the status of the Church is a call for justice that includes Christians and non-Christians, including Muslims' (Strømmen and Schmiedel, 2020, p. 63). In a way, these statements put into prose what the cases that Frykberg presents put into practice. Frykberg – like Allchorn whose reflections on Christian activism we will return to – picks up on our point that communities on the ground continue to respond to far-right movements. Frykberg demonstrates how community organization can confront far-right claims to Christianity in a way that creates solidarity across minority/majority divides, thus providing a visible presence on the ground that models justice. Frykberg's analysis makes a compelling contribution to our knowledge about what can be done if Christians join Muslims in countering the far right. Even under challenging conditions, community organization can make a difference. This *is* the semantic struggle that we refer to in *The Claim to Christianity*. While definitions and doctrines of theology continue to be perceived as the purview of those with dog collars or doctorates, Frykberg's cases demonstrate how theology plays out, how it is practised rather than preached.

Overall, then, practices of contact that counter the far right connect to ethical, political and theological issues that will be taken up in the following responses. While the people who are engaged in these practices might not perceive them as a 'semantic struggle' for the meaning of Christianity, the practices can still be characterized as such. In all the practices that our respondents present, claims to Christianity are embedded and embodied, ranging from statements to streets, from Bibles to barbecues, and from churches to city councils. What the responses make clear is a challenge to all theologians that we will have to keep at the top of our minds when engaging with the far right. Our own theologies are always provisional, which means that we have to approach them critically and self-critically. Ims suggests that laughing at ourselves might be a litmus test for whether we have this ability. We agree.

Notes

1 Historian of religion Kristina Myrvold points to the significance of the ritualization of sacred scriptures for the controversies stirred up by burnings of the Qur'an. See Kristina Myrvold, 2023, 'Paludan upprör men flera religioner förstör sina skrifter', *Sydsvenskan* 19 February 2023, https://www.sydsvenskan.se/2023-02-19/paludan-uppror-men-flera-religioner-forstor-sina-skrifter (accessed 5.4.24).

2 For a helpful overview, see Molly H. Bassett and Vincent W. Lloyd, 2015, 'Introduction', in Molly H. Bassett and Vincent W. Lloyd (eds), *Sainthood and Race: Marked Flesh, Holy Flesh*, London: Routledge, pp. 1–17. See also Shannon Sullivan, 2006, *Revealing Whiteness: The Unconscious Habits of Racial Privilege*, Bloomington: Indiana University Press.

3 See the Norwegian Bible Society's account of this event: https://bibel.no/nyheter/bibelfest-i-sápmi (accessed 5.4.24).

4 See Svenska kyrkan, 2022, *Handlingsplan: Åtaganden kopplade till Svenska kyrkans ursäkt till det samiska folket 2022–2031, Etapp 1*, Stockholm: Svenska kyrkan. The action plan, including a short English summary, is available online at https://www.svenskakyrkan.se/samiska/mal-och-handlingsplan (accessed 5.4.24).

5 See the summary by Daniel Lindmark and Olle Sundström (eds), 2017, *Samerna och Svenska kyrkan: Underlag för kyrkligt försoningsarbete*, Möklinta: Gidlunds Förlag. The English translation was published as Daniel Lindmark and Olle Sundström (eds), 2018, *The Sámi and the Church of Sweden: Results from a White Paper Project*, Möklinta: Gidlunds Förlag.

6 In *The Invention of the Biblical Scholar: A Critical Manifesto*, Stephen D. Moore and Yvonne Sherwood have highlighted the way modern biblical scholarship has tended to shy away from uncomfortable ethical and political questions raised by biblical texts (Moore and Sherwood, 2011, pp. 40, 116).

References

Ahmed, Sara, 2014, *The Cultural Politics of Emotion*, 2nd edn, Edinburgh: Edinburgh University Press.

Allport, Gordon, 1954, *The Nature of Prejudice*, Reading: Addison-Wesley.

Bassett, Molly H. and W. Lloyd Vincent, 2015, 'Introduction', in Molly H. Bassett and Vincent W. Lloyd (eds), *Sainthood and Race: Marked Flesh, Holy Flesh*, London: Routledge, pp. 1–17.

Batka, L'ubomír, 2014, 'Luther's Teaching on Sin and Evil', in Robert Kolb, Irene Dingel and L'ubomír Batka (eds), *The Oxford Handbook of Martin Luther's Theology*, Oxford: Oxford University Press, pp. 233–53.

Bednarz, Liane, 2009, *Die Angstprediger: Wie rechte Christen Gesellschaft und Kirchen unterwandern*, München: Droemer.

Black, Fiona C. and Jennifer L. Koosed, 2019, 'Introduction: Some Ways to Read with Feeling', in Fiona C. Black and Jennifer L. Koosed (eds), *Reading with Feeling: Affect Theory and the Bible*, Atlanta: SBL Press, pp. 1–12.

Bretherton, Luke, 2011, 'A Postsecular Politics? Inter-faith Relations as Civic Practice', *Journal of the American Academy of Religion* 79(2), pp. 346–77.

Bunglawala, Shenaz, in this volume, 'Chapter 5: Beyond the Far Right: "Respectable Racism" and British Muslims'.

Douglas, Kelly Brown, 2019, *The Black Christ: 25th Anniversary Edition*, Maryknoll: Orbis Books.

Dube, Musa, 2000, *Postcolonial Feminist Interpretation of the Bible*, St Louis: Chalice Press.

Frykberg, Henrik, in this volume, 'Chapter 2: From Prejudice to Pride – Towards an Organized Anti-racist Community'.

Henriksen, Marit B., 2020, 'Bibelen på samisk: Historisk blikk på samiske bibeloversettelser', *Kirke og Kultur* 1(125), pp. 68–84.

Ims, Steinar, in this volume, 'Chapter 1: A Norwegian Perspective'.

Jackelén, Antje, 2021, 'Speech of Apology', https://www.svenskakyrkan.se/samiska/speech-of-apology (accessed 5.4.24).

Johnsen, Tore, 2022, *Sámi Nature-centered Christianity in the European Arctic: Indigenous Theology beyond Hierarchical Worldmaking*, Lanham: Lexington Books.

Johnsen, Tore, 2023, 'Luthersk teologi, kolonial makt og Sámisk tradisjon – utkast til en dekolonial teologi', *Kirke og Kultur* 1(128), pp. 5–26.

Kirkelig dialogsenter, 2013, *Sier vi: Ressursmateriell om antisemittisme, islamofobi og antisiganisme til bruk i den norske kirke*, Oslo: Mellomkirkelig råd.

Lindmark, Daniel and Olle Sundström (eds), 2017, *Samerna och Svenska kyrkan: Underlag för kyrkligt försoningsarbete*, Möklinta: Gidlunds Förlag.

Lindmark, Daniel and Olle Sundström (eds), 2018, *The Sámi and the Church of Sweden: Results from a White Paper Project*, Möklinta: Gidlunds Förlag.

Lis, Julia, 2021, 'Kirche bewährt sich in der Geschichte: Zur Positionierung einer politischen Ekklesiologie', in Jan Niklas Collet, Julia Lis and Gregor Taxacher (eds), *Rechte Normalisierung und politische Theologie: Eine Standortbestimmung*, Regensburg: Friedrich Pustet, pp. 211–30.

Martinussen, Bente, 1992, 'Anders Porsanger – teolog og språkforsker fra 1700-tallets Finnmark', *Nordlyd: Tromsø University Working Papers on Language & Linguistics* 18, pp. 15–59.

Meir, Ephraim, 2019, *Faith in the Plural*, Tel Aviv: Idra Publishing.

Moore, Stephen D. and Yvonne Sherwood, 2011, *The Invention of the Biblical Scholar: A Critical Manifesto*, Minneapolis: Fortress.

Myrvold, Kristina, 2023, 'Paludan upprör men flera religioner förstör sina skrifter, *Sydsvenskan* 19 February 2023, https://www.sydsvenskan.se/2023-02-19/paludan-uppror-men-flera-religioner-forstor-sina-skrifter (accessed 5.4.24).

Paynter, Helen, 2023, *Blessed are the Peacemakers: A Biblical Theology of Human Violence*, Grand Rapids: Zondervan.

Piliawsky, Monte, 1984, 'Racial Equality in the United States: From Institutionalized Racism to "Respectable" Racism', *Phyton* 45(2), pp. 135–43.
Schaefer, Donovan O., 2015, *Religious Affects: Animality, Evolution, and Power*, Durham: Duke University Press.
Stålsett, Sturla J., 2018, 'Fearing the Faith of Others? Government, Religion and Integration in Norway', in Ulrich Schmiedel and Graeme Smith (eds), *Religion in the European Refugee Crisis*, New York: Palgrave Macmillan, pp. 105–20.
Stålsett, Sturla J., 2021, *Det livsynsåpne samfunn*, Oslo: Cappelen Damm Akademisk.
Strømmen, Hannah and Ulrich Schmiedel, 2020, *The Claim to Christianity: Responding to the Far Right*, London: SCM Press.
Sullivan, Shannon, 2006, *Revealing Whiteness: The Unconscious Habits of Racial Privilege*, Bloomington: Indiana University Press.
Svenska kyrkan, *Handlingsplan: Åtaganden kopplade till Svenska kyrkans ursäkt till det samiska folket 2022–2031*, Etapp 1, Stockholm: Svenska kyrkan, 2022.

PART 2

The Interfaith Perspective

4

A Lebanese Perspective on Religion-inspired Political Extremism

MARTIN ACCAD

I am a Lebanese of Arab and European descent, with dual citizenship in Lebanon (through my father) and in Switzerland (through my mother). But I was born and raised in Lebanon. As the son and product of an Evangelical pastor's home, but also as a child of the Lebanese civil war (1975–90), I have experienced first hand both the lifegiving and the lethal power of faith and religion. I also have five years of experience living in the UK while studying for my MPhil and DPhil between 1996 and 2001. I finally obtained my DPhil after a two-hour dissertation defence at the University of Oxford on what would become the fatal day of 11 September 2001, though when my examiners and I entered that room at the Oriental Institute it was just another peaceful and unsuspecting day of late summer.

But the ominous events of that day threw me straightaway into the role of interpreter, an interpreter of the West and Christianity to my region of birth origin, and an interpreter of the Middle East and Islam to the region of origin of my religious tradition. For the best part of the past 22 years, I have taught Islam and Christian-Muslim relations to Arab Christian leaders from the entire MENA region at the Arab Baptist Theological Seminary. And for a season of six years (2006–12) I also had the opportunity to teach Islam and Christian-Muslim relations for three months of each year to North American, European and global leaders at Fuller's Graduate School of Intercultural Studies in Pasadena, California. Throughout these 22 years of my career, I was also invited on numerous occasions to take part in both regional and international interfaith events.

I am invited to the present conversation primarily to offer a perspective from this Middle-Eastern-rooted Christian interfaith perspective. As I approach the theme of our conversation, I do not feel primarily part of a Christian majority in Europe, needing to address the influence of Christianity on far-right European politics and its negative impact on

Islam and Muslim displaced persons in Europe. I have always been part of a Lebanese society consisting of all-minority communities involved in a power struggle for survival vis-à-vis one another.

From about 1920 until its official independence in 1943, Lebanon would go through birth pangs and eventually be born to a large extent as a Maronite Christian state, designed originally as an extension of French interests in the region, and largely ignoring Muslim discontent with the young nation's Western inclination. Lebanese Muslim leaders had wanted to join their destiny to that of a 'greater Syria', as a transitory phase to the creation of a united Arab geopolitical entity. But demographics and sociopolitical realities would decide the fate of Lebanon otherwise. The overly confident 'political Maronitism', unwilling to share power fairly with other sects on that small geographic patch of the Eastern Mediterranean, would lead to a fratricidal civil war in 1975, exacerbated by the 'Palestinian problem'. The war would only gradually come to an end with the Taef Accord of 1988, brokered by Saudi Arabia, but it would take another two years until the official end. Taef tipped the balance of power to the Sunni sect, inaugurating the dominance of 'political Sunnism', under the business-like leadership of Prime Minister Rafik Hariri for the next 15 years.

But political Sunnism, driven by economic interests, did not think it important to address the past. Economic prosperity was thought sufficient to heal the wounds of a fratricidal conflict. In 1991, a general amnesty law was passed in parliament, by parliamentarians primarily consisting of former warlords, such that these criminals were seamlessly able to transition from their bunkers to their new fancy offices under the sponsorship of Saudi Arabia and the vigilant eye of Syrian security and military occupation. The country went through a feverish decade and a half of infrastructural reconstruction, glazing over any national soul searching. But another force had begun to emerge with the occupation of Lebanon by Israel, first in 1978 and again in 1982. The Shiite 'Movement of the Oppressed' (AMAL) had already begun to emerge in the early 1970s, and its militarized arm of Hezbollah would grow in power and influence because of Israeli occupation in South Lebanon. This 'culture of resistance' would only be kept in check by economic interest through the Sunni 'culture of affluence' until the assassination of Prime Minister Hariri in 2005.

On 14 February 2005, the assassination of Rafik Hariri was a watershed moment. The 'culture of resistance' had come head-to-head with the 'culture of affluence'. Through what became known as the Cedar Revolution, which led to the ousting of Syrian military power from Lebanon, the Lebanese population and its leaders had once more the unique opportunity to pause at the excitement of the moment and reconsider the past. But instead of reimagining a new order through a new social contract that would work for the common good of all, the dominant Shiite powers of the time grasped their opportunity and captured the moment to their own ends. The Hezbollah-Amal duo managed to ride the wave of the Syrian regime's grief at their humiliating ousting and managed to monopolize power, establishing what turned out to be another 15 years, this time of 'political Shiism'.

On 17 October 2019, because of a collapsing economy and near-total impossibility of civil participation in politics and in deciding their own fate, Lebanese citizens took to the streets in the hundreds of thousands. At least in its initial stages, the '17 October Revolution' was a non-sectarian call for the ousting of the entire corrupt political class that had led the country to its current desolate state through clientelist networks that functioned more like cartels than state structures. But with the onslaught of the Covid-19 pandemic in February/March 2020, the disastrous explosion at the Beirut port on 4 August 2020, and the prolonged financial and banking sector collapse, the non-sectarian movement soon folded back into sectarian patterns. Today Lebanon is in total disarray, all but the perfect manifestation of a 'failed state'.

So far, my chapter sounds more like a lesson in the history of modern Lebanon than a response to *The Claim to Christianity*. But here is the point: Lebanon's history should function as a parable of how unbridled sectarian conflict will lead to the collapse of the concept of the modern state. Sectarianism is all about identity. Observers of Lebanese society have long chastised the Lebanese for affirming their sectarian above their national identity. We have always known and observed that the Lebanese feel that they are Christian or Muslim – Maronite, Greek Orthodox, Catholic, Syriac, Armenian, Protestant, Sunni, Shiite or Druze – before they feel Lebanese. The collective identity observed in tribalism in most pre-modern-state peoples manifests itself in sectarianism in Lebanon. Fundamentally, sectarianism has little to do with religion and everything to do with community identity.

In Europe, the nationalisms that manifested themselves along the lines of race conflict were, for a time, kept in check by international human rights treaties, following two disastrous world wars. But, with the end of the bipolar world of the Cold War period, with the rise of globalization and social media, and with the exacerbation of people migration resulting from ruthless wars in Africa, the Middle East and Central Asia, it appears that this 'new racism' disguised as a 'clash of cultures' (as discussed in the book) is a return to the old human patterns of exclusivist identities vying for geopolitical control.

As we learn from the Lebanese model and from the field of psychology, the exclusive identity of one community is often affirmed through the identification of an anti-community and at its expense. The situation described in Europe, through the case studies of Norway, Germany and the UK, manifests the emergence of Islam and Muslims as the anti-community against which the 'European' seems to be pitting him/herself. And through the dangerous pitfalls of political correctness, races, ethnicities and even religions (among those still seeking to paint themselves as decent human beings), a 'clash of cultures' has emerged as the remaining acceptable moniker in the human search for exclusivist identity.

I am comfortable with *The Claim to Christianity*'s unwillingness to let Christianity off the hook by claims that 'Christianity is merely instrumentalized for popular appeal and political actions'; those who affirm that 'Claims to Christianity are not an interpretation of religion but an instrumentalization of religion', and that 'Christianity is a mere means to propagandistic and political ends'; those who claim that 'Christianity has been hijacked' (Strømmen and Schmiedel, 2020, p. 5). I am comfortable with this intransigence towards Christianity on the part of Christian theologians because I demand the same from Muslim theologians towards Islam. In the same way as in 'Christian' Europe, the 'Muslim' world too often reverts to this apologetic to distance itself from the responsibility to deal with religious fanaticism and extremism in its own camp. As an Arab Christian theologian and student of Islam and Muslim-Christian relations living in the Middle East, I affirm that Islamisms (the politically engaged extremist forms of Islam) tap copiously into Islamic history, theology and sacred texts. I also affirm, with Strømmen and Schmiedel, that 'far-right claims to Christianity are tapping into theologies of violence that Christians have actually practised' (Strømmen and Schmiedel, 2020, p. 6) and, I would add, into Christian sacred texts, including the Bible. In the introduction to my book *Sacred Misinterpretation*, I make the following affirmations:

> The claims of some Muslims, Christians, Jews, or members of any religion that violent people acting in the name of their religion are simply imposters, and that it is therefore not their problem to address, are suspicious. By doing so, they adopt the same tendency as violent extremists who essentialize religion, who claim that they hold the only correct interpretation of their texts, and who anathematize all others. (Accad, 2019, p. 3)

Let me affirm here as well that this remark is not transactional. I affirm that Christian theologians are responsible for addressing these interpretations and manifestations of Christianity regardless of whether Muslim theologians reciprocate.

Furthermore, as a Middle East Christian, I am less impacted – though of course greatly concerned – by the influence of Christianity on the far right, and by the ways that this negatively impacts social relations between various religious communities in Europe. On the other hand, I am significantly impacted by the influence of Christian biblical hermeneutics on evangelical Zionism, and by the ways that this negatively impacts relations between Palestinians and Israelis, Christians, Muslims and Jews. I consider it supremely important that Christian and Jewish theologians should engage in scriptural interpretation that challenges Zionist ideological hermeneutics. The pen of Muslim theologians may not be freed to carry out the task of revisiting some of their dangerous qur'anic hermeneutics until Christian and Jewish theologians freely, courageously and prophetically engage their pen for the cause of human justice in the Palestine conflict.

The weaponization of Islam by extremists against non-Muslims is paralleled by the weaponization of Christianity by extremists on the far right, and if we consider such weaponization as heresy, then it is the responsibility of theologians to dislodge it. Sometimes religions will only awaken to certain aspects of their hermeneutical responsibility when they are forced to do so. It would appear that Christianity in Europe is waking up to its responsibility to address the Christian roots of the political far right because interfaith conflict is beginning to reach a tipping point in Europe. But as transpires from the three case studies that Strømmen and Schmiedel offer, the voice of the Church remains shy and has not yet reached its true prophetic potential. In its challenge to religious essentialization and its proposal that Christianity (and religions in general) should be viewed as a 'project', *The Claim to Christianity* is a remarkable attempt to broaden and deepen the prophetic voice of the Church.

The Muslim world too, it would seem, reached a new tipping point as a result of *Daesh*'s (ISIS in Arabic) savage behaviour that emerged on the world stage in the summer of 2014. The ensuing months forced Muslim theologians of all brands to engage in an unprecedented soul-searching. In the 18 months that followed that fatal summer, I collected with a group of colleagues the closing statements of over 30 conferences organized globally by Muslim authorities and organizations, which had clearly been convened in response to ISIS. I was struck by some of the revolutionary conclusions and commitments surveyed in these documents.

Daesh's justification of its actions based on the Qur'an and other Islamic texts imposed some unprecedented interpretive challenges on traditional understandings of these texts that religious leadership circles had to address – some for the first time in such a context. The shame and embarrassment felt within the Muslim world is reflected in the abundance of documents of self-justification that emerged within those first 18 months of the ISIS phenomenon. My assessment is that *Daesh* administered a considerable blow to a certain brand of Islamic traditional authoritarianism that had dominated Muslim societies for centuries.

The themes that emerged from this introspection were not entirely new, but to my knowledge they had never been so broadly endorsed and vehemently affirmed. These included radically revisionist views of classical concepts of Jihad, the Caliphate, and the very notion of an Islamic state. There were calls for comprehensive revisions of school curricula in the Muslim world, invitations for initiatives aiming at the formation of religious scholars and experts in addressing issues of jurisprudence through social media, and a strong urging for a coordinated effort to dismantle *takfiri fatwas* (extremist jurisprudence that declares all those disagreeing with it as non-Muslims). Such statements stand in strong contrast to the continuing claims by many on the far right, such as Pegida's Bachman in Germany, but also by many evangelical Christians, that 'Once the Muslims are the majority – regardless in which country of the earth – they have the religious duty to rule this country' (Strømmen and Schmiedel, 2020, p. 69). The statement might not be wrong if it were only referring to a description of a medieval Muslim political doctrine. But recent conferences organized by Muslim theological authorities in Muslim lands against ISIS ideology have made it abundantly clear that they do not subscribe to such views. By perpetuating such beliefs, Christian theologians and far-right and not so far-right politicians are consolidating extremist Islamist views on a constantly transforming Islam.

Religions are heavy and deeply rooted institutions that will not be easily moved but, as this book affirms, they are not static phenomena either. The authors explain that 'what the far right has done … is to push a theology in which both religions are strong, stable and static sides that are by definition enemies' (Strømmen and Schmiedel, 2020, p. 34). To the sharp eye of the historian and social scientist, however, it is clear that religions are in fact always on the move, even if this is more difficult to observe for the untrained eye. Religions are constantly transforming and adjusting to the new demands of changing contexts. I'll mention two recent Muslim scholars who make this point rather sharply. The first is Shahab Ahmed, in his 2017 publication *What Is Islam? The Importance of Being Islamic,* and the second is Rumee Ahmed, in his 2018 book *Sharia Compliant: A User's Guide to Hacking Islamic Law.* The first argues, against essentializing theories, that Islam is whatever Muslims have made and continue to make of it in every place and time. The second playfully demonstrates – against any notion of Islam as a static religion – that Islamic Law is a sort of 'game' that allows, through a set of rules, for the admission or banning of beliefs and practices according to majority need reflected in consensus (*ijma'*).

It is interesting that the Norwegian Church's response has been the clearest in its rejection of violent Christianity. Is this because the 2011 terrorist attack by a far rightist was the clearest in its claim to Christianity in the perpetrator's manifesto? It was clear that Breivik's dangerous ideology had to be dismantled and, in a sense, the Church had no difficulty debunking it for this reason. In the German Church, the dangerous ideology is more subtle. It appears that Protestants and Catholics have both had a harder time debunking it because it has not been as obviously violent as in Norway. The authors point out that the EKD (Protestant Church in Germany) has been particularly ambiguous in its position on Islam, with a problematic 2006 statement making clear associations between Islam and anti-democracy and misogyny. Clearer statements on Islamic diversity, also seeking to explore the roots of this diversity, are necessary in Germany. The polemical approach to Islam, which tends to essentialism, is problematic. In the same way as with racism, anti-Islam polemics facilitates prejudice by lumping all Muslims into the single box of extremism by holding the many responsible for the actions of the one. The lethal consequences of the polemical approach of the likes of Bat Ye'or and Robert Spencer were the most obvious in the multiple references to them in Breivik's manifesto (Strømmen and Schmiedel, 2020, p. 39).

In a couple of places in the book, one would have wished to find more than simple affirmations by the authors. For example, on page 28 they agree with social anthropologist Sindre Bangstad that 'it would be an understatement to say that the work of Bat Ye'or fails to meet the basic standards of academic research when it comes to Islam'. They maintain that 'she mimics an academic style, giving her work a scholarly appearance'. I do not disagree, but I wish that they had discussed Bat Ye'or's thinking further, given that it is so influential in far-right circles. Later in the book, the authors affirm that 'Christians can learn a lot about theologies of liberation from reading the Qur'an' (p. 127). I was expecting that some discussion would ensue about liberation theology based on the Qur'an, but unfortunately this never comes. Much could be said of course, as the Qur'an is full of advocacy for the poor, the orphan and the widow. The Qur'an's teaching about the third pillar, *zakat*, is in fact foundational to our understanding of the centrality of the Qur'an's advocacy for the poor and marginalized.

As for the 'solutions' proposed by the book's authors to the problem of the far right, I am interested in two of these. The first is the 'contact theory', while the second is the idea of Christianity as a 'project'. I am very sympathetic to the importance of 'contact theory', and agree on the importance that it be *meaningful* and *conversational* contact that leads to collaborative *action*, rather than just two communities living side by side without meaningful engagement. On the other hand, I take exception to the claim that, although 'there can be Islamophobia with Muslims and Islamophobia without Muslims ... statistically, the more Muslims there are in a country, the less likely it is that Islamophobic prejudices can be shaped and sustained among the population' (Strømmen and Schmiedel, 2020, p. 133). This statement may be confirmed by statistics comparing Eastern and Western Europe, but it does not hold when comparing Europe on the one hand and the Middle East on the other. The dominant Muslim demographic in the Middle East does not diminish Christian prejudice against Islam. In fact, the opposite may be true, as Christians struggle as numeric minorities dominated by a majority population which, in most of these countries, feels little need to make space for non-Muslims in the public square. Meaningful contact that leads to collaborative action in society is therefore as important in the Middle East today as it is in both Eastern and Western Europe.

Finally, I concur with the authors about the importance of seeing 'the identity of Christianity as a project rather than a possession' (p. 137). I would add that hermeneutics is central to the idea of Christianity as a project, rather than a static essentialized reality. The same is true of Islam, the Qur'an, and its interpretation. As the authors affirm, 'biblical interpretation cannot be fixed and finished in a search for an unequivocal meaning waiting to be found in the text. Biblical interpretation is a project. Scripture is lived' (p. 139). The same can certainly be said about the interpretation of the Qur'an and the ensuing and continuously changing manifestations of both religions.

References

Accad, Martin, 2019, *Sacred Misinterpretation: Reaching across the Christian-Muslim Divide*, Grand Rapids: Eerdmans.
Strømmen, Hannah and Ulrich Schmiedel, 2020, *The Claim to Christianity: Responding to the Far Right*, London: SCM Press.

5

Beyond the Far Right: 'Respectable Racism' and British Muslims

SHENAZ BUNGLAWALA

Are problematic ideas and attitudes towards Muslims to be found more generally among Christians? I don't pose the question to be offensive or unduly provocative but to ask whether the 'Culture Christianity' that permeates the far right (Strømmen and Schmiedel, 2020, p. 42) is also present in the mainstream. It is perhaps all too easy to point to far-right manifestations of Islamophobia. From street protestors brandishing the cross[1] and handing out Bibles to Muslims,[2] to calls for Muslims to sign a 'Proposed Charter of Muslim Understanding'[3] which entreats them to render verses from the Qur'an that pertain to 'encouraging physical violence' as 'inapplicable, invalid and non-Islamic'[4] until such time as 'scholars find a solution for their interpretation',[5] to the election manifesto published by the UK Independence Party (UKIP) in 2017, which then leader Paul Nuttall pledged would 'cut out the cancer of Islamic fundamentalism' from the UK.[6] Less palatable perhaps is discerning the extent to which milder variations of the prejudices that inform these extreme hostile views about Muslims exist in spaces that we would not characterize as far right at all. And, assuming that they do, what do we do about it? That is, is the 'semantic struggle' that Strømmen and Schmiedel (2020, pp. 9–10) argue is necessary to reclaim Christianity from the far right a struggle of wider reach and deeper significance?

There is a reason why the prevalence of Islamophobia as 'respectable racism' (Wolfreys, 2018) has been termed the 'dinner table prejudice' (Jones and Unsworth, 2022), the type that slips by unnoticed and unremarked largely because those espousing such views would not regard themselves, or others who share their disposition, as racists or far-right sympathizers. Needless to say, there is a political gulf between 'dinner table' Islamophobia and the more rabid expressions of 'new racism' that is the stock in trade of the far right (Strømmen and Schmiedel, 2020, p. 20), but if Christians are to claim back Christianity from the far right and divest it of the ability to dress its anti-Muslim racism in Christian garb, addressing expressions of Islamophobia in the mainstream becomes as essential as ridding it from the clutches of opportunistic ideologues on the far right.

The focus of my chapter is my remodelling of data from a piece of research from a project I was involved in which, ironically, dealt with some of the tropes that sustain both Culture and Crusader Christianity (Strømmen and Schmiedel, 2020, p. 73): what messaging and messengers can effectively shift the dial on connections or conflations made between 'Muslim' and 'terrorism/extremism' and, consequently, how should British Muslims respond to terrorist incidents committed by Daesh/ISIS[7] who, like their Crusader counterparts, make 'claims' to Islam? The aim of my chapter is to engage with some of the questions that arise from Strømmen and Schmiedel's work, questions about whether Christians bear a 'special responsibility' (Strømmen and Schmiedel, 2020, p. 54) to respond to acts of political violence committed by their co-religionists, whether the 'openness of churches' is a viable approach to reclamation efforts, and how Muslims can support Christians, and indeed vice versa, in challenging those who conceive of the world in a simple binary where only one creed can legitimately dominate.

'Media-generated Muslims'

It was the Pew Research Center's report on 'Being Christian in Western Europe' (Sahgal, 2018, p. 22) that piqued my interest and prompted me to revisit survey data from a piece of market research that aimed to examine perceptions of Muslims in British society and communication tools that could help to shift the dial on the association made between 'Muslim' and 'terrorism/extremism'. The Pew report showed that both church-attending Christians (45 per cent) and non-practising Christians (47 per cent) more strongly held the view that Islam is fundamentally incompatible with the UK's culture and values than the general population (42 per cent) and those who self-identified as having no religious affiliation (30 per cent) (Sahgal, 2018, p. 19). The report also highlighted scores on the zero to 10 point NIM (nationalist, anti-immigrant and anti-minority views) scale which showed that, in the UK, Christians – church-going and non-practising – were more likely than religiously unaffiliated people to express negative views of immigrants, as well as of Muslims and Jews (Sahgal, 2018, p. 77).

The earlier piece of research, which was conducted in 2017, comprised focus groups in different parts of the UK and a nationally representative omnibus survey of 2,073 adults. The results made for difficult reading. The overall picture it painted revealed distressingly negative perceptions of Muslims in British society with Muslims held in far lower regard than all other religious groups. The research, consistent with the 'special responsibility' argument noted by Strømmen and Schmiedel, found that Britons felt Muslims had a particular responsibility to speak out against terrorism committed in the name of Islam.[8] The research also engaged in narrative testing of stylized responses to terrorism to test which styles worked best to cut through prejudice and 'land well' with a listening audience. The final phase of the project sought to assess the impact of the narrative by gauging for any change in attitudes among the sample groups, qualitative and quantitative, before and after reading the stylized tract. It showed that terrorism or extremism was just one of many negative conflations made and that any communication strategy undertaken by Muslims that aimed at driving a clear disconnect would have to go much further than just a focus on violence and extremism.

On reading the Pew report and looking again at the survey sample, I had the data cut by religious affiliation to examine the extent to which the findings reported by Pew resonated, or not, with the extant sample. Given that Christians comprised the largest group in the sample (1,052), compared to 'Nones' (852) and other religions, excluding Muslims (79), I was curious to learn the distribution of negative perceptions of Muslims among Christians and Nones, gain deeper insights, and to compare and contrast the results. I should add that given the research was conducted with market research insights in mind, and to aid the development of communication techniques and tools to foster a deeper disconnect between 'Muslim' and 'terrorism/extremism', the sample was further subdivided into categories of 'Sceptics', 'Neutrals' and 'Positives' with each comprising sub-groups based on scores on a zero to 10 scale on how positively or negatively they viewed Muslims, with zero being very negatively and 10 being very positively. Sceptics were those who scored 0–4, Neutrals scoring 5, and Positives those whose scores ranked 6–10. Most of what follows will focus on Sceptics and Positives in the Christian and Nones groups.

Interestingly, Muslims were the most well-known group among Christians; among Nones, they were the second-most well-known group after Christians. But the sample also showed that almost half of both Christians and Nones, 45 per cent per cent and 46 per cent respectively, lived in areas with a local Muslim population of less than 1 per cent. The survey does allude to quite superficial levels of familiarity with Muslims and one has to wonder at the extent to which media discourses on Islam and Muslims accounts for the disparity between claiming to know and actually knowing Muslims personally. Rane and colleagues argue that while there has been an exponential rise in media coverage of Islam and Muslims since 9/11, what the ordinary public are more familiar with is not knowledge of Islam per se, or of Muslims in their midst, but of a 'media version of Islam' and 'media-generated Muslims' (Rane, Ewart and Martinkus, 2014, p. 29). There are implications here for the contact theory hypothesis advanced by Strømmen and Schmiedel to which I will return later in the chapter. Suffice to note here is the relevance of the concept of 'media-generated' Muslims as an explanatory factor for the apparent incongruity between claims of knowing Muslims while being unable to demonstrate stated types of familiarity among friends, work colleagues or family members.

Changing the (Media) Narrative on Muslims

While there were more Christians who ranked as Positives in their view of Muslims than there were among the Nones, the larger part of whom were Neutral, there were also more Sceptics among the Christians than among the Nones. This was illustrated in responses to questions about integration, contributions to society, and in spontaneous word associations made with Muslims. More Christians than those of no religious affiliation felt that 'overall, Muslims make a very negative contribution to British society', and that 'Muslims cannot integrate into British society at all'. Word associations revealed stark differences between Christian Sceptics and Positives when thinking about Muslims while there were minor observable differences among Sceptics from both Christian and Nones groupings.

Among Christian sceptics, tropes that dominated their perception of Muslims were largely based around 'terrorism' and 'extremism' with both words occurring with the highest level of frequency. Other words that topped associations made with Muslims were 'fanatic(al)', 'danger-(ous)' and 'bomb/bombers/suicide bombing'. While terrorism was a strong driver of negativity, tropes of a cultural distinction were also prevalent with Muslims seen as 'arrogant', 'non-integrating' and 'sexist', with treatment of women and Muslim women's dress ('burka', 'veils') also showing high levels of frequency.

For Christian Positives, the contrast was significant with associations here focusing on Muslims as 'religious', 'devout', 'friendly', 'family-oriented', 'hard-working' and 'misunderstood' – traits that Christians would perhaps ascribe to Muslims as members of a faith community with values much like their own.

As with Christian sceptics, tropes around terrorism and fanaticism also dominated among sceptic Nones and the same associations were present in views of Muslims as 'intolerant', 'insular' and 'unwilling to integrate', but whereas Christian Positives associated Muslims with religiosity, this trait was more likely to be mentioned by sceptics among the religiously non-affiliated.

The study attempted to assess the extent to which Muslims addressing terrorism with language that powerfully and emotively condemned acts of violence committed in the name of Islam would alter perceptions among the most negatively inclined. The wording of the narrative scored strong positive responses when passionately and unapologetically framed; that is, with Muslims responding to terrorist incidents by issuing condemnations without excuse or caveat. The outcome, however, was negligible with little discernible overall change reported in attitudes towards Muslims.

Reasons given for the minor shift in attitudes emerged from both the survey data and focus group analysis that, though showing that terrorism was a strong driver of negativity, also highlighted the conflation of a number of other issues in the 'repertoire' of anti-Muslim perceptions. That is to say, responding to terrorist actions alone would not address the range of issues that influenced anti-Muslim sentiment. Among sceptics, those with the most pronounced negative views, issues beyond terrorism which explained the heightened negativity were found to be:

- a sense that Islam had distinct values and rules incompatible with British life
- a perceived lack of effort to integrate into the wider community
- a general perception that Muslims were a 'drain on resources'
- anecdotes about antisocial behaviour by young Muslims in local regions
- 'grooming' scandals occurring in parts of the UK.

I think all of these factors map neatly on to the 'Culture' and 'Crusader' typology of Christianity weaponized by the far right in service of their anti-Muslim racism that Strømmen and Schmiedel analyse. Tropes that draw sharp distinctions between Muslims and others in society; 'their' failure to integrate and 'our' goodwill and generosity that is taken for granted and trampled on; 'their' values and customs that impede on 'our' cultural norms, 'their' misogynistic ways that offend 'our' norms on equal rights between men and women. The difference here is that the survey sample was not majority far right at all. The vast majority of the sample identified with voting intentions for mainstream British political parties with only 7 per cent of Christians stating they would vote for UKIP.

The YouGov Islam Tracker poll, which posed a regular question on whether 'there is a fundamental clash between Islam and the values of British society' between January 2015 and February 2019, shows that while views supportive of a clash are more likely to be found among the far right (UKIP) and on the right generally, it is not entirely absent on the left with between a third and two-fifths of those on the left also subscribing to views of a clash.[9] The point here is that Islamophobia is not the preserve of the far right and that attempts to wrestle claims to Christianity must engage with tropes that are distinctive to those on the left as well as those on the right, those in the mainstream and those on the margins of our political spectrum. That is not to say that Islamophobia is an entrenched problem in British Christian communities whether left or right, any more than the Pew report analysis of scores on the NIM scale purports to show that 'Christian theology or religious teachings necessarily lead to anti-immigrant, anti-Muslim or anti-Jewish positions' (Sahgal, 2018, p. 78). What the survey and polling data does suggest is that anti-Muslim sentiment cuts across the spectrum and addressing it requires a more nuanced examination of tropes that proliferate on the left and centre, and not just those that are more common and widespread on the right.

To go back to the narrative testing and the negligible change that was seen in attitudes towards Muslims before and after reading the stylized statement in which Muslims condemn terrorism committed by members of their faith group, I should state that I have addressed in another publication my rejection of the 'special responsibility' argument. My chapter in the edited collection *I Refuse to Condemn* draws on this same research and reviews the burden Muslims are made to assume when asked to condemn the violent actions of others. My argument there is essentially a critique of why the burden is shifted on to Muslims when the exploration of causal factors explaining acts of terrorism are multifaceted, as Strømmen and Schmiedel duly acknowledge. There is a notable absence of reflective analysis on the part of the majority population as to causes of violence when the burden of blame is placed squarely on the shoulders of the Muslim minority and religion is made to occupy the singular frame of reference for causal explanation (Bunglawala, 2020, pp. 31–42). It seems to me people of faith do themselves and their co-religionists a disservice when they perform this part, and it is performative, because they crowd out the scope for clearer, sharper analyses of causal factors.

I am not saying that claims to Islam and claims to Christianity do not provoke soul-searching questions for Muslims and Christians alike when faced with individuals who purport to engage in violence for a cause whose justification is (erroneously) rooted in religion, I think they profoundly do. But I don't think that making a community 'responsible' for the actions of members within it is necessarily helpful, and in many ways it reinforces the divisive rhetoric that motivates those who seek to polarize societies into 'us' and 'them' camps, and for whom shifting the burden of responsibility serves merely to entrench notions of distinctive superiority over the other: 'if only they could be more like us!' I believe there is more thinking that needs to be done here, and I would recommend the essays in *I Refuse to Condemn* as a place from where a critical view of any 'special responsibility' borne by Christians might be re-examined. That is not to deny that there is room to examine the conflations that members of our faith groups make about the other that can shape, influence and act as causal factors in the move to violence. That goes without saying. But there is a notable difference between resisting the performativity inherent in demands to condemn, and displaying a lackadaisical attitude to violence committed by those purporting to act for or in the name of religion. It is not addressed by Strømmen and Schmiedel, but I would query the degree to which demands for Muslim condemnation of terrorism since 9/11 shaped the conditions (the expectation?) in which the Islamic Council of Norway and the Church of Norway issued their joint statement (Strømmen and Schmiedel, 2020, p. 55) following Breivik's attack in 2011 and the choice of wording.

Usurpation of 'Voice'

The Claim to Christianity's analysis of church responses to the far right by acknowledging Christianity's own troubled relationship with violence, past and present, is a helpful one. But there are areas where I feel it perhaps goes too far.

To take one example, in their criticism of the easy conflation of 'Muslims with terrorism' Strømmen and Schmiedel lament the media's failures in this regard as 'rarely attempt[ing] to suggest that terrorists are not in fact Muslim' (Strømmen and Schmiedel, 2020, p. 26). There are two objections that I would raise to this. The first is an argument advanced by Brian Klug, a philosopher cited in the book, about the usurpation of 'voice' (Klug, 2011, p. 11). Klug's argument is made in his critique of David Cameron's speech to the Munich security conference[10] in which he opined the need for a 'muscular liberalism' to counter the 'Islamist threat' – note the parallel with UKIP's 'Christian Manifesto' and the call for a 'more muscular Christianity' (Strømmen and Schmiedel, 2020, p. 102) – I don't think the borrowing of this parlance was an accident.

Klug takes issue with Cameron's speech on multiple fronts but the one that is pertinent here is this: Cameron refers to terrorist attacks in the UK 'some of which are, sadly, carried out by our own citizens', saying that the threat comes 'overwhelmingly from young men who follow *a completely perverse, warped interpretation of Islam*, and who are prepared to blow themselves up and kill their fellow citizens'.[11] Klug – and, I would concur, Cameron – is in no position to determine what Islam is, let alone pontificate on what 'a completely perverse, warped interpretation of Islam' might look like. Strømmen and Schmiedel's claim that the media is failing when there is 'rarely an attempt to suggest that terrorists are not in fact Muslim' invites the same criticism. It supports the challenge to Crusader Christianity, but are Christians, or indeed the media, the ones to make this argument, or Muslims?

The second objection, strongly related to the first, is that 'takfirism' – excommunication of Muslims – is a dangerous and slippery slope; a slope that is recognized in the book in another place where arguments are made about 'purity' and its never-ending pursuit, and in its question 'Can we call far right terrorists "Christian"? Why? Why not?' (Strømmen and Schmiedel, 2020, p. 65).

It is possible, in my view, to disassemble claims to Christianity (or Islam) without shouldering a 'responsibility', special or otherwise, for perpetrators of violence in both our religions. And by doing so we might be more successful in changing the narrative on religion and violence than performative acts themselves yield. Muslims can make common cause with Christians in this regard when it comes to tackling Crusader Christianity, and its mirror in Muslim contexts, but I would waver from the book's plea that the 'definition of Christianity cannot be done only by Christians' (Strømmen and Schmiedel, 2020, p. 141). I would argue that the definition of Christianity can *only* be done by Christians, just as challenging Muslims who abuse Islam to justify violence can only be done by Muslims. In fighting the semantic struggle we should be careful not to contaminate and dilute the essence of that over which the struggle is fought. Going back to Klug, it is important to be mindful of the usurpation of 'voice' if our attempts to challenge the far right are not to end up perversely stoking their efforts rather than defusing them.

Contact Theory and Cleavages in British Society

There is a further dimension to condemning violence that is alluded to but left unsaid by Strømmen and Schmiedel and that is this: if Christians knew Muslims better, and vice versa, would our personal knowledge and familiarity with one another obviate any need for our seeking explicit condemnation? Would knowing one another better enable us to look beyond the violence perpetrated by the few and see in other fellow people of faith continuing their semantic struggle to keep faith out of it?

Strømmen and Schmiedel make the case for contact theory (Strømmen and Schmiedel, 2020, p. 130) as a functional tool to eradicate the ignorance and lack of familiarity that allows for stereotyping and scapegoating of the other to persist. This is what they call the 'theological trap' (Strømmen and Schmiedel, 2020, p. 19) that confines us to binary and essentialized notions of ourselves and of others. Drawing on the work of Allport, Strømmen and Schmiedel posit the possibility of contact that reaches 'below the surface … the type of contact that leads people to *do* things together' (Strømmen and Schmiedel, 2020, p. 141) as a means of problematizing prejudice the better to respond to it while recognizing that the truth claims inherent in religions create fixed boundaries that can just as likely promote prejudice as undo it. But I concur entirely with the view that 'The gospel is strong enough to stand on its own legs' (Strømmen and Schmiedel, 2020, p. 57) and that contact can allow us to engage fully with the other without fearing the boundaries that distinguish us are becoming porous to the point of dissolving our differences. Contact can help us notice our boundaries better without feeling the need to over-police them. The Qur'an states the same in the verses 'There is no compulsion in religion: true guidance has become distinct from error …'[12] and 'Call [people] to the way of your Lord with wisdom and good teaching. Argue with them in the most courteous way, for your Lord knows best who has strayed from His way and who is rightly guided.'[13]

The Pew report 'Being Christian in Western Europe' certainly emphasizes the benign effect that contact with Muslims has on prejudicial views. The report states 'personally knowing someone who is Muslim tend[s] to go hand in hand with more openness to immigration and religious minorities' (Sahgal, 2018, p. 22).

I am a strong advocate of the contact hypothesis approach myself, but I am mindful of the very real challenges that contact presents when we are talking about cleavages in society that are not as easily addressed by just the 'openness of churches'. Where people make contact matters as much as how that contact translates into something more meaningful for both parties. *The Claim to Christianity* focuses on churches principally, but I wonder if there is not more that can be done, and explored in more detail, in relation to how contact can be made in other settings that might translate more easily into action.

In the survey research I revisited, contact was clearly a problem. The three main places where Christians did encounter Muslims were (a) friendship groups (b) workplaces, and (c) neighbourhoods, with more than half the sample saying they enjoyed no contact with Muslims at all.

Moreover, Christian women were more likely to have positive views of Muslims than males, and younger Christians were more likely to hold positive views than older groups. These cleavages, of age and gender, alongside geography, are worth noting. If contact theory is a possible and meaningful antidote to the 'Culture' and 'Crusader' Christianities popularized by the far right, then it is not just the quality and transference of the contact into action that is necessary, but a disaggregation of the groups between whom contact is most valuable to alleviate the harms of far-right rhetoric and Islamophobia.

An area where I think contact can be more benignly and productively exploited is in the workplace, where wider and deeper conversations about faith, the accommodation of religious practices in the workplace, and about making workplaces more 'faith-friendly' can occur. With church attendance in the UK in steep decline (Eames, 2023, p. 12), perhaps looking beyond the churches might prove more useful?

The Claim to Christianity refers copiously to 'who is my neighbour?' (Strømmen and Schmiedel, 2020, p. 7) but I think less well to the question of 'where is my neighbour?' Cleavages in society of age, gender and geography are very real sticking points to the practicality of contact theory. British Muslims have the youngest age profile of all religious groups in the UK and Christians the oldest, according to the most recent census data (Wood and Ransley, 2023). Muslims are also concentrated in cities while Christian communities are not. And far more Muslim women are economically inactive than those of other faith groups (Mayhew, Lindo and Windsor-Shellard, 2023). Bridging these challenges is vital if we are to put aspects of contact theory into practice.

'A Common Word Between Us and You'

I return to my earlier remarks about 'media-generated Muslims'. It seems to me physical contact is but one type of contact we should explore given the realities of our global communities, digital media platforms and lived realities. Benedict Anderson refers to a nation as an 'imagined community' where 'members … will never know most of their fellow-members, meet them or even hear of them, yet in the minds of each lives the image of their communion' (Anderson, 1991, pp. 6–7). The far right in Europe have successfully conjured up an image of Muslims in their societies, an 'imagined' fifth column that threatens the majority society with violence and subverts their cultural traditions. One might argue contact theory is a necessary but insufficient condition to redress the contrived Muslim other, as the authors acknowledge in their recognition of 'Islamophobia without Muslims' (Strømmen and Schmiedel, 2020, p. 133). The act of 'becoming and being neighbours to Muslims' (Strømmen and Schmiedel, 2020, p. 158) must take on more than just a physical dimension if a communion with Muslims in society (nation) is to be fostered. It seems to me the question 'where is my neighbour?', and not just 'who is my neighbour?', is a vital one. The effort to become and be a neighbour to Muslims must go beyond those with whom we have personal contact, it must also embrace those Muslims whom Christians may 'never meet'.

A final thought, in the style of questions posed at the end of each chapter in *The Claim to Christianity*, is this: Is there a Culture Christianity in which Muslims can be seen as equal partners – that is, imagining a Europe in which both the Christian and Muslim faiths can be bulwarks of democracy, freedom and equality for all? Is there a Crusader Christianity in which Christians and Muslims find common cause to disrupt the claims to violence that drive a wedge between our respective religions? Strømmen and Schmiedel, significantly, point to the inter-religious initiative 'A Common Word between Us and You' (Strømmen and Schmiedel, 2020, p. 159) as a platform to move forward conversations about enacting neighbourliness but don't sufficiently explore the responses of European churches to the invitation to which I can only respond with the hopeful rejoinder, 'to be continued …'.

Notes

1 'Exclusive: Britain First Planning Return to Luton after Controversial "Christian Patrol"', *Luton Today*, 27 January 2016.

2 H. Pidd and D. Lloyd, 2014, 'Police Investigate Far-right "Invasions" of Bradford and Glasgow Mosques', *The Independent*, 13 May 2014.

3 S. Solomon, 2006, *A Proposed Charter of Muslim Understanding*, https://www.theguardian.com/politics/interactive/2014/feb/04/charter-muslim-ukip-gerard-batten (accessed 5.4.24).

4 Solomon, *A Proposed Charter*, Article 5(b).

5 Solomon, *A Proposed Charter*, Article 5(d).

6 'UKIP Manifesto Summary: Key Points at-a-Glance', *BBC News*, 25 May 2017.

7 F. Irshaid, 2015, 'Isis, Isil, IS or Daesh? One Group, Many Names', *BBC News*, https://www.bbc.co.uk/news/world-middle-east-27994277 (accessed 5.4.24).

8 The research also found that when presented with instances where Muslims had responded to terrorist incidents, these were either unknown to, or doubted by, the respondents.

9 https://yougov.co.uk/politics/articles/14621-tracker-islam-and-british-values (accessed 5.4.24).

10 Cabinet Office, *PM's Speech at Munich Security Conference*, 5 February 2011, https://www.gov.uk/government/speeches/pms-speech-at-munich-security-conference (accessed 5.4.24).

11 Cabinet Office, *PM's Speech*, my emphasis.

12 M. A. S. Abdel Haleem, 2016, *The Qur'an*, English translation with parallel Arabic text, Oxford: Oxford University Press, 2.256, p. 43.

13 Haleem, *The Qur'an*, 16.125, p. 282.

References

Anderson, B., 1991, *Imagined Communities: Reflections on the Origin and Spread of Nationalism*, rev. edn, London: Verso.

Bunglawala, S., 2020, 'Remaking Rule #1: "I Utterly Refuse to Condemn ..."', Asim Qureshi (ed.), *I Refuse to Condemn: Resisting Racism in Times of National Security*, Manchester: Manchester University Press.

Eames, K., 2023, *Statistics for Mission 2022*, London: Church of England.

Jones, S. H. and A. Unsworth, 2022, *The Dinner Table Prejudice: Islamophobia in Contemporary Britain*, Birmingham: University of Birmingham, https://www.birmingham.ac.uk/documents/college-artslaw/ptr/90172-univ73-islamophobia-in-the-uk-report-final.pdf (accessed 5.4.24).

Klug, B., 2011, *An Almost Unbearable Insecurity: Cameron's Munich Speech*, University of South Australia: International Centre for Muslim and Non-Muslim Understanding, MnM Working Paper No. 6.

Mayhew, M., S. Lindo and B. Windsor-Shellard, 2023, *Diversity in the Labour Market, England and Wales: Census 2021*, London: Office for National Statistics, https://www.ons.gov.uk/employmentandlabourmarket/peopleinwork/employmentandemployeetypes/articles/diversityinthelabourmarketenglandandwales/census2021 (accessed 5.4.24).

Rane, H., J. Ewart and J. Martinkus, 2014, *Media Framing of the Muslim World: Conflicts, Crises and Contexts*, London: Palgrave Macmillan.

Sahgal, N. et al., 2018, *Being Christian in Western Europe*, Washington DC: Pew Research Center.

Strømmen, H. and U. Schmiedel, 2020, *The Claim to Christianity: Responding to the Far Right*, London: SCM Press.

Wolfreys, J., 2018, *Republic of Islamophobia: The Rise of Respectable Racism in France*, London: Hurst.

Wood, S. and J. Ransley, 2023, *Religion by Age and Sex, England and Wales: Census 2021*, London: Office for National Statistics, https://www.ons.gov.uk/peoplepopulationandcommunity/culturalidentity/religion/articles/religionbyageandsexenglandandwales/census2021 (accessed 5.4.24).

6

Contextualizing the Claim to Christianity: A Response to Martin Accad and Shenaz Bunglawala

HANNAH STRØMMEN AND ULRICH SCHMIEDEL

Shenaz Bunglawala's and Martin Accad's responses in Chapters 4 and 5 of this volume take *The Claim to Christianity* on a trip to new countries and new contexts. Together, they point to the pervasiveness and the persistence of the construct of the clash of civilizations that runs through the rise of the far right in Europe. We are grateful that the respondents took us on these trips. They show us that 'respectable racism' (Bunglawala, Chapter 5 in this volume) can be found anywhere, although its targets change according to one's place and perspective. Historian Rita Chin discusses the invention of what she interprets as 'new racism' in immigration and integration debates in Europe (Chin, 2017, pp. 138–90). While there is overlap between 'racism' and 'new racism', she suggests that what is new is a shift from categories of race to categories of religion.[1] This shift is what makes racism 'respectable'. In *The Claim to Christianity*, we drew on Chin's discussion to probe how we can counter this new racism (Strømmen and Schmiedel, 2020, pp. 18–21). Bunglawala offers an intervention from a Muslim perspective. In Chapter 4 of this volume Accad offers an intervention from a Middle Eastern perspective. In what follows, we address these interventions, taking them back to see what Christians in Europe can learn from them.

What Bunglawala calls and characterizes as 'the "special responsibility" argument' is crucial to both of our respondents (Bunglawala, Chapter 5 in this volume). The argument is that members of a community of faith have a special responsibility to condemn violence that is committed by somebody claiming to be a fellow member. In a way, *The Claim to Christianity* makes a special responsibility argument, albeit by going from condemning to characterizing and to countering anti-Muslim attitudes and anti-Muslim actions that cause violence in the name of Christianity.

Bunglawala highlights fascinating research results that point to the problems in this argument. Muslims who act as if they have a special responsibility for violence committed in the name of Islam are caught in a double-bind. Drawing on her insightful chapter 'Remaking Rule #1: "I ~~Utterly~~ Refuse to Condemn ..."' in *I Refuse to Condemn: Resisting Racism in Times of National Security*, Bunglawala argues that the acceptance of such a responsibility has a false assumption built in, namely that 'in the name of Islam' is indeed the cause for the violence (Bunglawala, 2020). Given the multi-faceted reasons that lead to violence, this assumption needs to be critiqued rather than confirmed. In *Beyond Religious Freedom: The New Global Politics of Religion*, political theorist Elizabeth Shakman Hurd makes a similar case, arguing that 'to declare religion the cause of particular political conflicts reduces complex questions of causation' (Hurd, 2015, p. 12). Bunglawala's point is essential for reflecting on how to address responsibility within communities of faith.

Even if condemnation is offered by Muslims, it will not protect them from Islamophobia because 'responding to terrorist actions alone would not address the range of issues that influenced anti-Muslim sentiment', the 'respectable racism' that can be found on the political right as well as the political left (Bunglawala, Chapter 5 in this volume).[2] What lurks in the background is 'the media-generated Muslim' (Bunglawala, Chapter 5 in this volume).[3] Perceptions about 'Islam' are generated through the media. In order to tackle Islamophobia, then, a much more sophisticated strategy is needed, countering in particular the stereotyping of Muslims in public discourse and political debate.

In *The Claim to Christianity*, we refrained from making recommendations for Muslim communities. Bunglawala's response makes clear why. The situation – particularly the mediatization of Islam – is very different from Christianity. In the countries we have covered, many people identify as Christian, so it's likely that perceptions of Christianity are also based on face-to-face encounters. In spite of the shrinking numbers of people who attend services, Christianity is in a position of privilege and power, with established or almost-established churches whose representatives are heard in public debate and political discourse (although they are perhaps not always listened to). Proposing a special responsibility for Christians, then, has a very different effect than for Islam. Given that Christianity is often presented as peaceful, the condemnation of violence in the name of Christianity has the potential to disturb the construct of the clash of civilizations in which one side is marked as violent and the other side is marked as non-violent. If a Christian takes special responsibility, these sides have to be considered again.

Similar – albeit less drastic – are cases where Christians join Muslims who condemn violence committed in the name of Islam, so that the message is turned into one about religion in general. 'Religion in general' is to be handled with care, for all sorts of reasons, academic and activist.[4] However, in this case, the condemnation of violence in the name of religion shows that violence is not – as it is often assumed – the purview of Islam, but that all religions struggle with it. Bunglawala's critique of the special responsibility argument, then, makes perfect sense for Muslims. Yet the difference in the perception and the portrayal of both religions in contemporary Europe means the critique doesn't travel smoothly to Christianity.

Accad's response is a case in point. When he suggests that Muslim theologians ought to condemn violence in the name of Islam, his suggestion is rooted in the Middle East. The distribution of privilege and power that faith communities have is not necessarily reversed from Europe, but it is different. Accad is clear that his suggestion is 'not transactional' (Accad, Chapter 4 in this volume). The point is not that each community of faith should condemn the violence committed in its name so that we get the equal amount of condemnation on each side. On the contrary, he argues that such condemnations could help with the relations between the communities: Muslims can enable Christians to develop their hermeneutics of scripture and Christians can enable Muslims to develop their hermeneutics of scripture in a way that counters violence by assessing their own understandings of the text. Accad's *Sacred Misinterpretation* (2019) skilfully shows the possibilities and the potentials here. 'The use of theological discourse to resolve differences is a common practice among groups with differing views within a single religion. But the idea that religious discourse can also contribute significantly to working toward peaceful relations between populations with rival ideologies is a relatively recent notion' (Accad, 2019, p. 6). Taking up this notion in the current geopolitical context, Accad argues, 'Christians will be urged to play a more active role of peacemakers' (Accad, 2019, p. 6).

Communities of faith can help one another. This brings us back to the tricky task of identifying who does and who doesn't count as a member of a community of faith. In *The Claim to Christianity* we critiqued the media reports on terrorists who self-identify as Muslims. We noted that there is 'rarely an attempt to suggest that terrorists are not in fact Muslims' (Strømmen and Schmiedel, 2020, p. 26). Bunglawala wonders whether we go too far here. Should such a suggestion, she asks, be made by people who are not themselves Muslim?

We are concerned with this scenario for Christians, which is – as mentioned above – very different when it comes to privilege and power. Our critique of reports on terrorism was triggered by the fact that the initial reports about the terror attacks in Norway assumed that the perpetrator was Muslim. Once it was clear that he was not, reports pointed to psychological and sociological factors. The fact that he self-identified as a 'monocultural Christian' – whatever that might mean – was only slowly and sporadically discussed (Strømmen and Schmiedel, 2020, pp. 38–9). The example shows that the difference in the standing and the situation of Christianity in Europe is so stark that suggestions for Christianity cannot be applied straightforwardly to Islam and suggestions for Islam cannot be applied straightforwardly to Christianity. None the less, Bunglawala's caution about the risk of obscuring complex causes that must not be pinned on 'religion' is important.

Accad would answer Bunglawala's question about whether people who aren't Muslims should be allowed to decide whether someone is or isn't a Muslim in the affirmative. He suggests that 'far-right and not so far-right politicians are consolidating extremist Islamist views on a constantly transforming Islam', if they refrain from challenging the definitions of Islam that traffic in public discourse and political debate (Accad, Chapter 4 in this volume). In other words, if the claim is made that Islam is a violent faith, so that terrorists who claim Islam for their terror are indeed Muslims, then the very definition of Islam that they follow is confirmed – namely, a violent one. But this definition needs to be countered both by inside and outside voices. As Accad argues, 'soul-searching' is what is needed on all sides (Accad, Chapter 4 in this volume).

Accad is correct that our attempt to criticize and counter views of Muslims that trap them in Islamophobic essentializations could have offered more detail. Bat Ye'or is a case in point. One of us has written on her extensively elsewhere because we agree with Accad that figures like her need to be challenged.[5] Describing herself as a historian of religious minorities under Muslim rule, Ye'or has been influential in popularizing conspiracies that are taken up in far-right ideology, both more mainstream versions and more marginal versions.[6] Many of the essays collected in Ye'or's *Understanding Dhimmitude: Twenty-One Lectures and Talks on the Position of Non-Muslims in Islamic Societies* (2013) are based on talks she delivered at universities in the USA and the UK. Her husband, David Littman, who shares her views, has represented various NGOs at the UN Commission on Human Rights in Geneva (Bangstad, 2014, p. 146). Resonating with Accad, scholars have suggested that studies of terrorism are often oriented around analyses of the perpetrators, thus losing sight of the worldviews that enable terrorism.[7] There are background voices to terrorist violence who communicate 'knowledge' about Islam from respectable channels. As Accad indicates, it is vital to investigate the people and places that enable particular perceptions and prejudices to take hold.

The stress on the significance of the hermeneutics of scripture in Accad's response is spot-on. In a way, such hermeneutics runs through *The Claim to Christianity* as it revolves around the parable of the Good Samaritan (Luke 10.25–37). Our suggestion that Christianity could be approached as a project rather than a possession is a way of pointing to the hermeneutical circle that cannot be escaped. We wrote about the notion of 'lived scripture' because we wanted to indicate that ancient texts that are canonized as sacred for a faith community are not static but dynamic. They aren't simply texts to be read. Scripture is lived out in a variety of ways, not all of which are centred on reading.[8] Attending to what anthropologist James Bielo (2009) has called the 'social life of scriptures' is about recognizing the way interactions with the Bible are on-going. The interaction with scripture cannot even be confined to one's own faith. Our suggestion that the Qur'an can teach Christians a lot about theologies of liberation is rooted in the work of Muslim theologians, such as Shadaab Rahemtulla's *Qur'an of the Oppressed* (2017). One of us has explored the problems and potentials of multi-faith theologies of liberation that allow Christians to work with Muslims elsewhere.[9]

The question of the interaction between faiths is raised by Bunglawala's critique of our suggestion that Christians cannot be alone in defining what can or cannot count as Christianity. Bunglawala pushes back: 'The definition of Christianity can only be done by Christians' (Bunglawala, Chapter 5 in this volume). Yet, we cannot agree with her on this pushback.

Historically, it is very difficult to pin down when and where Christianity started. The movement that gathered around Jesus of Nazareth was a Jewish movement following a Jew. Research into the process in which Christianity 'separated' from Judaism shows that both religions were shaped by each other.[10] Judaism shaped Christianity directly when Christians confirmed Jewish customs and Jewish concepts. Judaism shaped Christianity indirectly when Christians critiqued Jewish customs and Jewish concepts. Hence, neither the start nor the shape of Christianity can be conceptualized without Judaism.

These processes didn't stop in antiquity.[11] When children meet in their neighbourhoods, what Christian children learn from Muslim children about their faith will influence how they see themselves and what Muslim children learn from Christian children about their faith will influence how they see themselves. Already in such day-to-day meetings, people reconsider their identity by learning where they converge and where they diverge from one another. Bunglawala's point that the workplace is promising for multi-faith encounters is helpful here. Christianity did not fall from the heavens, ready-made. There is no moment in its history that allows us to see a pure Christianity, untouched by contact with others. Why should we shun such contact now?[12]

Systematically, theologian Klaus von Stosch (2012) has taken the fact that Christianity revolves around the Jew Jesus of Nazareth as a point of departure for his comparative theology. He argues that the acknowledgement of Christianity's opening to Judaism allows Christianity to be opened up to a variety of faiths, because it revolves around the acceptance of a concrete other from whom one can learn precisely because of their otherness (Von Stosch, 2012, pp. 281–2). As a result of the persecution of Jews by Christians, it is crucial to keep in mind that the openness we are pointing to here has been held up as a feature of Christianity that is lacking in Judaism. Supersessionist claims that an open Christianity that is inclusive rather than exclusive emerged out of a Judaism that was closed in on itself have been hugely damaging, furthering stereotypes of Jews. Von Stosch's point is precisely that such supersessionism and such stereotypes are not only problematic but would miss the purpose of a comparative theology that aims to listen and to learn from the other (Von Stosch, 2012, pp. 269–75).

Finally, the idea of a pure or purified Christianity would be a bit like a cat that bites its tail. In order to define Christianity, one needs to identify Christians. In order to identify Christians, one needs to define Christianity. Here too, then, the moment of purity is impossible. As mentioned above, the hermeneutical circle cannot be escaped. It's therefore not so helpful to ask how we can get out of it. We can't. We need to ask 'How do we get in?' The initiative of *A Common Word between Us and You* is a moment that allows churches to get into the hermeneutical circle. While Bunglawala is correct that we have not explored how churches in Europe responded to this initiative, it's clear that it has triggered some change in how Christians see themselves.[13]

When it comes to practical recommendations, Gordon Allport's contact hypothesis that runs through *The Claim to Christianity* is confirmed by both respondents. Building on the contact hypothesis, Bunglawala challenges us to go beyond churches. Once we go beyond churches to look for opportunities for contact, the parable of the Good Samaritan takes on a new meaning. As Bunglawala argues, the question of this parable moves from '*who* is my neighbour?' to '*where* is my neighbour?' (Bunglawala,

Chapter 5 in this volume). 'Cleavages in society ... are very real sticking points to the practicality of contact theory' (Bunglawala, Chapter 5 in this volume), which means that the contact that Allport recommended requires structural change. We have discussed the dialectic of racist structures and racist stereotyping in our response to Steinar Ims and Henrik Frykberg. We agree with Bunglawala that for change to come about, 'the effort to become and be a neighbour to Muslims must go beyond those with whom we have personal contact, it must also embrace those Muslims whom Christians may "never meet"' (Bunglawala, Chapter 5 in this volume).

Accad's comparison between Muslim majority and Muslim minority contexts confirms this call to go beyond. In *The Claim to Christianity*, we discussed statistics that demonstrate that there is 'Islamophobia without Muslims' – which means that anti-Muslim stereotypes have a stronger hold in societies in which one is less likely to meet Muslims (Strømmen and Schmiedel, 2020, pp. 132–3). As Accad points out, these statistics are rooted in countries with Muslim minorities rather than Muslim majorities. The fact that the 'dominant Muslim demographic in the Middle East does not diminish Christian prejudice against Islam' (Accad, Chapter 4 in this volume) confirms that contact is not a catch-all cure. As our conversation with Ims and Frykberg made clear, the key to many contexts is that '*meaningful* contact' can lead to 'collaborative *action* in society' (Accad, Chapter 4 in this volume).

The Muslim and the Middle-Eastern perspectives, then, have pushed our analysis and our arguments further than we anticipated. It seems to us that the comparative work that the two respondents have started – comparing churches in Europe to Muslim and Middle-Eastern communities – is a promising point of departure in challenging the rise of the far right both here and there. This might be a point of departure for collaborative action. Hence, we can only join the hopeful rejoinder: 'to be continued ...' (Bunglawala, Chapter 5 in this volume).

Notes

1 Anya Topolski, 2018, 'The Race-Religion Constellation: A European Contribution to the Critical Philosophy of Race', *Critical Philosophy of Race* 6(1), pp. 58–81, presents connections between the categories of race and religion in the history of Europe, pointing in particular to the impact that Christian theology has had on the construction of racism. See also Anya Topolski, 2020, 'The Dangerous Discourse of the "Judaeo-Christian" Myth: Masking the Race-Religion Constellation in Europe', *Patterns of Prejudice* 54(1–2), pp. 71–90.

2 Bunglawala draws on Jim Wolfreys, 2016, *Republic of Islamophobia: The Rise of Respectable Racism in France*, Oxford: Oxford University Press. See also Monte Piliawsky, 1984, 'Racial Equality in the United States: From Institutionalized Racism to "Respectable" Racism', *Phyton* 45(2), pp. 135–43.

3 Bunglawala draws on Halim Rane, Jaqui Ewart and John Martinkus, 2014, *Media Framing of the Muslim World: Conflicts, Crises and Contexts*, New York: Palgrave Macmillan.

4 For a succinct summary of the debate, stressing the social and political significance of the conceptualization of religion, see Jayne Svenungsson, 2020, 'The Return of Religion or the End of Religion? On the Need to Rethink Religion as a Category of Social and Political Life', *Philosophy and Social Criticism* 46(7), pp. 785–809.

5 See Hannah M. Strømmen, 2017, 'Biblical Blood-Lines: From Foundational Corpus to Far Right Bible', *Biblical Interpretation* 25(4–5), pp. 555–73. The analysis is developed in Hannah M. Strømmen, 2024, *The Bibles of the Far Right*, Oxford: Oxford University Press.

6 See Matt Carr, 2006, 'You Are Now Entering Eurabia', *Race and Class* 48(1), pp. 1–22, and Liz Fekete, 2017, *Europe's Fault Lines: Racism and the Rise of the Right*, London: Verso, pp. 60–1.

7 See Paul Jackson, 2013, 'The License to Hate: Peder Jensen's Fascist Rhetoric in Anders Breivik's Manifesto 2083: A European Declaration of Independence', *Democracy and Security* 9, pp. 247–8; and Matts Ekman, 2015, 'Online Islamophobia and the Politics of Fear: Manufacturing the Green Scare', *Ethnic and Racial Studies* 38(11), pp. 1986–2002.

8 See Hannah M. Strømmen, 2022, 'Sacred Scripts of Populism: Scripture-Practices in the European Far Right', in Ulrich Schmiedel and Joshua Ralston (eds), *The Spirit of Populism: Political Theologies in Polarized Times*, Leiden: Brill, pp. 85–101. The concentration on the usage of scripture in this chapter is taken up by Fatima Tofighi, 2022, 'Hermeneutics, Politics, and Liberalism in Islamic Modernity: Beyond Populism', in Ulrich Schmiedel and Joshua Ralston (eds), *The Spirit of Populism: Political Theologies in Polarized Times*, Leiden: Brill, pp. 101–16; and Mattias Martinson, 2022, 'Populism, Christianity, and the Role of the Theologian', in Ulrich Schmiedel and Joshua Ralston (eds), *The Spirit of Populism: Political Theologies in Polarized Times*, Leiden: Brill, pp. 132–47.

9 See Ulrich Schmiedel, 2021, *Terror und Theologie: Der religionstheoretische Diskurs der 9/11-Dekade*, Tübingen: Mohr Siebeck, pp. 365–97.

10 See Paula Fredriksen, 2019, *When Christians Were Jews: The First Generation*, New Haven: Yale University Press; and Peter Schäfer, 2014, *The Jewish Jesus: How Judaism and Christianity Shaped Each Other*, Princeton: Princeton University Press.

11 See the contributions to Marianne Bjelland Kartzow (ed.), 2021, *The Ambiguous Figure of the Neighbor in Jewish, Christian, and Islamic Texts and Receptions*, London: Routledge.

12 A particularly instructive publication for these interactions is Adele Berlin and Mordechai Z. Cohen (eds), 2016, *Interpreting Scriptures in Judaism, Christianity and Islam: Overlapping Inquiries*, Cambridge: Cambridge University Press.

13 See Vebjørn L. Horsfjord, 2018, *Common Words in Muslim-Christian Dialogue: A Study of Texts from the Common Word Dialogue Process*, Leiden: Brill, for a detailed discussion of the dialogue that 'A Common Word' triggered.

References

Accad, Martin, 2019, *Sacred Misinterpretation: Reaching Across the Christian-Muslim Divide*, Grand Rapids: Eerdmans.

Accad, Martin, in this volume, 'Chapter 4: A Lebanese Perspective on Religion-inspired Political Extremism'.

Bangstad, Sindre, 2014, *Anders Breivik and the Rise of Islamophobia*, London: Zed Books.

Berlin, Adele and Z. Cohen Mordechai (eds), 2016, *Interpreting Scriptures in Judaism, Christianity and Islam: Overlapping Inquiries*, Cambridge: Cambridge University Press.

Bielo, James (ed.), 2009, *The Social Life of Scriptures: Cross-Cultural Perspectives on Biblicism*, New Brunswick: Rutgers University Press.

Bunglawala, Shenaz, 2020, 'Remaking Rule #1: "I Utterly Refuse to Condemn ..."', in Asim Qureshi (ed.), *I Refuse to Condemn: Resisting Racism in Times of National Security*, Manchester: Manchester University Press, pp. 31–42.

Bunglawala, Shenaz, in this volume, 'Chapter 5: Beyond the Far Right: "Respectable Racism" and British Muslims'.

Carr, Matt, 2006, 'You Are Now Entering Eurabia', *Race and Class* 48(1), pp. 1–22.

Chin, Rita, 2017, *The Crisis of Multiculturalism in Europe: A History*, Princeton: Princeton University Press.

Ekman, Mats, 2015, 'Online Islamophobia and the Politics of Fear: Manufacturing the Green Scare', *Ethnic and Racial Studies* 38(11), pp. 1986–2002.

Fekete, Liz, 2017, *Europe's Fault Lines: Racism and the Rise of the Right*, London: Verso.

Fredriksen, Paula, 2019, *When Christians Were Jews: The First Generation*, New Haven: Yale University Press.

Horsfjord, Vebjørn L., 2018, *Common Words in Muslim-Christian Dialogue: A Study of Texts from the Common Word Dialogue Process*, Leiden: Brill.

Hurd, Elizabeth Shakman, 2015, *Beyond Religious Freedom: The New Global Politics of Religion*, Princeton: Princeton University Press.

Jackson, Paul, 2013, 'The License to Hate: Peder Jensen's Fascist Rhetoric in Anders Breivik's Manifesto 2083: A European Declaration of Independence', *Democracy and Security* 9(3), pp. 247–8.

Kartzow, Marianne Bjelland (ed.), 2021, *The Ambiguous Figure of the Neighbor in Jewish, Christian, and Islamic Texts and Receptions*, London: Routledge.

Martinson, Mattias, 2022, 'Populism, Christianity, and the Role of the Theologian', in Ulrich Schmiedel and Joshua Ralston (eds), *The Spirit of Populism: Political Theologies in Polarized Times*, Leiden: Brill, pp. 132–47.

Piliawsky, Monte, 1984, 'Racial Equality in the United States: From Institutionalized Racism to "Respectable" Racism', *Phyton* 45(2), pp. 135–43.

Rahemtulla, Shadaab, 2017, *Qur'an of the Oppressed: Liberation Theology and Gender Justice in Islam*, Oxford: Oxford University Press.

Rane, Halim, Jaqui Ewart and John Martinkus, 2014, *Media Framing of the Muslim World: Conflicts, Crises and Contexts*, New York: Palgrave Macmillan.

Schäfer, Peter, 2014, *The Jewish Jesus: How Judaism and Christianity Shaped Each Other*, Princeton: Princeton University Press.

Schmiedel, Ulrich, 2021, *Terror und Theologie: Der religionstheoretische Diskurs der 9/11-Dekade*, Tübingen: Mohr Siebeck.

Stosch, Klaus von, 2012, *Komparative Theologie als Wegweiser in der Welt der Religionen*, Paderborn: Ferdinand Schöningh.

Strømmen, Hannah M., 2017, 'Biblical Blood-Lines: From Foundational Corpus to Far Right Bible', *Biblical Interpretation* 25(4–5), pp. 555–73.

Strømmen, Hannah M., 2022, 'Sacred Scripts of Populism: Scripture-Practices in the European Far Right', in Ulrich Schmiedel and Joshua Ralston (eds), *The Spirit of Populism: Political Theologies in Polarized Times*, Leiden: Brill, pp. 85–101.

Strømmen, Hannah M., 2024, *The Bibles of the Far Right*, Oxford: Oxford University Press.

Strømmen, Hannah and Ulrich Schmiedel, 2020, *The Claim to Christianity: Responding to the Far Right*, London: SCM Press.

Svenungsson, Jayne, 2020, 'The Return of Religion or the End of Religion? On the Need to Rethink Religion as a Category of Social and Political Life', *Philosophy and Social Criticism* 46(7), pp. 785–809.

Tofighi, Fatima, 2022, 'Hermeneutics, Politics, and Liberalism in Islamic Modernity: Beyond Populism', in Ulrich Schmiedel and Joshua Ralston (eds), *The Spirit of Populism: Political Theologies in Polarized Times*, Leiden: Brill, pp. 101–16.

Topolski, Anya, 2018, 'The Race-Religion Constellation: A European Contribution to the Critical Philosophy of Race', *Critical Philosophy of Race* 6(1), pp. 58–81.

Topolski, Anya, 2020, 'The Dangerous Discourse of the "Judaeo-Christian" Myth: Masking the Race-Religion Constellation in Europe', *Patterns of Prejudice* 54(1–2), pp. 71–90.

Wolfreys, Jim, 2016, *Republic of Islamophobia: The Rise of Respectable Racism in France*, Oxford: Oxford University Press.

Ye'or, Bat, 2013, *Understanding Dhimmitude: Twenty-One Lectures and Talks on the Position of Non-Muslims in Islamic Societies*, New York: RVP Press.

PART 3

Politics of the Far Right and the Church

7

Encountering and Countering the Far Right in the UK Today

JAMES CROSSLEY

The Claim to Christianity by Hannah Strømmen and Ulrich Schmiedel is an impressive achievement as an assessment of the state of the far right. It raises many important questions, not all of which can be covered in a comparatively brief response. In this chapter, I want to use the insights of Strømmen and Schmiedel to reflect on issues relating to the contemporary far right and related movements in the UK, including their understanding of religion. Here I define 'far right' in general, popularly understood terms to cover known nationalist, anti-leftist, and often anti-liberal movements ranging from those whose object of hate is typically Muslims and Islam (e.g. English Defence League, Tommy Robinson, For Britain) to those who are more fascistic and overtly racist (e.g. Patriotic Alternative, National Action, British National Party). Most of these groups, we might add, typically make some claim to Christianity, even if not always to the theatrical extent of Britain First from their regular prayer offerings to carrying crosses in Muslim areas as part of their 'Christian Patrol'. This is an imperfect definition, not least because there are some significant differences among far-right groups (which will not be ignored here) but overlaps in ideas remain. I will briefly outline some of the ways the far right currently function and offer some modest suggestions regarding how their influence can be countered. Indeed, given the ever-changing nature of the far right, such an exercise should be seen as part of the significance of a book like *The Claim to Christianity*: it helps us constantly to rethink the challenges posed in new circumstances, what lessons can be learned, and what can be done next.

JAMES CROSSLEY

Why We Love to Hate the Far Right

A central issue raised in *The Claim to Christianity* concerns how ideas about Islam and the West (Christianity/Europe/nation) are presented as a clash of civilizations in far-right discourses. But the authors are aware that these ideas are not restricted to the far right. They are also found leftwards on the political spectrum and are a common enough feature of mainstream political discourse. This point is, I think, crucial, including for reasons the authors discuss in the book, such as mainstream politicians constantly trying to capitalize on the potential for votes through interrelated discourses (e.g. immigration, anti-Islam, 'Cultural Christianity'). We might keep thinking about how far into the centre and left such thinking goes. Is far-right thinking symptomatic of a broader trend? Is the far-right version of this idea of a clash of civilizations a rhetorical heightening of fairly common tropes?

As *The Claim to Christianity* discusses how such rhetoric is a wider cultural and political phenomenon, I want to push the discussion further along the lines of why hating the far right is so common in mainstream political discourse despite their overlaps in some key areas. Slavoj Žižek argued that the populist right can act as the common enemy of the mainstream and established political spectrum as a means of bolstering the idea that the official system is ultimately benevolent. He added that a corollary of this is that any radical alternative, especially involving class struggles and anti-capitalist movements, becomes delegitimized by tainting such alternatives with the concerns of the populist or far right (Žižek, 2000).

One of the most infamous examples of the far right bolstering the benevolence of the official system in the twenty-first century was the controversial appearance of Nick Griffin on the BBC's flagship political programme *Question Time* in 2009. Griffin was predictably erratic and self-damaging as expected, and the opposing politicians were united in their condemnation of someone who was then the UK's most well-known far-right figure. Among the mainstream political figures was Jack Straw who was a cheerleader of the Iraq War, a supporter (then) of Uzbekistan despite its human rights record, and a leading figure in the Labour Party which was beginning its embrace of austerity measures. The presence of a bigot like Griffin meant Straw was presented among the voices of moderation and received generous applause in his condemnation of the far right.

In the following decade, Tommy Robinson (ex-English Defence League) became the most prominent figure associated with the far right to be universally condemned across the political mainstream, whether in Parliament or in the media. Robinson is of further significance because he shows one key area where ideas about loving to hate the far right have been updated. Robinson has focused on 'religion' rather than 'race', in line with the shifting rhetoric of the far right as Muslims became the focus of their disdain, as shown amply in *The Claim to Christianity*. One of the distinctive features of some parts (certainly not all) of the British far right is a peculiar concern for antisemitism and love for Israel, the most prominent figure to express such views being Robinson. Some of the reasons for this seemingly surprising concern are obvious enough: a subset of the far right think Israel is taking a heroic stand against Islam and Muslims. As I write (autumn 2023), Israel is currently invading Gaza, and such familiar ideas are easy enough to find in social media venues such as Telegram and X/Twitter.

One of the notable features of mainstream political discourses concerning Robinson is that he is typically presented as vaguely unsavoury, bigoted or racist rather than focusing too much on his anti-Muslim or anti-Islamic views. One reason is precisely because there are striking overlaps between Robinson and leading politicians on the issue of Islam and Muslims, even if the rhetoric is typically softened when associated with politicians. To take one example, Tony Blair's claim, following the murder of the soldier Lee Rigby in 2013 by two Muslim men, that there is 'a problem within Islam' was something with which Robinson agreed, commenting publicly on (what was then) Twitter, that Blair 'confirms everything we say'. Blair's office responded that Blair was made aware of the English Defence League tweet and 'totally disagrees with what they have said'. The closest we got to a reference to the details of disagreement was the Tony Blair Institute for Global Change claiming that Robinson 'obviously' had not 'read the article properly' (reported in *Mail on Sunday*, 1 June 2013; *Huffington Post*, 6 June 2013). More examples from politicians even more explicitly 'hating' Robinson could be given and the point would be the same: the common enemy of Robinson allows the more liberal mainstream to be presented as the benevolent actor – even or especially when there are comparable or potentially comparable views – in an attempt to deflect accusations of racism, Islamophobia or bigotry (for more examples, see May, 2011; Cameron, 2011; and reports in *Daily Mail*, 1 March 2016; *Telegraph*, 8 April 2017).

The association of the far right and extremism with any potentially anti-capitalist or class-based alternative has been most obviously seen in the case of Jeremy Corbyn. As Labour leader, Corbyn represented what was effectively a social democratic alternative from the left and (probably more threatening to the British ruling class) a considerably less belligerent foreign policy. But this was too much of a stretch for much of the political establishment. Consequently, the most prominent anti-racist campaigner in Parliament in recent decades has been associated (by the press, the Labour Party establishment, and the then government) with totalitarianism, al Qaeda, terrorism, antisemitism, Donald Trump, Nigel Farage, Charles Manson, cults, fundamentalism, zealotry, fanaticism, etc. (for discussion, see, for example, Crossley, 2018, pp. 132–61).

The dual-edged nature of the attitude towards the far right among the ruling class and the mainstream political spectrum soon becomes clear: while the far right were to be condemned, they take on their historic role as an attack dog to help deal with other opponents of the status quo. Anyone familiar with some sections of the British far right in recent years will know that Corbyn is one of the main figures of their derision, including claims that he is associated with both communism and fascism (indistinguishable in some contemporary far- and alt-right rhetoric). Other common features of such discourses include ideas that Hitler was really a socialist and the left are the real antisemites, or anyone to the left of the far right are communists and socialists (including Boris Johnson, presumably to his surprise). This is, of course, part of familiar, American-led discourses about 'cultural Marxism' taking over everything classified on the right as a threat to inherited values (e.g. Black Lives Matter, Critical Race Theory, social liberalism).

The love-hate relationship between the political mainstream and the far or alt right is seen in the renewed hostility to 'communism', 'socialism' and 'lefties'. In the mother of all horseshoe theories, the EU Parliament, for instance, has equated fascism and communism (reported in, for example, *Morning Star*, 1 September 2019; 30 September 2019; 19 October 2019; 26 January 2020). Certainly, there was opposition among some mainstream politicians in the UK and elsewhere and the EU has its own less-than-reputable record on far-right MEPs, but it is nevertheless a striking overlap between the political mainstream and far-right rhetoric. In the UK, even a phrase like 'cultural Marxism' was used by the prominent Conservative MP (and very recently ex-Home Secretary at the time of writing) Suella Braverman in a manner popularized on the far/alt right: 'As Conservatives,' she claimed, 'we are engaged in a battle against cultural Marxism,' later adding that it was a 'culture evolving from the far left which has allowed the snuffing out of freedom of speech, freedom of thought', and that the 'ongoing creep of cultural Marxism … has come from Jeremy Corbyn' (reported in the *Guardian*, 26 March 2019). Again, this statement was not without opposition (particularly as the cultural

Marxism conspiracy theory has historic links with antisemitism) but, as with the rhetoric about the clash of civilizations and Islam, it is another instance where the far right represent the reactionary end of some mainstream ideas.

A Mass Audience?

Why would sections of the British far or alt right, and some mainstream politicians, be so keen to claim that the left are the real fascists and real racists? Scratch beneath the surface and it is not difficult to find old-fashioned antisemites of the far right. It will come as no surprise that the ostensibly pro-Israel, pro-Jewish far right is using this rhetoric for purposes other than combating antisemitism (for discussion see, for example, Crossley, 2018, pp. 65–98). Probe a bit more and the various far-right groups are not clued up on Marxist dialectics and are not reading the works of Marx and Engels or thinking about historical materialism, modes of production, alienation of the worker, and so on. In the case of so-called cultural Marxism, it is typically used to denote an alleged leftist conspiracy dominating the establishment and its institutions and designed to undermine traditional values relating to, for instance, gender, sexuality, nationality and free speech. None of these issues are specifically Marxist of course (let alone the oddity of Marxists somehow running the capitalist world) but that the blame is put on Marxism and related ideas hardly needs spelling out.

Why then? One reason is because the left are obviously among their main historic enemies. But another is to muster support, and not just from wealthier right-wing organizations. Research into (limited) support for the English Defence League has highlighted the significance of social and economic dislocation, precarious employment, low pay, community neglect, the loss of relatively stable employment in industry, and exclusion from representation in the hierarchies of politics, culture and higher education. The liberal complicity in this social and economic settlement has become epitomized by the Labour Party, the party that has betrayed the working class and its working-class roots, at least according to such perceptions (for discussion, see, for example, Winlow, Hall and Treadwell, 2017). In this context, the allegation of Marxism as a theory not about class but about the values (real or not) of the cultural elite is being used by the far right to gain adherents.

Yet beyond armchair, online gossip, there is no mass audience in the UK for the far or alt right. Certainly, far-right elements will try to stir up local troubles over (say) issues relating to immigration or fears (real or not) about grooming gangs. But as things currently stand, there is minimal potential for a mass, overtly racist or fascistic street movement. At the moment, the closest phenomenon has taken place within the sporadic actions of football-related hooligans for whom a day of physical confrontation fuelled by drink, cocaine and nationalism is as important an issue as anything else, as seen in the 2023 counter demonstration against a pro-Palestine march in London (see, for example, *Morning Star*, 12 November 2023). The far right is not organized in the sense of becoming a mass political party, at least not to the extent that they could successfully capitalize on the decline of church influence, trade union power, or mainstream party-political affiliation.

Furthermore, the UK has become increasingly progressive over the decades on issues of race. Not many today would openly proclaim that they are racist or actively hate an ethnic minority. This is not to deny that racists and racism exist or that racist attacks happen – of course they do. Rather, the popular credibility for 1930s fascism or the far-right street movement of the National Front of the 1970s is not what it was, while it would be highly unusual for even a maverick politician to utter some of the words Enoch Powell once did (such as the claim he attributed to a constituent that 'in 15 or 20 years' time the black man will have the whip hand over the white man'). In my home town of Barrow-in-Furness (to which we will return below), the Nazi-sympathetic Patriotic Alternative have constantly tried to recruit and stir up trouble, but the number of Barrovian recruits appears to be tiny. This is partly why some far-right groups in the UK stress that they are against an ideology or religion and not a race – race does not work as it once did and so the rhetorical emphasis on 'religion' is a deliberate, mostly opportunistic, move in their navigation of contemporary cultural shifts.

Indeed, the popular audience associated with the far right in the UK has changed. Over the past five years, I would say that characteristic features (in addition to immigration and Islam/Muslims) include ideas or perceptions of free speech and shutting down free speech, encroaching authoritarianism, anti-vaxx and conspiracy theories like QAnon and the 15-Minute City. Again, with a little investigation, it won't take long to find racist views associated with some proponents. But equally these are shared views among people who would not see themselves as racist – and are not necessarily far-right views in and of themselves. Lockdown during the Covid-19 pandemic, and the accompanying intensification of social atomization and the boredom some people felt, no doubt contributed to the popularity of conspiracy theories. I have monitored such ideas across social media accounts (e.g. Facebook, Twitter, Telegram) over the past few years and such ideas were being entertained by people with no particularly strong political affiliations or interests, and even among those who were openly anti-racist and vaguely liberal and leftish. We should not automatically assume that this is a right-wing tendency. Nevertheless, such people are a recurring target of far-right interest and opportunistic online propaganda of an inherently conspiratorially minded far right.

Barrow-in-Furness: A Case Study

Some of these issues were at play in Barrow-in-Furness, a town that has become of interest to the far right in recent years. In the spring of 2020, a story made national news concerning Eleanor Williams and her claims about an Asian/Muslim (depending on who retold the story) grooming gang who had trafficked her (for an overview of key events, see, for example, McCann, 2023). Williams shared horrific pictures of injuries she had allegedly received which went viral. Despite the police claiming there were no such gangs in Barrow, there was an immediate reaction, including a fundraising campaign and boycott of the local newspaper. What got little traction in the media was that there was a relatively well-organized Justice4Ellie campaign prompted by far-right activists in Barrow (and from outside) associated with Britain First. Rumours had circulated for some time that there was a grooming gang active in Barrow and Tommy Robinson echoed these claims in a public speech in Barrow when running in the European elections of 2019. By the time the Williams story went viral, local far-right activists were able to whip up interest in Facebook groups and public demonstrations against grooming gangs in the interests of recruitment (among other things), though carefully avoiding the use of the words 'Britain First' where possible. There were two sizeable protests in a town centre car park (including one where Robinson himself appeared, which did get media traction), a convoy of cars driving in support of Williams, and attacks on local restaurants and takeaways associated with Asian owners.

By the end of the summer of 2020, it soon became clear to the Barrovian public that Williams herself had actually been arrested and, as the trial later made clear, she had invented some fantastical stories about grooming (among other things) and inflicted wounds upon herself. The Britain First-linked activists continued, with ever-dwindling numbers, to support Williams while the overwhelming majority of the town (certainly on social media and in any conversations I heard) no longer believed her.

To the surprise of some (including on the far right), Robinson had shifted to opposing Williams's story, even to the extent of producing a documentary exposing the claims of the Williams's camp and befriending a local Muslim man at the centre of the allegations. As expected, Williams was eventually (winter 2022) found guilty of various counts of perverting the course of justice and is currently serving an eight-and-a-half-year sentence. The diehard believers of Williams ended up on obscure conspiracy theory pages on social media with a minimal audience.

In terms of the far-right influences, what can be learned from this? The far right certainly punched above their weight at first and produced sizeable protests and interest. The hostilities towards the alleged groomers as Islamic, Muslim or Asian had some support and no doubt played their part in attacks on restaurants. Despite occasional attempts to invoke Christianity as the shield against Islam and the liberal left, there was (as expected) no real take-up of this idea. Nevertheless, as we might have learned from *The Claim to Christianity*, this had the function of emboldening the Clash of Civilizations claim, or at least highlighting Islam and Muslims as the 'problem'. However, the far right appear to have gained virtually no new followers, and the lack of a support base soon became clear despite their concerted efforts. Despite continuing to claim that such grooming gangs exist and that Williams was wrongly imprisoned as a result of some nefarious establishment conspiracy, the local far right were soon happy enough to move on to the next issues (in this case, hotels for migrants and anti-vaxx).

This points to another feature of the contemporary far right in the UK today: opportunism. Robinson is an excellent and typical example of this in his own way. But, for those more associated with Britain First, the case of Williams and then moving on to the next issue was one example among many. Indeed, there has been a consistent inconsistency among their few members: from pro-Boris to anti-Boris, from criticisms of Hitler and Nazism to carefully worded support for the neo-Nazi Patriotic Alternative (of the 'they raise some important points' variety) and the invocation of Oswald Mosley. In one sense, this is a sign of their weakness as they search for the next thing that might stir things up; in another sense, this is a sign of their potential – they *might* spark something again.

Compared with, say, the 1930s or the 1970s, the far right are historically weak in numbers, popular support and take-up of overtly racialized ideas. But this understanding of the contemporary far right should not be misunderstood as complacency. As all this implies, elements of the far right still have the potential to inflict serious harm. In recent years, we only need think of the murder of the MP Jo Cox, the foiled plan of

National Action to kill the MP Rosie Cooper, and the Finsbury Park attack on Muslims which killed Makram Ali and had Corbyn as one of the targets.[1] Individuals or small groups can still be stirred up to attempt murderous acts. If nothing else, this is a warning that vigilance is needed, no matter how weak the far right is as a mass movement.

What to Do?

Strømmen and Schmiedel have pointed to some of the issues relating to churches, including the issue of the lack of church authority on this and other matters. This lack of authority is a wider problem. As mentioned above, there is no serious, mass party looking out for and belonging to working-class interests and providing a strong counter to far-right ideas. Trade unions lack the strength of yesteryear. This weakness is exploited in far-right social media activity (and mainstream centre-right discourse today) with the claim that the left is made up of the middle classes, university types and journalists, as are the political, religious and cultural establishment – indeed, this is part of the reason why the left and establishment are conflated in far-right and right-wing discourses.

So, what to do? While it is easy to pick holes in such thinking (a Conservative government for over a decade perhaps being the most obvious counterargument), there is an element of truth in such claims. This means that building a strong working-class movement among communities and representative of their material interests is going to be central to dealing with far-right ideas. This is a long-term project. The nature of such a project is obviously beyond a chapter like this but it would have to involve trade unions and political representation to be effective. It has been done before in the twentieth century and, in the 1930s, such a movement most famously challenged fascism on the streets when fascism was at its strongest and most dangerous.

And if it has been done before, it can be done again. If providing a detailed blueprint is beyond this chapter, then some of the more immediate possibilities are worth noting. The churches have well-documented problems with declining attendance and a loss of public authority in the UK, but they do have plenty of experience working in communities and are acutely aware of the problems of social isolation. In addition to their important and culturally respected work in the provision of foodbanks, we might add the further possibilities they offer. Where churches act as hubs of community support, they have individuals better equipped than most to deal with, or act as a point of contact for, disillusioned and isolated individuals attracted to far-right ideas, particularly in their Christianized forms (I owe this point to a discussion with Helen Paynter).

In the recent rail strikes, Mick Lynch and Eddie Dempsey have emerged as credible figures representing working-class interests with popular appeal and support. They have shown how working-class leaders exposing ruling-class interests and focusing on the material concerns of their members can work. While material interests are central to providing a better future for all, the battle of ideas cannot be neglected or misdirected (and nor have they been by Lynch and Dempsey). Plenty of well-meaning colleagues likely to read this book would reply that they have acted otherwise. But we only need look at the example of Brexit to show how polarizing the debate relating to class issues became and how some working-class communities were cast aside by professional thinkers in favour of supporting the neoliberal trading bloc and the cheap labour it provides (e.g. fruit-picking, lorry driving). We might point to nearly 90 per cent of university staff supporting Remain and related issues, and constant pressure for a second referendum in the centre-left *Guardian* to see how the EU was seen as representing the interests of the liberal, often globally oriented middle classes – all of which reflected the dominant attitude of the Labour Party membership (see, for example, *Times Higher Education*, 16 June 2016; *Independent*, 15 October 2018; *Guardian*, 2 January 2019). This was hardly the attitude of some of post-industrial England.

Whatever the rights and wrongs of the EU and the referendum, the period inaugurated by the 1975 referendum on joining the then EEC roughly coincided with the beginning of the long-term decline in industry in parts of England that voted Leave. That may or may not be coincidental, but the regular claims that Brexit would have serious consequences for the economy rang hollow in certain areas where industries were being destroyed while the country was in the EU. Claims of racism and hostility to immigration in Brexit-voting communities likewise rang hollow. Well-meaning support for immigrants and immigration was certainly voiced by Remainers but with little sustained concern for the fate of migrants crossing the Mediterranean and dealing with the EU's strict borders. Seemingly unlikely heroes emerged among liberal-minded Remainers. The retired Conservative Michael Heseltine was lauded in the *Guardian* for his pro-EU arguments (*Guardian*, 19 October 2019). We might recall that when Heseltine was President of the Board of Trade, he was involved in closing deep coal mines and the loss of 30,000 jobs in what would become Leave country. We even saw the bizarre spectacle of a privately educated Oxford graduate journalist for the *Guardian* calling a Labour MP and a veteran of the Miners' Strike of 1984–5 a 'scab' on Twitter for holding pro-Brexit views (@zoesqwilliams, 17 October 2019). The disconnect between some parts of the post-industrial UK and the liberal middle classes and intelligentsia was, to say the least, often stark.

I travelled weekly to Sheffield, London and Cambridge while living in Barrow-in-Furness during the referendum year and the following years when the demand for a second referendum was common. In a (semi-)post-industrial town like Barrow, I never saw one EU flag, but I did see a few England flags. By contrast, in the world of universities, there were countless EU flags, with England flags extremely rare. This is no surprise as English identity was one factor behind the Leave vote in England and Europhilia was a standard identity marker of Remainers. Certainly, parts of the far right have tried to exploit the English flag and concerns about English identity. But we should not oppose issues simply because the right and far right use them opportunistically. Once progressive patriotism was part of the (successful) opposition to fascism. In the 1930s, when fascism was at its most powerful, the opposition to it involved pageants, literature, history and music extolling the progressive English and British heritage and incorporated people no matter what their ethnic background (see, for example, Crossley, 2022, pp. 345–61).

The liberal-left have largely abandoned this tradition rather than updating it. But, again, there are exceptions worth noting. In the admittedly niche world of folk music, the idea of an egalitarian and non-racialized understanding of English identity has continued to thrive. One such group, The Young'uns, have promoted such ideas of English identity and tied them in with the example of how a mosque in York dealt with an English Defence League protest in 2013 through offering up two widely acknowledged symbols of English identity to the protestors: tea and biscuits (Dishman, 2014).

Churches might take some inspiration from this, but they (especially the nonconformist ones) also have their own vast tradition of alternative understandings of what England might be, from John Ball through the various dissenting groups of the seventeenth century to the Chartists and trade unionists. Even the Church of England produced the church in Thaxted which, in the twentieth century at least, celebrated and promoted such a history as much as any other church in the country. Contemporary interest in the English progressive tradition may need to downplay its retired geography teacher chic and repackage it accordingly, but promoting this tradition has been done before and can be done again. England, English identity and Englishness should never have been surrendered to the far right and the reactionary end of the ruling class.

Note

1 Jo Cox was murdered on 16 June 2016 by a far-right, white nationalist. In 2018, a National Action activist was found guilty of preparing an act of terrorism which involved planning to murder Rosie Cooper. On 19 June 2017, a man with an interest in far-right figures and anti-Muslim propaganda drove a van into a gathering of Muslims and later told a court that he wanted to kill Corbyn and others.

References

Cameron, David, 2011, 'Public Disorder', Hansard: House of Commons, 11 August, Column 1086, https://www.publications.parliament.uk/pa/cm201011/cmhansrd/cm110811/debtext/110811-0001.htm (accessed 5.4.24).

Crossley, James, 2018, *Cults, Martyrs, and Good Samaritan: Religion in Contemporary English Political Discourse*, London: Pluto.

Crossley, James, 2022, *Spectres of John Ball: The Peasants' Revolt in English Political History, 1381–2020*, Sheffield: Equinox.

Dishman, Mark, 2014, 'The Young'uns': David Eagle on New Album Never Forget, Anti-fascism, Dodgy Reviews and Biscuits', *Folk Witness*, 19 March.

McCann, Phil, 2023, 'Eleanor Williams: The Grooming Gang Lies that Sparked Outrage', *BBC News*, 3 January, https://www.bbc.co.uk/news/uk-england-cumbria-64150026 (accessed 5.4.24).

May, Theresa, 2011, 'English Defence League', Hansard: House of Commons, 24 January, vol. 522, https://hansard.parliament.uk/Commons/2011-01-24/debates/1101248000029/EnglishDefenceLeague (accessed 5.4.24).

Strømmen, Hannah and Ulrich Schmiedel, 2020, *The Claim to Christianity: Responding to the Far Right*, London: SCM Press.

Winlow, Simon, Steve Hall and James Treadwell, 2017, *The Rise of the Right: English Nationalism and the Transformation of Working-Class Politics*, Bristol: Policy Press.

Žižek, Slavoj, 2000, 'Why We All Love to Hate Heider', *New Left Review* 2, pp. 37–45.

8

'Stop waving crosses around and making them a symbol of hate': Localized Christian Responses to the Populist Radical Right in the UK

WILLIAM ALLCHORN

At 1.40 pm on 15 March 2019, a far-right terrorist, Brenton Heston Tarrant, approached the Al-Noor Mosque in Christchurch, New Zealand. Greeted by a septuagenarian usher at Friday prayers, Tarrant opened fire on worshippers for six minutes. He only stopped to reload and to gather more ammunition and weapons from his car outside before continuing his bloody rampage. Returning to his vehicle at 1.46 pm, the terrorist then drove for seven minutes (6.5 km) across town to the Linwood Islamic Centre, where he began firing through the Centre's windows at worshippers gathering inside (Bostock, Corcoran and Logan, 2019). Challenged by one congregant, Tarrant then fled the scene of his second massacre at 1.56 pm before being arrested at 1.59 pm.

While the use of a manifesto, video livestreaming over the internet and the transnational nature of the attacker's networks set a trend of far-right terrorism in 2019 and 2020,[1] a vital detail remains unique to Christchurch: it is the site of the deadliest far-right terror attacks the world has witnessed in recent years. In total, 51 people were killed and another 50 seriously wounded, with the attacker foiled from targeting a third location and setting fire to the Muslim places of worship (Fattal, 2019). A week after the first anniversary of his shooting spree, Tarrant unexpectedly pleaded guilty to 51 charges of murder, 40 charges of attempted murder, and one charge of terrorism, thereby denying himself a public platform for his views that a trial would provide (*BBC News*, 26 March 2020). Several months later, he was given a sentence of life without parole – the first of its kind in New Zealand (*BBC News*, 27 August 2020).

This attacker used existing tropes (or 'grand narratives') circulating among the online and globally networked far right to justify his actions. Most important of these were the conspiracy theory that became the title of Tarrant's manifesto ('The Great Replacement'); and the use of anti-Muslim ideology that received worldwide attention when, on 22 July 2011, Anders Behring Breivik engaged in a mass shooting spree at a Labour Party summer camp on the island of Utøya, Norway – motivated by his belief in the fable that Europe was becoming a 'Eurabia', aided and abetted by left-wing politicians, and a book of a similar name was released by far-right thinker Renaud Camus.[2] The perpetrator of the 1995 Oklahoma City Bombings Timothy McVeigh (with his accomplice, Terry Lynn Nichols) was similarly inspired by a work of far-right fiction – with a highway patrol officer finding an excerpt from the far-right anti-government polemic, *The Turner Diaries*, in McVeigh's car as he fled the scene (CNN, 28 April 1997).

The events of March 2019, however, started a cumulative (Macklin, 2019) (or what others have called a 'hive' (Koehler, 2018) or 'stochastic' (Hamm and Spaaij, 2017)) effect that would reverberate around the globe in 2019 and early 2020, providing an inspiration for other attacks.[3] From El Paso, to Halle and Hanau, several far-right terror attacks began a new wave of global far-right terrorism embedded in anti-Muslim and anti-foreigner prejudice (Augur, 2020; Weinberg and Eubank, 2015).

Context: Anti-Islamic Protest in the UK – 'Hating Globally, Acting Locally'

Anti-Islamic protest is one pillar of far-right activism that has grown up in the UK over the past ten years.[4] This has been the result of the electoral decline of the neo-fascist British National Party (BNP) and the rise of a broader group of 'new' far-right street movements. In the UK context, two groups are of particular importance: the English Defence League (EDL) and Britain First. The former started in 2009 in response to the picketing of a military homecoming parade in the South Bedfordshire town of Luton. The latter started in 2011 as a website but then quickly spread its activities to the streets in June 2014 onwards – with its Christian patrols, Mosque invasions, protests and marches stoking tensions and jeopardizing community cohesion. Both have moved in the same circles as far-right terrorists and attackers. Anders Behring Breivik, for example, wrote in his 2083 manifesto how he was 'impressed' with the EDL's campaigns against the spread of Islam and Sharia Law in the UK (McDevitt,

25 July 2011). Furthermore, Darren Osborne – a UK far-right terrorist who drove a van into worshippers at the Finsbury Park Mosque in June 2017 – was influenced by the 'drip effect' of Britain First's anti-Muslim activism; both online and in the Rochdale area (Dearden, 2018).

My research involved 58 interviews with a mixture of politicians, police officers and behind-the-scenes officials in five key cases of EDL and Britain First activism: Luton, Leicester, Birmingham, Bradford and Tower Hamlets (Allchorn, 2019). These explored the local drivers of anti-Islamic protest but also tracked the 'what, how and why' of policy-makers' preparations and responses to these protests. I found that localized drivers revolved around high levels of deprivation, the presence of industrial decline, social polarization between religious communities, the current or past presence of extreme right or extreme Islamist groups, and a credibility attached to these groups by marginalized local populations (Allchorn, 2020). As a Christian layperson of the Baptist confession, I found their use of Christian symbols, scripture and faith artefacts to be both worrying and disturbing.

Scholarship, however, on anti-Islamic protest movements has largely focused on questions of Islamophobia, support bases and the trajectory of these groups.[5] Little has been written about how responses – and in particular Christian responses – have dealt with the consequences and impacts of this form of populist radical right protest.[6] In this chapter, I will attempt to address both – outlining how we arrived at this 'new' iteration of the far right (what I and others term as the 'populist radical right' (Mudde, 2007)),[7] the particular 'Christianist' inflection of their discourse and current Christian responses and what these might look like going forward. My argument is that – to stave off the prejudicial and populist (and potentially violent) barbs of these movements – we need to combat polarization, marginalization and religious bias that such groups feed off at the local level in order to foster resilience against the apparently plausible theological logic of the populist radical right.

Origins of the Populist Radical Right: A (Not-So) Silent Backlash?

Where has the populist radical right come from? What are the origins of this particularly aggressive and antagonistic form of politics?

Intellectual origins

The intellectual origins of the far right can be traced to the French New Right (Nouvelle Droite) which emerged in the 1960s. The brainchild of Alain de Benoist and the *Groupement de recherche et d'études pour la civilisation européenne*, the New Right opposed multiculturalism and the mixing of different cultures – seeing this as a form of ethnocide. It sought to influence the cultural climate in the 1970s and went on to inform the ethno-differentialist policies of the Front National, which like the segregationist policies of the US Deep South saw individuals of different ethnic groups as 'separate but equal' (Bar-On, 2013).

Social origins

Second, from the 1980s onwards, the radical right has distinctive social origins in places such as France and Austria. The primary driver of this initial success was what one Italian political scientist, Piero Ignazi, called a silent counter-revolution against left-liberal, postmaterialist values of the 1970s, towards a more socially conservative, xenophobic and strongly authoritarian set of positions along the ideological spectrum in the 1980s (Ignazi, 2003). As mainstream parties began to adopt a left-liberal values consensus, this created a new electoral niche on the right which Ignazi (1992) suggests has been taken up by new right-wing parties – keen to exploit this gap in the electoral market and to prey on anxieties around sociocultural issues concerning race, ethnicity and religion.

Political origins

A third source that has seen the rise of the radical right is what Richard Katz and Peter Mair (1995) have termed the cartelization of party politics in Western democracies. While their analysis is separate from the academic scholarship on the populist radical right, both authors suggest that an increasing focus on the political centre ground and capture of established parties by the state has left more radical options open to exploitation by populist radical-right parties. This centralization in terms of ideology also feeds into the 'elite critique' of the radical right – putting forward the populist notion of a corrupt elite, unrepresentative of the people making decisions against the general will of the population.

Economic origins

A fourth source – which is the usual causal model associated with right-wing extremism – is destabilization of low-skilled labourers by the onset of economic globalization. Scholars such as Ignazi (1992), Betz (1994) and Minkenberg (2003) argue that post-industrial capitalism has led to the creation of a contemporary cross-European equivalent of Germany's middle-class extremists in the 1930s. Unable to keep up with the revolutions in education and technology, the new extreme right 'precariat' is composed of an unskilled, under-educated working class (Betz, 1994, p. 4). '[A]nxious, bewildered, and insecure' (Betz, 1994, p. 33), these individuals become disenchanted with their individual life chances, the direction of societal developments and the political system in general, and look to populist radical-right voices as a means of empowerment and liberation through the blaming of the other.

Christianism and the Populist Radical Right: The Logics of a Cultural Form of Christianity

When exploring how Christianity manifests itself within the populist radical right, it can be suggested that it is a nominal but no less disturbing manipulation of Christianity by these movements, what Strømmen and Schmiedel in *The Claim to Christianity* (2020, p. 44) call Culture Christianity, whereby a golden age can be reclaimed through a return to tradition. More broadly, this can be treated under the umbrella of Christianism,[8] which, according to Rogers Brubaker (2017), denotes 'not a substantive Christianity ... [but] a secularized Christianity as culture ... It's a matter of belonging rather than believing' that appeals to emotive issues around tradition, culture and the nation. It is 'as a distinct, ideological perversion of Christianity' (Feldman, 2021) which weaponizes Christianity for performative, exclusionist ends and strategic political advantage, rather than sincere belief.[9] Here, I suggest that the logics of this cultural form of Christianity work at an ideological, practical and sociological level within the populist radical right.

Ideological logics of Cultural Christianity

At the ideological level, such groups expect an *imminent* clash between the Christian West and the Muslim East. They also entertain conspiracy theories around Eurabia that suggest resident populations are being invaded or replaced by Muslim migrants, what Breivik refers to as 'Islamic Colonization of Europe through demographic warfare' (2011, p. 9). The far right also use Christianity as a device to stress the positives of in-group identity, particularly as a way of promoting themselves as the protectors of tradition. The most seminal example of recent times has been the aforementioned attack by Norwegian radical-right terrorist in Oslo and Utøya in July 2011. Before this lone-wolf attack, Breivik self-published a manifesto entitled, '2083: A European Declaration of Independence', that following a European Civil War there will be a 'third' Muslim expulsion completed in Europe by 2083. In the manifesto, Breivik declares himself to be a supporter of a monocultural Christian Europe and fashions himself as a 'cultural Christian'. Defined by Strømmen and Schmiedel (2020, chapter 3) as an example of what they call Crusader Christianity, Breivik also saw himself as an example of a resurrected order of the medieval Knights Templar, riding out to suffer the glory of Christian martyrdom in the process. In a rather crude way, Breivik uses Christianity and broader crusader rhetoric to justify his slaughter of 76 (mainly non-adult) Norwegians on 22 July 2011 and asks members of a fictional Knights Templar Europe to join him as part of a renewed crusade 'against the ongoing European Jihad' (Breivik, 2011, p. 817).

Practical logics of Cultural Christianity

At a more practical level, the populist radical right uses Christian iconography in its campaigns and rhetoric, mainly as a means of othering Muslim communities. Britain First is a key example of the populist radical right using Christian symbols and rhetoric to further its own form of anti-Muslim extremism. Formed in 2011 using the website 'British Resistance', Britain First was founded by former BNP fundraiser Jim Dowson, and BNP Sevenoaks councillor Paul Golding. As a June 2014 report on the group by anti-fascist collective, Hope not Hate, has suggested, the group distinguishes itself ideologically from the BNP by eschewing 'the scientific racial hatred and ideas of racial supremacy in favour of dire biblical warnings ... in the face of the supposed "Islamification" of Britain' (Hope Not Hate, 2017, p. 5). Looking beyond ideology, however, Britain First is most famous for its direct-action tactics – whether that be invading mosques, driving ex-military Land Rovers down Brick Lane, or conducting 'Christian patrols' in predominantly Muslim areas. Britain First's Jim Dowson is also a Calvinist Scottish priest, anti-abortion activist and founder of the Knights Templar International group.

In Eastern Europe, Viktor Orbàn, the Hungarian Prime Minister, is also a Christian ideologue of the populist radical right. Head of the right-wing populist and national-conservative party Fidesz, Orbàn has been busy dismantling key institutions, building a wall on the border with Serbia and Croatia, and implementing his own form of illiberal 'Christian' democracy. After being re-elected as Prime Minister (133/199 seats) in April 2018, Orbàn put forward his main goal as preserving Hungary's Christian culture and security by enforcing checks on migrant NGOs and a 25 per cent tax on foreign donations. These were largely targeted at Jewish philanthropist and financier George Soros. Again, and like Breivik, this is a 'crusader' form of Christianity that plays on identity politics and is meant to look symbolically tough (or authoritarian) on the issue of migration – at least to his most ardent of followers.

Sociopolitical logics of Cultural Christianity

One of the key paradoxes is that while these groups are increasingly using Christianity to further a type of anti-Muslim populism, they still struggle to attract Christian voters. Although they may be able to attract socially conservative individuals, these individuals are not regular church-goers. Some of the reasons given for the absence of Christians within populist radical-right electorates include the so-called 'vaccination effect' of religiously active voters already being 'firmly attached' to Christian Democratic or conservative parties (Arzheimer and Carter, 2009) but also the 'pro-social' aspects of being part of a church organization – thus, moderating effects of individualism, powerlessness, loneliness and negative feelings towards immigrants through inter-group contact (Billiet, 1995). Generally, Christians – on the whole – tend to conform to the existing social order, which contradicts populist radical-right parties' anti-elite and anti-establishment populist ideologies (Montgomery and Winter, 2015). Although Christians are neither more nor less hostile towards ethnic minorities and thereby neither more nor less prone to vote for a radical-right party, the populism characteristics of populist radical-right parties therefore are less likely to be appreciated by Christians.

This is not to say that regular church attendance has some magical effect on congregants, rather that most Christianists – like Islamists – lie on the fringes and outskirts of mainstream confessions of Christianity, with very limited and superficial regard for the core tenets of their faith (see Wilkinson, 2018, for key distinctions). It also seems that given the increasing de-alignment away from established parties, the 'vaccine effect' is likely to become weaker with time (Arzheimer and Carter, 2009). Just as the parties of the mainstream left can no longer count on a traditional base of working-class voters, Christian Democratic and conservative parties are today faced with fewer religious voters than they once were. Thus, in spite of still being able to 'encapsulate' Christians as their main voting base, this natural reservoir of support is shrinking. All other things being equal, therefore, this points to an increase in the potential of populist radical-right parties as European societies become more secularized (Arzheimer and Carter, 2009, p. 1005).

Christian Responses to Anti-Islamic Protest in the UK: The Examples of Tower Hamlets and Luton

Turning to Christian responses to this phenomenon in the UK, I will suggest examples of attempts to foster resilience towards the populist radical right. While my research has largely explored localized responses by police, politicians and behind-the-scenes officials in five UK locations, I have also interviewed two clergymen who have taken it upon themselves to challenge these groups but also engage in exercises of consolidation. As pointed out by Strømmen and Schmiedel (2020, chapter 6) these two phenotypes – challenge and consolidation – provide us with a roadmap for how the Church can respond to the Christianism in its midst.

Examples of Christian responses: 1 Tower Hamlets

Tower Hamlets has been the centre of far-right activity since the early twentieth century. From Mosley's Blackshirts in the 1930s, to the BNP in the 1990s, and the EDL and Britain First post-2010, there have been significant waves of far-right and populist radical-right activism in the East End of London. Less well known is the significant role of the local church in combating these groups. For example, in the 1930s at Christ Church Watney Street in the East End of London, its vicar, the Reverend John Grosner, became what historian Tom Lawson called one of 'the most famous Christian opponents of fascism' (Lawson, 2010). Grosner could be seen marching ahead of anti-fascist demonstrations with a crucifix and other Christian symbols when the British Union of Fascists came in 1936, as well as speaking out against fascist propaganda in his Watney Street Parish. Furthermore, Grosner was on the frontline remonstrating with police who wouldn't allow him to confront fascist propagandists directly (i.e. Mosley's Blackshirts).

Another example from Tower Hamlets and the East End of London came again in the 1990s with those resisting the re-election of BNP councillor Derek Beackon in 1994 in the Millwall ward of the Isle of Dogs. It was significant here that efforts by established anti-fascist movements, such as Anti-Fascist Action and Anti-Nazi League, had failed (Copsey, 2017, chapter 5). Instead, churches assisted in a practical and straightforward manner. They set about helping the main parties translate their electoral literature for the Bangladeshi minority in the area, aided housebound voters to register for postal votes and organized minibuses to transport voters to polling stations on Election Day (Copsey, 2017, chapter 5). In a more religious mode, they also provided a public witness of their faith, with the local Catholic church of St Edmunds hosting Bible readings every half-hour and Anglican Christ Church holding a prayer vigil on polling day. The effect of this dual-pronged strategy was devastating for the BNP. The BNP made no gains and Derek Beackon lost his seat (Copsey, 2017, chapter 5).

Britain First came to Tower Hamlets on five occasions between 2014 and 2016 to perform Christian Patrols and 'invade' the East London Mosque. One key figure of Britain First's sustained attempts to intimidate and sometimes provoke the local Muslim community into reaction for the group, and later film, was Anglican priest of St John on Bethnal Green, the Reverend Alan Green. When the group initially came to the borough in February 2014, Green appeared in the local media to suggest Britain First did not 'represent' the local community and weren't 'welcome here' (RT, 12 February 2014). Moreover, when Britain First appeared outside of the East London Mosque, Green mediated between them and an angry crowd of Muslim worshippers assembling in opposition to the group – demanding that they should 'stop waving crosses around and making them a symbol of hate'. According to Green, this caused him 'a lot of grief' with Britain First, who did a lot to attack him on the internet and social media (Green, 24 May 2017). Unperturbed, he publicly condemned the group's final demonstration outside the East London Mosque, stating that: 'They seek to incite a violent reaction to justify their Islamophobia. Until this incitement is prevented by legal means it is vital that the whole community stands together peacefully' (Enfield, 2016). Unfortunately, violence did occur on that day when a fight broke out between Britain First activists and local youths – with one flying kick delivered to a Britain First supporter making the national newspapers (Flynn, 2016). None the less, returning to Strømmen and Schmiedel's (2020) terminology of the 'Challenge' phenotype, this story does show powerfully how some clergy have attempted to fight back at the misappropriation of Christian symbols by far-right groups.

Examples of Christian responses: 2 Luton

Luton, just north of London, does not have such a storied history of far-right extremism and populist radical-right activism but is salutary for its Christian responses towards this more recent anti-Muslim populist brand of street protest. Apart from hat-making, its automotive industry and the airport, the town has now become indelibly linked with the EDL which emerged in June 2009, and its leader Tommy Robinson. After this, it had two of the group's largest protests in 2011 and 2012, attracting over 2,000 supporters from all over the UK to the doorstep of the East Bedfordshire town in the former instance (Adams, 7 June 2017). More recently, Britain First has protested there, organizing a mosque invasion, a march, and a Christian patrol in the space of two years.

One of the leading organizations involved in the community's response to these two groups has been St Mary's Church. In particular, interfaith worker and Christian Peter Adams has created cross-community solidarity in the face of these protests through their Centre for Peace and Reconciliation. Rather unusually, Peter has also taken it upon himself to meet with leaders of the EDL and Britain First in a conciliatory manner. For example, in the early period of the EDL's emergence, he built relationships with Tommy Robinson and his cousin Kevin Carroll. He asked them about their problems and why they were organizing this movement as well as talking to those on the fringes of the movement. The idea was not simply to oppose, but rather to listen to their concerns in a non-judgemental way (Adams, 7 June 2017).

When Britain First came for its main protest in 2015, Adams also met with the (then) leaders of Britain First, Paul Golding and Jayda Fransen, to (again) try and understand their concerns and stop their demonstration plans. This second meeting, which lasted two hours, tried to flesh out their concerns (Adams, 7 June 2017). He also explained that local Christians were engaged in such dialogue to demonstrate their opposition to anything that divided the community (Adams, 7 June 2017). Unsurprisingly, Britain First's leadership did not make many concessions, and they subsequently went to one of the mosques and staged the protest. As a response to this, when the group came the following February Adams handed out flowers to the local community as a sign of peace (*Luton Today*, 2016).

Compared to Tower Hamlets, then, Luton has shown a more conciliatory form of Christian anti-fascism – trying to engage in dialogue with these groups as a way of de-escalating their concerns and disrupting their plans. On top of this there has been an emphasis of working across different faith communities to reduce the inevitable tensions caused by these protests – baking in expressions of resilience before anti-Muslim activism rears its ugly head.

Conclusion: Towards a Christian Response to the Populist Radical Right

In conclusion, this chapter has surveyed how the populist radical right has risen, what can be said of its engagement with Christianity, and how Christians have responded to it in the UK at the local level. It has identified the key ideological, practical and sociopolitical logics to the populist radical right's engagement with Christianity (what Strømmen and Schmiedel, 2020, call 'Culture Christianity'). This examination also unearthed that their theological interpretation was one of tradition, culture and the nation. It also found that its logics (of othering the East) were positioned to eliminate the Muslim 'other' by violent means (what Strømmen and Schmiedel, 2020, chapter 3) call 'Crusader Christianity'). Moreover, in the case studies, we find that the most common phenotype of response in the UK Church locally tends towards a challenger role rather than a consolidation one (again see Strømmen and Schmiedel, 2020, chapter 6).

Though in the Luton case this consolidatory phenotype has recently become more pronounced, we can also see the challenger response phenotype occupying the main centre of gravity when it comes to Christian responses in the UK nationally. Taking the broader Christian community together, some of the most effective recent responses have been seen when denominations have actively debunked or disrupted the Christianist narratives of the populist radical right. In January 2016, for example, every major Christian denomination in the UK condemned Britain First's so-called 'Christian Patrols' as 'hi-jacking the name of Jesus Christ to justify hatred and spread fear' (York, 2016). Moreover, a similar joint condemnation was served at the 2009 European Elections when the BNP used Christian imagery in response to a ban on clergy joining the party – stating that 'The Christian vision of society is one where each person is treated with dignity and respect, whatever their race or religion. It is a vision of hope. The Christian churches are totally opposed to the BNP' (Ashworth, 2009).

That being said, at the level of the local church, there is scope for us to improve the consolidatory response as a way of boosting resilience to the entreaties of the populist radical right. For example, we can see how, through greater cross-community dialogue and the sharing of the same spaces and places with Muslims, migrants and other religious allies, the prejudicial barbs of radical-right populism can be prevented through greater inter-community contact (Pettigrew, 1998; Allport, 1954). At the lowest common denominator, it also means looking at ourselves as followers of Christ and combating the temptations of populist identity politics – of a 'persecuted' or 'victimized' mindset versus other faith communities – from within; this can be done through a greater familiarity with members and the overlapping theological tenets of other faith communities in the UK and their own particular struggles.

Looking beyond the UK and these case studies, then, what can Christians do to respond to the populist radical right in their midst? One broad approach best suited to engaging with the current *Zeitgeist* could be termed a holistic form of Christian anti-fascism that is informed by the drivers of the populist radical right and seeks to avoid tapping into its narratives, particularly on identity politics. This resonates with a distinction made by scholars of anti-fascism between liberal versus militant approaches (Copsey, 2017, introduction). Under this distinction, the former approach takes a more indirect or legal approach that seeks to undermine the presence of the far right through understanding its drivers, versus more militant forms that take a more confrontational, direct-action approach of attacking the far right – usually on the streets. It also adjoins with Strømmen and Schmiedel's (2020, p. 14) consolidatory phenotype and their call for non-neutrality when standing up for those affected by the far right (i.e. 'the other' as instructed in the parable of the Good Samaritan, Luke 10.25–37) and Christian duty towards the least, the last and the lost (Matt. 20.16; Matt. 25.40; Matt. 18.11).

Notes

1 See the following: G. Macklin, 2019, 'The Christchurch Attacks: Livestream Terror in the Viral Video Age', *CTC Sentinel* 12(6), July, https://ctc.usma.edu/christchurch-attacks-livestream-terror-viral-video-age/ (accessed 5.4.24); G. Macklin, 2019, 'The El Paso Terrorist Attack: The Chain Reaction of Global Right-wing Terror', *CTC Sentinel* 12(11), December, https://ctc.usma.edu/el-paso-terrorist-attack-chain-reaction-global-right-wing-terror/ (accessed 5.4.24).

2 Such conspiracy theories have become staples of what some scholars have termed as the culturally nationalist end of the contemporary far right, which depict 'Muslim culture as backward and repressive' (Bjørgo and Ravndal, 2019, p. 3) and cleave to the radical-right element of the broader far-right galaxy which calls for the maintaining of democracy but also petition for the replacement of liberal elites who are seen as part of 'a conspiracy to "Islamise" Europe through the stealthy

implementation of Islamic Sharia [and Islamist government]' (Meleagrou-Hitchens and Brun, 2013, p. 1).

3 For an in-depth look at the enabling factors and trigger events of modern-day terrorism, see M. S. Hamm and R. Spaaij, *The Age of Lone-Wolf Terrorism*, New York: Columbia University Press, chapters 5 and 7.

4 Here, 'anti-Islamic' is used to describe the EDL and Britain First's particular form of protest. This is a slightly altered version of Pilkington's, 2016, 'anti-Islamist' characterization of the EDL and aims at the groups' main area of grievance: not just radical Islam or 'Islamism', but the beliefs, tenets and theology of Islam itself.

5 For some early examples, see D. Alessio and K. Meredith, 2014, 'Blackshirts for the Twenty-first Century? Fascism and the English Defence League', *Social Identities* 20(1), pp. 104–18; C. Allen, 2011, 'Opposing Islamification or Promoting Islamophobia? Understanding the English Defence League', *Patterns of Prejudice* 45(4), pp. 279–94; C. Allen, 2014, 'Britain First: The "Frontline Resistance" to the Islamification of Britain', *Political Quarterly* 85(3), pp. 354–61; J. Bartlett and M. Littler, 2011, 'Inside the EDL: Populist Politics in a Digital Age', London: Demos; J. Busher, 2015, *The Making of Anti-Muslim Protest: Grassroots Activism in the English Defence League*, London: Routledge; A. Brindle and C. MacMillan, 2017, 'Like & Share if You Agree: A Study of Discourses and Cyber-activism of the Far Right British Nationalist Party Britain First', *Journal of Language Aggression and Conflict* 5(1), pp. 108–33; N. Copsey, 2010, *The English Defence League: Challenging Our Country and Our Values of Social Inclusion, Fairness, and Equality*, London: Faith Matters; J. Garland and J. Treadwell, 2010, '"No Surrender to the Taliban": Football Hooliganism, Islamophobia and the Rise of the English Defence League', Conference Paper for the British Criminological Society, vol. 10, pp. 19–35; P. Jackson, 2011, 'The EDL: Britain's "New Far-right Social Movement"', Northampton: Radicalism and New Media Group; G. Kassimeris and L. Jackson, 2015, 'The Ideology and Discourse of the English Defence League: "Not Racist, Not Violent, Just No Longer Silent"', *British Journal of Politics and International Relations* 17(1), pp. 171–88.

6 For some examples, see: W. Allchorn, 2018, *Anti-Islamic Protest in the UK: Policy Responses to the Far Right*, London: Routledge; L. E. Berntzen and M. Weisskircher, 2016, 'Anti-Islamic PEGIDA Beyond Germany: Explaining Differences in Mobilization', *Journal of Intercultural Studies* 37(6), pp. 556–73; A.-S. Heinze, and M. Weisskircher, 2022, 'How Political Parties Respond to Pariah Street Protest: The Case of Anti-Corona Mobilization in Germany', *German Politics*, doi: 10.1080/09644008.2022.2042518 (accessed 5.4.24).

7 Here, the 'populist radical right' is defined as a particularly nativist, authoritarian and populist form of politics that divides society into a native in-group and out-group, appeals towards strong authoritarian leadership and policy solutions, and divides politics between the 'pure' people and a self-serving 'corrupt' political class (Mudde, 2007).

8 The term was coined by Matthew Feldman in 2011, see: https://www.independent.co.uk/voices/commentators/dr-matthew-feldman-slaughter-was-killer-s-appetiser-it-is-the-trial-that-is-his-main-course-2325910.html (accessed 7.8.24).

9 For more on the far right's strategic use of exterior belief systems, see W. Allchorn, 2020, 'Free Speech Defenses and the Far Right: The Cases of Tommy Robinson, Geert Wilders and Milo Yiannopoulos', *EuropeNow*, January.

References

Adams, P., 7 June 2017, interview with author, telephone, Leeds.
Allchorn, W., 2019, *Anti-Islamic Protest in the UK: Policy Responses to the Far Right*, London: Routledge.
Allchorn, W., 2020, 'Political Responses to Anti-Islamic Protest: Responses, Rationales and Role Evaluations', *British Politics* 15, pp. 393–410, https://doi.org/10.1057/s41293-019-00127-2 (accessed 5.4.24).
Allport, G., 1954, *The Nature of Prejudice*, New York: Basic Books.
Arzheimer, K. and E. Carter, 2009, 'Christian Religiosity and Voting for West European Radical Right Parties', *West European Politics* 32(5), pp. 985–1011, doi: 10.1080/01402380903065058 (accessed 5.4.24).
Ashworth, P., 2009, 'BNP Puts Jesus on its Poster', *The Church Times*, 1 April, https://www.churchtimes.co.uk/articles/2009/3-april/news/uk/bnp-puts-jesus-on-its-poster (accessed 5.4.24).
Augur, V. A., 2020, 'Right-wing Terror: A Fifth Global Wave?', *Perspectives on Terrorism* 14(3), June, pp. 87–97, https://www.universiteitleiden.nl/binaries/content/assets/customsites/perspectives-on-terrorism/2020/issue-3/auger.pdf (accessed 5.4.24).
Bar-On, T., 2013, *Rethinking the French New Right: Alternatives to Modernity*, London: Routledge.
BBC News, 26 March 2020, 'Christchurch Shootings: Brenton Tarrant Pleads Guilty to 51 Murders', https://www.bbc.co.uk/news/world-asia-52044013 (accessed 5.4.24).
BBC News, 27 August 2020, 'Christchurch Mosque Attack: Brenton Tarrant Sentenced to Life without Parole', https://www.bbc.co.uk/news/world-asia-53919624 (accessed 5.4.24).
Betz, H.-G., 1994, *Radical Right-wing Populism in Western Europe*, London: Palgrave Macmillan.
Billiet, J., 1995, 'Church Involvement, Ethnocentrism, and Voting for a Radical Right-wing Party: Diverging Behavioral Outcomes of Equal Attitudinal Dispositions', *Sociology of Religion* 56(3), pp. 303–26, https://doi.org/10.2307/3711825 (accessed 5.4.24).
Bjørgo, T. and J. A. Ravndal, 2019, 'Extreme-right Violence and Terrorism: Concepts, Patterns, and Responses', The Hague: International Centre for Counter-Terrorism, https://icct.nl/publication/extreme-right-violence-and-terrorism-concepts-patterns-and-responses (accessed 15.5.24).
Bostock, B., K. Corcoran and B. Logan, 2019, 'This Timeline of the Christchurch Mosque Terror Attacks Shows how New Zealand's Deadliest Shooting Unfolded', *Insider*, 19 March, https://www.insider.com/christchurch-shooting-timeline-49-killed-new-zealand-mosques-2019-3 (accessed 5.4.24).
Breivik, Anders, 2011, '2083 – A European Declaration of Independence' (no longer online).
Brubaker, R., 2016, 'A new "Christianist" Secularism in Europe', The Immanent Frame: Secularism, Religion and the Public Sphere, *Social Science Research Council*, https://tif.ssrc.org/2016/10/11/a-new-christianist-secularism-in-europe/ (accessed 5.4.24).
CNN, 28 April 1997, '"Turner Diaries" Introduced in McVeigh Trial', http://edition.cnn.com/US/9704/28/okc/ (accessed 5.4.24).

Copsey, N., 2017, *Anti-Fascism in Britain*, 2nd edn, London: Palgrave Macmillan.

Dearden, L., 2018, 'Finsbury Park Attacker Turned Violent by Far-right Posts from Tommy Robinson and Britain First, Police Say', *The Independent*, 26 February, https://www.independent.co.uk/news/uk/crime/finsbury-park-terror-attack-tommy-robinson-far-right-britain-first-mark-rowley-speech-police-a8229936.html (accessed 5.4.24).

Enfield, L., 2016, 'Two Men Arrested in Connection with Alleged Attacks at the East London Mosque', *The Wharf*, 20 April, http://www.wharf.co.uk/news/local-news/two-men-arrested-connection-alleged-11217266 (accessed 5.4.24).

Fattal, I., 2019, 'New Zealand Went More Than 20 Years Between Mass Shootings', *The Atlantic*, 15 March, https://www.theatlantic.com/politics/archive/2019/03/new-zealands-history-mass-shootings-christchurch/585052/ (accessed 5.4.24).

Feldman, M., 2021, 'Christianism: The Elephant in the Extremism Room', *Fair Observer*, 1 July, https://www.fairobserver.com/politics/matthew-feldman-religious-extremism-christianity-history-violence-christianism-news-37281/ (accessed 5.4.24).

Flynn, E., 2016, 'Britain First Demonstrator is Booted with Flying Kick after Right-wing Mob Provokes Muslims outside mosque', *The Sun*, 12 April, https://www.thesun.co.uk/archives/news/1124975/britain-first-demonstrator-is-booted-with-flying-kick-after-right-wing-mob-provokes-muslims-outside-mosque/ (accessed 5.4.24).

Green, A., 24 May 2017, interview with author, telephone, Leeds.

Hamm, M. S. and R. Spaaij, 2017, *The Age of Lone Wolf Terrorism*, New York: Columbia University Press.

Hope Not Hate, 2017, 'Britain First: Army of the Right', https://hopenothate.org.uk/wp-content/uploads/2017/11/Britain-First-Army-of-the-Right.pdf (accessed 5.4.24).

Ignazi, P., 1992, 'The Silent Counter-Revolution: Hypotheses on the Emergence of Extreme Right-wing Parties in Europe', *European Journal of Political Research* 22(1), pp. 3–34, https://doi.org/10.1111/j.1475-6765.1992.tb00303.x (accessed 5.4.24).

Ignazi, P., 2003, *Extreme Right Parties in Western Europe*, Oxford: Oxford University Press.

Katz, R. S. and P. Mair, 1995, 'Changing Models of Party Organization and Party Democracy: The Emergence of the Cartel Party', *Party Politics* 1(1), pp. 5–28, https://doi.org/10.1177/1354068895001001001 (accessed 5.4.24).

Koehler, D., 2018, 'Recent Trends in German Right-wing Violence and Terrorism: What Are the Contextual Factors behind "Hive Terrorism"?', *Perspectives on Terrorism* 12(6), pp. 72–88, https://www.jstor.org/stable/26544644 (accessed 5.4.24).

Lawson, T., 2010, '"I was Following the Lead of Jesus Christ": Christian Anti-Fascism in 1930s England', in N. Copsey and A. Olechnowicz (eds), *Varieties of Anti-Fascism*, London: Palgrave Macmillan, London.

Luton Today, 2016, 'Exclusive: Britain First Planning Return to Luton after Controversial "Christian patrol"', 27 January, https://www.lutontoday.co.uk/news/politics/exclusive-britain-first-planning-return-to-luton-after-controversial-christian-patrol-1274156 (accessed 5.4.24).

Macklin, G., 2019, 'The El Paso Terrorist Attack: The Chain Reaction of Global

Right-wing Terror', *CTC Sentinel* 12(11), December, online at: https://ctc.usma.edu/el-paso-terrorist-attack-chain-reaction-global-right-wing-terror/ (accessed 5.4.24).

McDevitt, J., 25 July 2011, 'EDL Influence over Breivik-linked Group Revealed', *Channel 4 News*, https://www.channel4.com/news/edls-connections-with-breiviks-norwegian-cell (accessed 5.4.24).

Meleagrou-Hitchens, A. Y. and H. M. Brun, 2013, 'A Neo-Nationalist Network: The English Defence League and Europe's Counter-Jihad Movement', London: International Centre for the Study of Radicalisation, https://kclpure.kcl.ac.uk/portal/en/publications/a-neo-nationalist-network-the-english-defence-league-and-europes- (accessed 15.5.24).

Minkenberg, M., 2003, 'The West European Radical Right as a Collective Actor: Modelling the Impact of Cultural and Structural Variables on Party Formation and Movement Mobilization', *Comparative European Politics* 1, pp. 149–70, https://doi.org/10.1057/palgrave.cep.6110017 (accessed 5.4.24).

Montgomery, K. A. and R. Winter, 2015, 'Explaining the Religion Gap in Support for Radical Right Parties in Europe', *Politics and Religion* 8(2), pp. 379–403.

Mudde, C., 2007, *Populist Radical Right in Europe*, Cambridge: Cambridge University Press.

Pettigrew, T. F., 1998, 'Intergroup Contact Theory', *Annual Review of Psychology* 49(1), pp. 65–85.

RT, 12 February 2014, 'MP Condemns "Christian Patrols" in London's East End', https://www.rt.com/news/muslim-christian-uk-patrol-734/ (accessed 5.4.24).

Strømmen, H. and U. Schmiedel, 2020, *The Claim to Christianity: Responding to the Far Right*, London: SCM Press.

Weinberg, L. and W. Eubank, 2015, 'An End to the Fourth Wave of Terrorism?', *Studies in Conflict and Terrorism* 33(7), pp. 594–602, doi: 10.1080/1057610X.2010.483757 (accessed 5.4.24).

Wilkinson, M., 2018, *The Genealogy of Terror: How to Distinguish between Islam, Islamism and Islamist Extremism*, London: Routledge.

York, C., 2016, 'Britain First Denounced by Every Major Christian Denomination in the UK', *Huffington Post UK*, 30 January, https://www.huffingtonpost.co.uk/2016/01/29/britain-first-denounced-every-christian-group_n_9111138.html (accessed 5.4.24).

9

Probing Challenges and Chances in UK Politics: A Response to James Crossley and William Allchorn

HANNAH STRØMMEN AND ULRICH SCHMIEDEL

In their responses to *The Claim to Christianity* in Chapters 7 and 8 of this volume, James Crossley and William Allchorn provide fascinating insights from the context of the UK. These insights allow us to zoom in on problems and possibilities in politics that we grappled with in our book, even though we could from time to time only gesture towards them. Taken together, they showcase the potential of Christian communities to counter hidden and not-so-hidden racism, stressing the challenge of concentrating on extreme examples that blindside us from more mainstream manifestations of racism. In what follows, we would like to focus on this political potential of Christian communities.

Allchorn presents cases of Christian activism that we haven't covered in *The Claim to Christianity*. While our focus was on statements of churches that allowed for cross-church and cross-country comparisons, we agree with Allchorn that it's crucial to highlight such activism in order to show how solidarity has been practised between Christians and non-Christians. In emphasizing the claims to Christianity that are exclusive, we might miss the prophetic power that religions have. As scholars of religion Atalia Omer and Joshua Lupo point out in their account of 'The Cultural Logic of White Nationalisms', we all too easily lose sight of subversive solidarities (Omer and Lupo, 2023, pp. 2–3).

The Bible is a case in point. It has been taken up in ways that confirm and in ways that challenge the racisms that were seen as justifying colonialism throughout Euromerican history. Uses of the Bible underscore how Christianity is lived out. Perhaps the most illustrative and the most instructive examples of such conflicting usages of scripture come from the campaigns regarding slavery. In the British West Indies, a special abridged Bible was produced, called *Parts of the Holy Bible, Selected for the Use of the Negro Slaves, in the British West-India Islands*. In this version, which became known as the 'Slavery Bible', parts of the Bible that might prompt resistance and rebellion were removed.[1] Other tactics involved leaving the Christian canon of scripture intact but certain passages were emphasized. The exhortation for slaves to obey their masters (Eph. 6.5; Col. 3.22) was one way for slave-owners to justify their actions. Frederick Douglass, a leading abolitionist in the USA, learnt to read through exposure to biblical texts when he was a slave, despite the fact that his master forbade him from accessing the Bible. Douglass gathered pages of a Bible from the gutter (Stuckey, 2000, pp. 251–65). He claimed the Bible back, turning its texts against those who assumed authority over who is and who isn't allowed to read them.

Of course, we don't have to turn to slavery to see examples of conflicting Bible-use. As we will discuss in our response to Nick Spencer and Chris Wilson, Spencer's *The Political Samaritan* demonstrates the uses to which the parable of the Good Samaritan (Luke 10.25–37) has been put in the politics of the United Kingdom (Spencer, 2018). We return and refer to this parable throughout *The Claim to Christianity*. Our point is not so much that the Bible contains a variety of texts that can be read in different and diverse ways. Rather, our point is that uses of the Bible are at the core of the 'semantic struggle' over Christianity that we already wrote about in our response to Steinar Ims and Henrik Frykberg. In *The Claim to Christianity*, we emphasized this struggle as something that is both urgent and usual (Strømmen and Schmiedel, 2020, pp. 1–14, 146–60). Everybody who identifies as a Christian contributes to the semantic struggle for what Christianity means, consciously or unconsciously. Hence, we could not be happier to learn from the examples Allchorn explores in his response.

Drawing on extensive fieldwork, Allchorn highlights examples from Tower Hamlets, in the East End of London, ranging from the 1930s, when the Reverend John Grosner rallied against the British Union of Fascists, to the 2000s, when the Reverend Alan Green rallied against Britain First. North of London, in the town of Luton, Allchorn points to Peter Adams's work in combating the English Defence League (EDL) and Britain First through his Christian activism, and also by attempting to engage in dialogue with them. Allchorn shows where these responses resonate with the strategies of the 'consolidating church' and the 'challenging church' that we outlined in *The Claim to Christianity* (Strømmen and Schmiedel, 2020, pp. 92–117). He underscores our suggestion that these strategies mustn't be seen as mutually exclusive. There is a lot of mixing and matching going on.

Taking up a suggestion that Helen Paynter made in our conversations, Crossley adds to Allchorn's point about anti-racist activism, proposing that Christian churches have experience and expertise in community-work that is hard to find elsewhere. Churches can be harnessed as 'hubs of community support' to address both racist politics and the roots of racist politics (Crossley, Chapter 7 in this volume). Frykberg's account of community organizing against the far right in Sweden is a case in point (Frykberg, Chapter 2 in this volume). According to Crossley, churches can also be spaces for practising a Christianity that connects to a patriotism that is inclusive rather than exclusive. Whether strategic or spontaneous, such practices might not be headline-grabbing in the way far-right acts of terrorism are, which is enough of a reason to put a spotlight on them. Shifting the attention to cases of successful solidarity in anti-racist campaigns is vital but should not come instead of the difficult work of exposing the features, forms and functions of racism. This work of exposure, as philosopher George Yancy (2012) has argued, is necessary before questions about how to move forward can be asked or answered. Understanding the embeddedness and the effects of racism is essential in order to begin thinking about the challenges involved in countering it (Yancy, 2012, p. 158).

While adding to our own analysis with examples of 'Culture Christianity' and 'Crusader Christianity' (Strømmen and Schmiedel, 2020, pp. 40–6, 46–50), Allchorn seems to shy away from suggestions that far-right claims to Christianity could *in fact* be Christian. He draws on scholarship that describes and defines Christians 'generally' or 'on the whole' as less attracted to the far right (Allchorn, Chapter 8 in this volume). Of course, as we also pointed out, many Christians will not recognize their faith in the claims to Christianity we identified in the margins and the mainstream of contemporary far-right politics. It's crucial for Christians to make clear that a Christianity that is claimed to conjure up hate and hate crimes is not Christianity.

We were, however, motivated to push back against arguments that have sought to draw a strong and stable distinction between a Christianity that is presumed to be honest (revolving around authentic 'believing') and a Christianity that is presumed to be hijacked (revolving around inauthentic 'belonging'). Sociologist Rogers Brubaker comes up with such a distinction in his very influential conceptualization of Christianism that Allchorn cites (Brubaker, 2017).[2] Brubaker introduces 'Christianism' to make sense of the references to religion in populist politics, particularly in Europe. He suggests that these references have very little to do with a return of religion into politics. On the contrary, Brubaker stresses that the

Christianity that is referenced by populist politicians is 'not a substantive Christianity', as he puts it (Brubaker, 2017, p. 1199). Here the distinction between a substantive Christianity and a nonsubstantive Christianity emerges, a 'Christianity' and a 'Christianism'. Crucially, the terms that make up Brubaker's distinction are neither properly defined nor properly described. But one can get at them by looking at the way Brubaker draws the distinction.

'Christianism' captures 'secularized' references to the Christian faith that see Christianity as a 'culture' or a 'civilization' (rather than a religion), by emphasizing 'belonging rather than believing' in an 'identitarian' way (Brubaker, 2017, p. 1199). There is no 'practice of worship' since Christianity is not an end in itself but a means to an end (Brubaker, 2017, p. 1199). 'Christianity', by contrast, captures non-secularized references to the Christian faith that see Christianity as a religion (rather than a culture or a civilization), by emphasizing believing rather than belonging in a non-identitarian way. There is a practice of worship since Christianity is not a means to an end, but an end in itself. Christianism is non-doctrinal, non-organizational and without ritual, while Christianity is doctrinal, organizational and with ritual (Brubaker, 2017, p. 1199). Brubaker's contrast is crystal clear: Christianism means style over substance. Although Brubaker offers no explicit evaluation of Christianism in contrast to Christianity, it's almost impossible to avoid the conclusion that he takes Christianism to be inauthentic rather than authentic – hijacked rather than honest.

However, the contrast between honest Christianity and hijacked Christianity that Brubaker constructs is so pure that scholars who work with it will be hard-pressed to find any Christians at all. If all those who reference Christianity in a secularized, non-doctrinal and non-organizational way without ritual are 'Christianists', then who is *not* (at least from time to time) a Christianist? In the Europe that Brubaker writes about as 'the most secularized region on earth' with 'about 5 per cent' worship attendance (Brubaker, 2017, p. 1199), how many people can be considered Christians according to Brubaker's standard? Would it be 3 per cent, 2 per cent or 1 per cent? The Christianity that Brubaker constructs is too nice and too neat to be convincing. As we contend in *The Claim to Christianity*, taking such a construct of Christianity as a lens to study how far-right protesters and far-right politicians lay claim to Christianity is problematic for a variety of reasons.

One reason is historical. In our book, we were keen to push back against arguments that seek to distinguish between legitimate and illegitimate Christians. Christianity has a track record of internal and external violence that makes it difficult to assume that Christianity always already stands on the side of justice. There are many cases in which Christians cut across categories of believing and belonging. Take the example of Martin Luther. When Luther raged against 'the Jews' and 'the Turks' (Miller, 2014),[3] was he a Christian or was he a Christianist? Even the appeal to 'Christians generally' – the majority or perhaps the silent majority of Christianity – that Allchorn cites is tricky. Who are 'Christians generally'? Is it about numbers? Numbers inside Euramerica or outside Euramerica? Are we speaking about the past or the present? How do we capture the continuities that run throughout the history of Christianity? Who has been authorized to define what counts as continuity or as discontinuity? Given that Christianity's history of violence has gone hand in hand with the enforcement of authority over who does, and who doesn't, count as a Christian, we want to caution against taking any such claim for granted.

Another reason why we pushed back was sociological. To return to the US examples of racist and anti-racist campaigns, proponents of the Ku Klux Klan are likely to consider *their* interpretation of Christianity authentic, while opponents of the Ku Klux Klan are likely to consider *their* interpretation of Christianity authentic.[4] Of course, we would say that Christianity is found among civil rights leaders, such as Fannie Lou Hamer who sang parts of the Bible in her campaigning.[5] Yet we still stress the ambiguity of Christianity because it is easy to act as if we all know what we are talking about when we talk about Christianity. The 'we' buckles under the weight of the assumptions that are loaded on to it.

While Allchorn is careful 'not to say that regular church attendance has some magical effect on congregants' that saves them from the far right, he draws on 'church attendance' and 'regular church attendance' as a criterion to distinguish between Christians and Christianists (Allchorn, Chapter 8 in this volume). To be sure, church attendance can be a helpful criterion. However, it is not enough to get rid of the ambiguity of Christianity. Which church are we talking about attending? The church of the proponents of the Klan or the church of the opponents of the Klan? What does or doesn't count as attendance? Does one have to be there every Sunday? And even if one is there every Sunday, what does one have to do for one's attendance to count? If one's mind wanders during the sermon, is one still attending?[6]

This brings us to theology. A reason we cautioned against the distinction between honest and hijacked Christianity in our book is that theology has to grapple with its own diversity. It may be offensive to many Christians that Britain First cites the Bible alongside conspiracies about the 'great replacement' on Telegram.[7] However, in many churches, the idea that the Bible is a collection of texts that everyone can read and relate to is celebrated. The fact that there is a diversity of theologies that we have to acknowledge and address when making claims about what does or what doesn't count as Christianity is not the same as saying 'anything goes'. Quite the contrary. As theologian Jan Niklas Collet argues, the question ought to be: which tropes and which themes from the history of theology do far-right movements promote and propagate? According to Collet, scholarship that asks such questions cannot but scrutinize assumptions about 'theological and ecclesiological normality' (Collet, 2021, p. 182, our trans.).

Theologically, the fact that Christianity can neither be fixed nor frozen is not a shortcoming but a strength in response to the far right because it opens Christianity up to the other. As we stressed in our response to Henrik Frykberg and Steinar Ims, as well as to Shenaz Bunglawala and Martin Accad, openness is about a porous 'we' that claims Christianity. If the God whose call Christians claim to hear and heed is greater than the theologies that they come up with to think and talk about this God, then the 'we' has to be porous. Christianity is open and open-ended.

Since we concentrate on theology in the response to Nick Spencer and Chris Wilson (Chapters 10 and 11 in this volume), we would like to move on by adding one more reason here – a strategic one. It is not clear what shapes Christianity might or might not take in the future. The semantic struggle for Christianity is indeed a struggle. It's possible to imagine scenarios in which the far right succeeds in laying claim to Christianity in a way that is supported by many or even most Christians. As we suggested in *The Claim to Christianity*, the future of Christianity is open. This has to do with history, sociology and theology. If Christianity is a lived and living religion, embodied and embedded in people's day-to-day lives, then it also depends on us. Allchorn's analysis of Christians who have fought racist politics is crucial because it helps to imagine a scenario in which Christianity stands up against the hate of the far right.

Turning up on streets and in squares to stand in solidarity with Muslims against Islamophobic movements is key. However, here Crossley's caution against the dangers of falling into thinking of *the* far right as *the* problem comes in. This is not a cop-out or complacency in the face of far-right radicalization. It is, however, a crucial corrective to the tendency – as Crossley so effectively shows – to love to hate the far right. If the far right is invoked as a demon to be exorcised from contemporary society, there is a risk of making racisms, such as Islamophobia, invisible during this exorcism. Because of this risk, we chose to study a variety of actors – reaching from perpetrators through protesters to parliamentarians – in

The Claim to Christianity. Drawing on Sturla Stålsett's insight about the 'stealth normalization' of Islamophobia in Europe (Stålsett, 2019), we signalled that it is no accident that Islamophobia spills over from the margins to the mainstream (Strømmen and Schmiedel, 2020, pp. 60–1). On the contrary, the spill-over is rooted in attitudes about Islam that are apparent on the political right as well as the political left, the 'respectable racism' that Bunglawala writes about (Bunglawala, Chapter 5 in this volume). Crossley's questions, then, are apt: 'Is far-right thinking symptomatic of a broader trend? Is the far-right version of this idea of a clash of civilizations a rhetorical heightening of fairly common tropes?' (Crossley, Chapter 7 in this volume)

Crossley's examples of Nick Griffin and Tommy Robinson are clarifying. He shows how the condemnation of extremists is reinforcing the 'reasonableness' of the status quo. Drawing on Susan Harding's discussion of fundamentalism (Harding, 1991), Thomas Lynch has convincingly criticized the tendency to construct populists as the 'culturally repugnant other' in ways that pathologize the populist in contrast to us and present us in contrast to the populist (Lynch, 2022, p. 40). As Lynch argues, there are 'genuinely felt frustrations with long standing, historically rooted, systemic problems' that people labelled populists pick up on (Lynch, 2022, p. 53). Again, this is not a cop-out or complacency in the face of racism. It is a way of making sense of the critique of populism that concentrates on the style rather than the substance of populist politics. This critique is common inside and outside the academy. But Lynch argues convincingly that the *substance* is what ought to be challenged. Such a challenge, however, is also a challenge of the status quo. Focusing on style over substance risks reinforcing the very divisions that fuel populist politics in the first place. As Crossley points out, the danger is that we exonerate the practices and policies of established mainstream politicians and parties.

Overall, then, what we might miss if we focus too intently and too insistently on the dangers of the extremes is the hidden racism that animates slow violence across societies inside and outside Europe. This focus might keep us from imagining alternatives for Christian and non-Christian communities. As Allchorn and Crossley indicate, Christians can contribute to practices that counter racism, thus imagining new ways of living together that go beyond the status quo.

Notes

1 *Parts of the Holy Bible, Selected for the Use of the Negro Slaves, in the British West-India Islands* was published in 1807. There are only a few copies of this Bible still in existence. Historian of religion Sam Kocheri is researching its use.

2 Our critique of Brubaker draws on the analyses and arguments developed in Ulrich Schmiedel, 2021a, 'The Cracks in the Category of Christianism: A Call for Ambiguity in the Conceptualization of Christianity', in Cecilia Nahnfeldt and Kaia S. Rønsdal (eds), *Contemporary Christian-Cultural Values: Migration Encounters in the Nordic Region*, London: Routledge, pp. 164–82; and Ulrich Schmiedel, 2021b, 'Introduction: Political Theology in the Spirit of Populism – Methods and Metaphors', in Ulrich Schmiedel and Joshua Ralston (eds), *The Spirit of Populism: Political Theologies in Polarized Times*, Leiden: Brill, pp. 1–22.

3 See also Thomas Kaufmann, 2017, *Luther's Jews: A Journey into Anti-Semitism*, Oxford: Oxford University Press.

4 Juan O. Sánchez, 2016, *Religion and the Ku Klux Klan*, Jefferson: McFarland and Co., covers what he calls the 'biblical appropriation' of the Ku Klux Klan, concentrating on how themes and tropes from the Bible come up in their songs and symbols. See also Kelly J. Baker, 2011, *Gospel According to the Klan: The KKK's Appeal to Protestant America, 1915–1930*, Lawrence: University of Kansas Press.

5 See Vincent Harding, 2000, 'The Anointed Ones: Hamer, King, and the Bible in the Southern Freedom Movement', in Vincent L. Wimbush (ed.), *African Americans and the Bible: Sacred Texts and Social Textures*, Eugene: Wipf & Stock, pp. 537–45.

6 For a careful and critical take on the so-called vaccine effect of the Church, see Joseph Sverker, 2022, 'Confessing Christ in "Christian Europe": The Death of the Church as a Theological Response to Populism', in Ulrich Schmiedel and Joshua Ralston (eds), *The Spirit of Populism: Political Theologies in Polarized Times*, Leiden: Brill, pp. 263–76.

7 See Hannah Strømmen, 2023, 'Crusades, Christ and Christmas: Islamophobia and the Bible in the European Far-Right after 9/11', *Zeitschrift für Religion, Gesellschaft und Politik* 7, pp. 711–28.

References

Allchorn, William, in this volume, 'Chapter 8: "Stop waving crosses around and making them a symbol of hate"': Localized Christian Responses to the Populist Radical Right in the UK'.

Baker, Kelly J., 2011, *Gospel According to the Klan: The KKK's Appeal to Protestant America, 1915–1930*, Lawrence: University of Kansas Press.

Brubaker, Rogers, 2017, 'Between Nationalism and Civilizationalism: The European Populist Moment in Comparative Perspective', *Ethnic and Racial Studies* 40(8), pp. 1191–226.

Bunglawala, Shenaz, in this volume, 'Chapter 5: Beyond the Far Right: "Respectable Racism" and British Muslims'.

Collet, Jan Niklas, 2021, 'Rechte Normalisierung und kirchlich-theologische Normalität: Möglichkeiten und Folgen einer Inanspruchnahme "orthodoxer

Kirchlichkeit" durch rechte Christ*innen für Prozesse rechter Normalisierung', in Jan Niklas Collet, Julia Lis and Gregor Taxacher (eds), *Rechte Normalisierung und politische Theologie: Eine Standortbestimmung*, Regensburg: Friedrich Pustet, pp. 159–81.

Crossley, James, in this volume, 'Chapter 7: Encountering and Countering the Far Right in the UK Today'.

Frykberg, Henrik, in this volume, 'Chapter 2: From Prejudice to Pride: Towards an Organized Anti-racist Community'.

Harding, Susan, 1991, 'Representing Fundamentalism: The Problem of the Culturally Repugnant Other', *Social Research* 58(2), pp. 373–93.

Harding, Vincent, 2000, 'The Anointed Ones: Hamer, King, and the Bible in the Southern Freedom Movement', in Vincent L. Wimbush (ed.), *African Americans and the Bible: Sacred Texts and Social Textures*, Eugene: Wipf & Stock, pp. 537–45.

Kaufmann, Thomas, 2017, *Luther's Jews: A Journey into Anti-Semitism*, Oxford: Oxford University Press.

Lynch, Thomas, 2022, '"Just because You're Paranoid Doesn't Mean They're Not after You": Populism, Political Theology, and the Culturally Repugnant Other', in Ulrich Schmiedel and Joshua Ralston (eds), *The Spirit of Populism: Political Theologies in Polarized Times*, Leiden: Brill, pp. 40–56.

Miller, Gregory, 2014, 'Luther's Views of the Jews and Turks', in Robert Kolb, Irene Dingel and L'ubomír Batka (eds), *The Oxford Handbook of Martin Luther's Theology*, Oxford: Oxford University Press, pp. 427–34.

Omer, Atalia and Joshua Lupo, 2023, 'Introduction: The Cultural Logic of White Christian Nationalisms', in Atalia Omer and Joshua Lupo (eds), *Religion, Populism, and Modernity: Confronting White Christian Nationalism and Racism*, Notre Dame: University of Notre Dame Press, pp. 1–20.

Sánchez, Juan O., 2016, *Religion and the Ku Klux Klan: Biblical Appropriation in Their Literature and Songs*, Jefferson: McFarland and Co.

Schmiedel, Ulrich, 2021a, 'The Cracks in the Category of Christianism: A Call for Ambiguity in the Conceptualization of Christianity', in Cecilia Nahnfeldt and Kaia S. Rønsdal (eds), *Contemporary Christian-Cultural Values: Migration Encounters in the Nordic Region*, London: Routledge, pp. 164–82.

Schmiedel, Ulrich, 2021b, 'Introduction: Political Theology in the Spirit of Populism – Methods and Metaphors', in Ulrich Schmiedel and Joshua Ralston (eds), *The Spirit of Populism: Political Theologies in Polarized Times*, Leiden: Brill, pp. 1–22.

Spencer, Nick, 2018, *The Political Samaritan: How Power Hijacked a Parable*, London: Bloomsbury.

Stålsett, Sturla J., 2019, 'Ekstreme holdninger pakkes inn som norske verdier', *Dagbladet*, 5 September, www.dagbladet.no/kultur/ekstreme-holdninger-pakkes-inn-som-norske-verdier/71558550?fbclid=IwAR3CJawO3UIsyWfN-duTXjPvzv8uyO61ARezZqnkbsGURHyWiOBiEaKGdSUo (accessed 5.4.24).

Strømmen, Hannah, 2023, 'Crusades, Christ and Christmas: Islamophobia and the Bible in the European Far-Right after 9/11', *Zeitschrift für Religion, Gesellschaft und Politik* 7, pp. 711–28.

Strømmen, Hannah and Ulrich Schmiedel, 2020, *The Claim to Christianity: Responding to the Far Right*, London: SCM Press.

Stuckey, Sterling, 2000, '"My Burden Lightened": Frederick Douglass, the Bible, and Slave Culture', in Vincent Wimbush (ed.), *African Americans and the Bible: Sacred Texts and Social Textures*, Eugene: Wipf & Stock, pp. 251–65.

Sverker, Joseph, 2022, 'Confessing Christ in "Christian Europe": The Death of the Church as a Theological Response to Populism', in Ulrich Schmiedel and Joshua Ralston (eds), *The Spirit of Populism: Political Theologies in Polarized Times*, Leiden: Brill, pp. 263–76.

Yancy, George, 2012, *Look, a White! Philosophical Essays on Whiteness*, Philadelphia: Temple University Press.

PART 4

Christian Theologians Respond

10

The 'Semantic Struggle' against the Christian Far Right: Learning from the Good Samaritan

NICK SPENCER

Introduction

In 2002, I conducted a series of research groups among UK adults who had ticked the 'no religion' box in the previous year's census. That year, 2001, had been the first time that religion had been included on the decadal UK census and it was the cause of some controversy. The rumour was that New Labour had wanted its inclusion primarily to get an accurate idea of the Muslim population in the UK, but it was the non-religious organizations that were getting most vexed at what they thought would be an undue inflation of the number of self-affiliating Christians.

In the end, 71 per cent of adults in England and Wales ticked the Christian box in that census, while only 15 per cent said they were of no religion. Whatever you make of those figures (and there is some reason to believe the census *does* inflate the Christian numbers), the point I want to make here is that to call yourself non-religious in the 2001 census really meant something. You were in a clear minority, and it was a serious, conscious and deliberate statement; anything but a default option.

So it was that, in my research groups, the people I spoke to were usually hostile, and sometimes very hostile to religion in general, and to Christianity in particular. Hostility was rarely matched by a comparable level of knowledge, and statements about the religion were sometimes breathtakingly ignorant: 'Isn't the Vatican made of gold?', 'Is *War and Peace* part of the Bible?' But even if my respondents had difficulty in pinpointing precisely what philosophical, scientific, historical, social or ethical objections to Christianity they had, they knew they were strong none the less.

So it was all the more interesting and remarkable, then, when the conversation turned to other religions in the UK, and what (if anything) distinguished one religion from another, that one participant said the following: 'Jesus or whatever name ... other religions use the same sort of person. I mean the Muslims have got Muhammad, haven't they? It is very similar to ours.'

The key word in that sentence is the last one: 'ours'. Jesus was 'ours', just as Muhammad was 'theirs', despite the fact the interviewees in question not only had no meaningful connection to Jesus or to Christianity but were often actively hostile to them. His comments were not challenged or even questioned by other respondents, many of whom nodded their agreement. Jesus is 'ours'.

It is engagement with this confusion, this tension, perhaps even this hypocrisy, that runs through the heart of Hannah Strømmen and Ulrich Schmiedel's *The Claim to Christianity*, responding to the Christian far right in Europe – albeit that the authors encounter it in rather uglier forms (none of my interviews was politically far right). The language and imagery and personae of Christianity are 'ours' simply by dint of the fact that the UK (or Europe) has a deep Christian history, and I live there. Treating the two as coterminous leaves other religions as, by definition, non-European – perhaps even anti-European – a threat to be tolerated (at best), or an enemy to be eradicated (at worst). Christianity is weaponized and sent off to fight a culture war.

Sometimes, this military language is horrifyingly literal. Strømmen and Schmiedel's third chapter recounts the dreadful events of July 2011 when Anders Breivik, a self-proclaimed crusader in defence of Christian Europe, murdered nearly 80 people, most of them under the age of 20, in one of Europe's most violent terrorist encounters. Breivik had assembled an absurdly long manifesto explaining and justifying his beliefs. He described himself as 'a supporter of a monocultural Europe' (Strømmen and Schmiedel, 2020, p. 41), damned the accommodationist passivity of mainstream churches, and lauded the cross as 'the symbol in which every cultural conservative can unite' (p. 41). However much Christians of every stripe denounced Breivik, his toxic rhetoric and murderous actions leave a poisonous taste in the mouth.

Sometimes the military language is more obviously metaphorical, in a way that is less morally repellent but still deeply troubling. Strømmen and Schmiedel's fourth chapter examines the way in which the so-called 'populist right' has used Christian language for ideologies that stretch from the inhospitable and intolerant to the aggressive and violent. Pegida[1] in Germany often collapses the difference between Islamism, Islamization and Islam (despite protestations to the contrary) and then defines the resulting gestalt entity as against, and therefore a threat, to Christian Europe.

Non-church members of Pegida outweigh church ones by about 70:30. The major Catholic and Protestant churches in Germany have issued denunciations of the movement. The churches have sought to resist the collapse of a plural public into the allegedly unitary 'people' favoured by populists, and also to 'protect the corridor in which political positions ... can be communicated' (Strømmen and Schmiedel, 2020, p. 80), resisting the foreclosure of political debate. Nevertheless, albeit in a less acute form than Norway experienced, if groups of people pursue policies of hatred, fear, enmity and inhospitality on the grounds of a belief system that is supposed to promote love, generosity and self-sacrifice, there is a similar nasty residue of taste, and a similar problem to be faced.

The Semantic Struggle

How, then, does one face this problem and defuse the situation? When Christian rhetoric, symbols, language, history and identity are deployed to ends that appear in direction tension with Christian ethics, and especially with the figure of Christ himself, how should we respond?

Strømmen and Schmiedel foreground what they call the 'Semantic Struggle' in these efforts. This is a struggle for 'the *meaning* of Christianity', wresting the faith from the hands that would use it for nefarious ends by asking (and answering) questions of who can (and can't) lay claim to Christian traditions, and who decides on what claims can and can't be made. 'We advocate for both Christians and non-Christians to lay claim to Christianity' (Strømmen and Schmiedel, 2020, p. 10).

There is a certain logic to this. When someone is learning to speak a language and they use a word in a way that isn't grammatically standard in that language, you tend to correct them. That is how we learn languages. In a similar vein, if someone deploys a big, weighty category like Christianity in a way that sits ill with the grammar of that religion, you correct them.

Of course, it is not as simple as that, as Strømmen and Schmiedel recognize. In the first instance, those who are 'misappropriating' and 'misusing' Christianity – I'll leave those words in scare quotes for now as they are so question begging – are not doing so because they are learning the language. Their actions are quite deliberate, indeed highly calculating, and they are unlikely to take to correction with patient humility. Even if we could definitively show the Christianity definitely meant this and not that for the range of complex, plural, late-modern, post-Christian, liberal democracies of Europe, it is highly unlikely that those who have been deploying Christian rhetoric would turn round and say, 'OK, that's a fair theological cop. You've got me there. I won't try and hijack this ideology again.' There is something much more intentional going on here.

More substantively, disagreement over the meaning of words, particularly deep, sprawling, socially mediated and ethically and culturally loaded words like Christian or Christianity, is always going to be inconclusive. Having just completed a project on, and am currently working on a monograph about, the meaning of the words 'science' and 'religion', I can confidently say that anyone who imagines they will reach a satisfactorily concrete and settled definition is liable to be disappointed.[2] Indeed, there are good philosophical reasons to believe that no such solution exists.

It is important to acknowledge that Strømmen and Schmiedel recognize this. They acknowledge that 'we can't own Christianity' (Strømmen and Schmiedel, 2020, p. 137), and that 'the distinction between hijacked and honest Christianity is too nice and too neat to convince' (p. 138). This leads them to their 'suggestion' that 'we see the identity of Christianity as a project rather than a possession' (p. 137). They argue that Christianity is 'neither fixed nor finished [but] something we're working on' (p. 137), and they do this, among other ways, by drawing on the parable of the Good Samaritan.

This is an approach to which I have much (though, as we shall see in the conclusion, not complete) sympathy. I would give, as it were, two and a half cheers, and I want to use the rest of this chapter to explain those cheers, by building on the parable, which is so familiar in recent theo-political rhetoric, and indeed so important to Strømmen and Schmiedel's book, before turning to my reservation at the end.

The Slippery Samaritan

Strømmen and Schmiedel cite a number of uses of the parable of the Good Samaritan throughout the book and, in doing so, make one thing very clear: the Samaritan has not always been deployed on the side of the political angels.

The authors report how Beatrix von Storch, one of the leaders of AfD (Alternative für Deutschland), interpreted the parable in the volume *Confessions of Christians in the AfD*. 'When the Samaritan found the victim of the accident on the roadside, he provided care and organized on-site support in a hostel,' she claimed. 'But,' she continued, 'he did not take him home to Samaria, and he did not allow him to bring his family with him either' (p. 76).

This, it is fair to say, seems to be deploying the parable in a rather forced way. It reminds me of an occasion in which I heard a prominent, and publicly Christian, senior Conservative politician in the UK claim that the parable legitimized the ownership of large cars, as only that way would modern-day Good Samaritans be able to carry the equipment needed to serve the one in need. Hermeneutics can be a broad circle sometimes.

We can laugh at this, but it does underline a rather serious point, which I tried to examine in my short book *The Political Samaritan* (2017), which explored the uses (and abuses) of that parable in (predominantly British) political rhetoric over the last 50 years. The parable had been used with remarkable frequency, by some very high-profile politicians, and from some very high-profile platforms. More interesting than this, however, was the *way* in which it had been used. Given that the story has been referenced by pretty much every major British political leader of the last two generations, from Margaret Thatcher at one end to Jeremy Corbyn at the other, you can imagine that it had not been used in the same way or to the same ends.

The question I was invariably asked whenever I spoke on the subject was 'who got it right?' Who came closest to the 'real' meaning and, by implication, what is the right interpretation of the parable? It is, alas, impossible to answer, and not simply because of legitimate hermeneutical differences. Like the logic of the semantic struggle itself, the question ignores the deliberately creative, provocative and polyphonous nature of stories themselves. Parables provoke as many questions as they answer.

To be clear, this is not to say that I don't think that some interpretations were distinctly more far-fetched and therefore less credible (and tenable) than others. When the Labour front bench parliamentarian Hilary Benn referenced the parable in an argument for the bombing of Syria in 2015, I think he might be stretching it a bit far. Similarly, when Margaret Thatcher said to a TV interviewer in 1981 that 'no one would remember the Good Samaritan if he'd only had good intentions; he had money as well' as a justification for accepting greater levels of inequality in the country, you can't help feeling the parable is being deployed beyond its proper remit.

We might not be able to say definitively who gets it right, but we can venture an opinion about who gets it wrong. Being polyphonous does not mean having no voice. Rather, it means that we need to be cautious, self-reflective and humble in pronouncing on that meaning. The semantic struggle for a parable is as difficult as that for a religion as a whole, an agonistic struggle, denying foreclosure, as good stories and complex categories always do.

Using the Good Samaritan

What, then, are we to do? I would suggest the parable can help us with this. Any semantic struggle must attend to the fact that words don't float free but draw their meanings from the forms of life, from the language games, in which they are embedded. To know what love is, is to know what love looks and feels like. Success in any semantic struggle necessarily demands attention being paid to the behaviours of those who claim to be able to define what Christianity is. And it is here that the parable of the Good Samaritan does offer an instructive contribution that goes beyond the 'he-said-she-said' of interpretation.

As already mentioned, in writing on the political use of the parable of the Good Samaritan, I was struck by how widely and variously the parable has been used over the last 50 years, not least given how much British (and other) politics has secularized over this period. However, time and again, these readings seemed to miss two important details that can really shape what we take away from the parable (in their defence, despite having read the parable more times than I can count, I too missed one of them until I started reading ancient commentaries on it).

As we know, the beginning of the parable sees an expert in the Law stand up to 'test' Jesus. It is, to the best of my recollection, the only time one of Jesus' parables is located in a specific encounter of this nature. The expert respectfully asks, 'What must I do to inherit eternal life?' (Luke 18.18) and Jesus dutifully directs him to what is written in the Law. 'How do you read it?' (Luke 10.26), he says, turning the tables on the lawyer.

The answer seems to be that he reads it well, answering correctly as Jesus confirms. 'Love the Lord your God with all your heart and with all your soul and with all your strength and with all your mind,' and 'Love your neighbour as yourself' (Luke 10.27). This, after all, was how Jesus himself had summarized the Law when asked in Mark 12.30–31.

The encounter seems over, and Jesus affirms his interpretation and tells him, 'Do this and you will live' (Luke 10.28). There is a key word in this response that we sometimes overlook but to which Jesus returns at the end, not least because the lawyer isn't done. We have reached one concluding point of definition – we have defined what we need to do to inherit eternal life – but that has only brought us to the start of a second definitional question. 'And who is my neighbour?' the lawyer asks, 'want[ing] to justify himself' (Luke 10.29).

Jesus then recounts the story with which we are familiar. Right at the end, he turns back to the expert in the Law and says, 'Which of these three do you think was a neighbour to the man who fell into the hands of robbers?' (Luke 10.36). The lawyer replies, 'The one who had mercy on him' (Luke 10.37). Jesus says to him, 'Go and do likewise.' And then the encounter genuinely is over.

Through the medium of the story, two things have happened, both of which are relevant to our issue at hand. The first is that the semantic struggle over meaning – of eternal life, of neighbour – is redirected. From having been an issue of being, neighbourliness has become one of action.

Recall that Jesus' advice to the lawyer once he got the definition right was 'Do this and you will live' – 'do', of course, being the crucial little word I mentioned above. The point is reinforced at the end. Although Jesus' final question, 'Which of these three do you think was a neighbour?', could be read either way; coming after the action-packed story he has just told, it seems that the right way to read his question is 'Which of these three do you think acted as the man's neighbour?' And this impression is underlined by these final parting words, 'Go and do likewise.' One cannot, it seems, define one's neighbour so much as simply behave as one. You don't have neighbours; you behave as a neighbour.[3] The semantic struggle over eternal life and neighbour identity can only be answered by doing, by action; the meaning of the words is given by their embeddedness in a form of life.

This is the first twist the parable presents us with – redirecting the semantic struggle to the arena of practical help and action. The second twist is even more interesting and in its own way even more subversive. From having been, at least implicitly, a passive figure, the neighbour is now active, the subject rather than the object of compassion.

At the start of the encounter, the lawyer is the agent, who wants to know upon whom he should bestow his love. He is the actor; the neighbour is the recipient. But the story Jesus tells, or at least the manner in which he interprets it at the end, is not one in which the lead character gets to choose which of the three people he is right to bestow his largesse upon.

On the contrary, the lead character is the victim in the ditch, who is ignored or treated by passers-by. This was one of the reasons why the Church Fathers almost unanimously interpreted this parable as depicting the entirety of salvation history, with humankind mugged by Satan and fallen into the ditch of sin, tragically unaided by the Law but rescued by Christ and brought to health at the inn, which is the Church (the interpretations could even be more elaborate!).

We do not interpret the parable in this salvation historical way any more but that does not mean we should ignore its important twist in agency. Jesus' concluding question – 'Which of these three do you think was a neighbour to the man who fell into the hands of robbers?' – is very powerful, because from having been the one who waits to receive kindness, the neighbour at the end is the one who exercises it. In the words of theologian Ian McFarland:

> Jesus does not so much answer the lawyer's question as turn it around. His counter-question forces the lawyer to apply the term 'neighbour' not to the victim of the assault, but to 'the one who showed (literally, 'did') compassion to him' ... Jesus asks lawyer and reader alike to consider the possibility that the question of their own status as neighbours might be anthropologically prior to any reflection on the status of other people. (McFarland, 2001, p. 60)

In other words, not only does Jesus subvert expectations when it comes to law, ethics, religion and ethnicity in his story, but the way he then frames the ensuing question appears to subvert the idea of there being an ethical subject and object. It's not a question of who is the neighbour to whom I should give my love and attention, but whether I am ready to receive help from one who is a neighbour.

In this way, if we are to pivot our discussion of responding to the 'Christian' far right on the parable of the Good Samaritan, as so much of this conversation often does, we might want to take both of these points into consideration.

First, the semantic struggle will always be with us. It is important and necessary. Many commentators now see this whole incident as a first-century 'halakhic' debate: in effect, a rabbinical debate over biblical law and oral law, and its subsequent elucidation and clarification. But semantic struggle will only get you so far, and to make any progress with it words need to be embedded in forms of life, actions and practices that give meaning to the terms we are trying to establish.

Second, the nature of that action may call upon more than simply dispensing largesse to those that need it. It's not that there is anything wrong with this, of course. However much the tables of agency are turned at the end of the parable, there is no doubt that the actions of the Samaritan are to be commended and followed. But that table turning also invites a question that is hardly less challenging than the obvious one of 'What will you now do?', which is 'Who are you prepared to accept help *from?*'

The neighbour we are commanded to help may be the one who helps us from the ditch. It's not necessarily solely a case of welcoming others – though there is surely much of that – but also receiving from them to achieve goods you value. What might this look like today?

Making Multiculturalism Work

A few years ago we (at Theos) conducted a research project that was ambitiously titled *Making Multiculturalism Work*. It drew on more than a decade of academic research and political rhetoric that pointed out that 'multiculturalism' had not worked and that it had, to reference Professor Ted Cantle, inadvertently essentialized people's identities and facilitated the development of 'parallel lives' within communities. This was not a project about the far right or immigration or Christian rhetoric but, somewhat more prosaically, how different communities did, or did not, live alongside one another.

This failure of multiculturalism led academics and politicians on a journey to find a new framework or a way of understanding community life that could restore a sense of common identity and endeavour. Cantle developed the idea of 'Interculturalism', 'the creation of a culture of openness that effectively challenges the identity politics and entrenchment of separate communities' (Cantle, 2012, p. 142). At the same time, the Labour government refocused its rhetoric on 'British values' as a means of fostering a sense of commonality among divergent communities, a path adopted by the subsequent Coalition government, or at least the Conservative element of it.[4]

Whatever the merits of these approaches, there was a sense that such new paradigms rested implicitly on a 'trickle down' theory of social change, in which getting the model right and changing the approach of academic and political elites was judged the best way of bringing about meaningful change. In effect, the debate around, and in the wake of, multiculturalism was its own kind of semantic struggle, in which the implicit assumption was that if we could just identify and correctly define the right kind of multiculturalism or interculturalism or set of values, the rest would fall into place. In the words of one of the interview participants in our research project, 'multiculturalism has become an elite discourse, it's what the elite tell people we should have'.

The same interviewee went on to say that 'that is really unhelpful because that is not how people experience their everyday life'. Now, to be clear, this is not to claim that all attempts to define how to live together well are pointless or unnecessary. The semantic struggle is not senseless. Rather, it is simply not sufficient, unlikely to be satisfactorily resolved in itself and unlikely to be a solution to problems around integration, and living together if it were. We need more than simply accurate definitions to address the question of how we live together.

The research amounted to a study not of what community cohesion should look like in theory, but what actual neighbourliness did look like in practice. In its own words, 'cohesive society is not in the end an abstract goal pursued through an intellectual exercise in conforming to an ideal or discovering sameness, but rather a relational process of working together in spite of differences'.

The project studied the Near Neighbours initiative and Citizens UK. Near Neighbours was a £5 million government programme that was established in 2011 with the aim of '[bringing] people together in religiously and ethnically diverse communities, creating friendships, building relationships of trust and helping people to transform their neighbourhoods together'.[5] In a similar vein, Citizens UK was and is a grassroots 'Community Organizing' project that aimed to 'develop the capacity and skills of the members ... to participate more fully in society'.[6] By looking at these interview participants, and evaluating the success or otherwise of initiatives, the report argued that it was in, what it called, localized 'political friendships' that people learned to live and work together, in spite of religious, cultural and other differences.

I do not wish to rehearse the entire project here, and the report is available online (Barclay, 2013), but I do want to highlight two factors that emerged in the study, factors that correlate well with the reading of the parable of the Good Samaritan outlined above, and that are relevant to the wider discussion of this chapter.[7]

The first point was the centrality and significance of *action* in political friendship, even to the point of being more important (certainly at the first stage) than conversation:

All interviewees expressed a belief that working together was more powerful than simply having 'dialogue'. What made the biggest difference, particularly at first, was the identification of common projects and the willingness to work towards them, before anyone attempted to define in any theoretical way what kind of model of cooperation this looked like. Political friendships were forged 'not by a widespread adherence to abstract national values or an idea of what multiculturalism should look like, but rather by common action'. (Barclay, 2013, p. 9)

The second point was the willingness to receive help from others who were different from you. The study showed that 'political friendships' needed to circumvent orthodoxy or 'right thinking', and set aside any 'progressive test' that sought to verify that potential partners were politically sound or acceptable (i.e. liberal). Rather, in place of the standard 'progressive test', the report favoured a 'relational test', whereby 'the central criterion for participation is that an organization must show that it is willing and able to work with people from different backgrounds and perspectives' (Barclay, 2013, p. 9). Put another way, political friendships were constructed not through one group doing something for, or on behalf of, another group, but by differing groups working together to achieve a common end; being willing to receive help from neighbours who were offering to help.

The parallel with the reading of the parable offered earlier should be clear. Placing any semantic struggle (over the meaning of 'neighbourliness' or 'multiculturalism', or indeed 'eternal life' or 'Christianity') within the context of practical action is essential. And locating that action within a wider context of being willing to *receive* help, and to see oneself as a neighbour, is also important. These two approaches might help inform our wider response to the (non-Christian) 'other', and all the questions of identity, hospitality, social harmony and the far right with which they are tied up.

Conclusion: The Samaritan, 'Political Friendship' and the Fight Against the 'Christian' Far Right

On the surface, and indeed quite a long way down, the argument of this chapter is consonant with that of Strømmen and Schmiedel's *The Claim to Christianity*.

I have argued that, following the flip from definition to action inherent in the parable of the Good Samaritan, action should be central to the Christian response to the far right, and this is broadly in line with Strømmen and Schmiedel's argument that 'If Christianity is a practical project, it is open to all – Christians and non-Christians' (Strømmen and Schmiedel, 2020, p. 120).

In a similar vein, following the flip from agency to receipt inherent in the parable, I have argued that the action is not (exclusively) a question of whom I give my support to, but also whom I receive it from, whom I am prepared to work with and alongside in achieving shared goods. Again, this is, I believe, broadly in line with Strømmen and Schmiedel's contention that that 'contact with Muslims is central to reclaiming Christianity in response to the rise of the far right' (p. 121).

Countering the Christian far right is done most effectively not simply by positive rhetoric around Islam or asylum, nor just by positive interfaith dialogue, nor by trying to define what Christianity is in such a way as excludes those who hijack it for far-right causes – though all of these do have a role – but by *acting alongside*, in partnership with, and *receiving assistance from* precisely those groups whom the far right wish to demonize, alienate and exclude. That was, as our research showed, how true 'political friendships', and a stronger and more robust sense of shared interest and identity, are formed.

Having said all that, I mentioned earlier that this chapter constitutes two and a half cheers, rather than the traditional full-throated three, and it would be dishonest to give the impression that the agreement is all the way down, and so I want to end with a short provocation.

For all that Jesus challenged the lawyer to act rather than define, and to see himself as a possible neighbour rather than solely a moral agent, he did concur with the lawyer's reading of the Law; indeed, he summarized the Law himself in the same way. He did not shirk from all attempts at what we might call the semantic struggle of the Law. He did not tell the lawyer that the Law didn't matter or that it was wholly superseded by action.

In a similar vein, while the research in *Making Multiculturalism Work* emphasized openness and cooperation, and the relationship test over and above any theoretical models of multiculturalism or formal progressive tests as a way of building 'political friendships', it was equally clear that dialogue between different parties can, indeed should, occur once those 'political friendships' had been established. It was not that different cooperating groups could or should ignore their differences, which were sometimes quite deep. There was no intention of using the idea of political friendship to turn religions into a spiritual grey-wash. Rather, it was a case of using the friendships constructed by action and openness to build a sufficiently secure basis on which these more definitional, theological and 'semantic' discussions could take place.

In other words, both of these sources underline that however much we might want to define Christianity as a project, it is also about a person, a set of beliefs and convictions that inspire the action we have been talking about. However difficult and ultimately Sisyphean the task of semantic struggle is, it cannot be ignored altogether. However much we have problems pinpointing definition, and however much we ultimately have to point to actions to give them their meaning, the actions to which we gesture are not those of ourselves but of Christ, who did and said certain things.

This is important as it guards against the problem underlying the project- or process-based approach to Christianity. When the authors say that 'churches have to become open to others' (Strømmen and Schmiedel, 2020, p. 52), that can mean very different things. Being open can mean accessible, hospitable and welcoming, a sentiment with which I imagine few actual church-goers would disagree. But open can also mean in the sense of abolishing credal or confessional hurdles to membership (which is rather more contentious).

And to that end, I wonder whether the authors of *The Claim to Christianity* are sometimes oversensitive to attempts to talk about Christianity in public, or indeed to identify the UK as a historically Christian nation. To pick up on a couple of examples from the book: Theresa May was, in reality, extremely reluctant to talk about her genuine Christian faith; indeed, far more reluctant than the rather more nominally Christian David Cameron. In the light of this, the idea that Theresa May 'played into notions of Britain as Christian, particularly in speaking of her background as a vicar's daughter' (Strømmen and Schmiedel, 2020, p. 102) is, I think, hard to sustain.

In a similar vein, criticizing Justin Welby for reimagining a UK in which 'Islam is welcome *on Christian terms only*' (p. 115) rather invites the question 'What other terms did you expect the Archbishop of Canterbury to use?' It seems to imagine that there is an objective, value-neutral, universally agreed set of terms on which the diverse, plural public agrees.

This is not, of course, to defend everything May or Welby or indeed any other publicly Christian figure did or said. Rather, it is to underline the fact that for all Christianity may be helpfully seen as a 'project' or a 'process' to be nurtured, developed and shared rather than defined, owned and defended, it is still a project about something, about someone. Its content is always open to discussion and contestation, and any foreclosure of such discussion is always premature. But that does not mean that it has no content, or that that content has not proved enormously pervasive in and through British history and politics.

In a similar way, the Christian faith may seek to be known 'through actions that are sincere, not through empty words' (1 John 3.18, GW) and Christ's commands may have been to 'go and do likewise', but that did not preclude reading, studying, weighing, and even being prepared to summarize the Law.

In short, we should not allow our understandable desire to avoid exclusionary theo-politics to lead us to a conceptualization of the Christian faith that empties it of content, even of content that risks being weaponized by others. That may be an uncomfortable place to stand but it is an honest one.

Notes

1 Standing for 'Patriotische Europäer gegen die Islamisierung des Abendlandes or Patriotic Europeans Against the Islamization of the West [or Europe]': the authors deal with the complex issues of translation.

2 Nick Spencer and Hannah Waite, forthcoming, *The Landscape of Science and Religion: What Exactly Are We Disagreeing About?*, Oxford: Oxford University Press.

3 I am grateful to Natan Mladin for this felicitous phrasing.

4 David Cameron, Speech at Munich Security Conference, 5 February 2011, http://www.number10.gov.uk/news/pms-speech-at-munich-security-conference/ (accessed 5.4.24).

5 http://www.cuf.org.uk/near-neighbours (accessed 5.4.24).

6 London Citizens Annual Report, 2009, p. 3, http://www.charitycommission.gov.uk/Accounts/Ends74%5C0001088174_ac_20090331_e_c.pdf (accessed 5.4.24).

7 This project preceded my work on the political Samaritan by a number of years, so there is no sense in which the findings were in any way informed by those hermeneutics; the Samaritan was entirely absent from *Making Multiculturalism Work*.

References

Barclay, David, 2013, *Making Multiculturalism Work: Enabling Practical Action Across Deep Difference*, London: Theos, www.theosthinktank.co.uk (accessed 5.4.24).
Cantle, T., 2012, *Interculturalism – the New Era of Cohesion and Diversity*, London: Palgrave Macmillan.
McFarland, I. A., 2001, 'Who Is My Neighbor?: The Good Samaritan as a Source for Theological Anthropology', *Modern Theology* 17(1), pp. 57–66.
Spencer, Nick, 2017, *The Political Samaritan: How Power Hijacked a Parable*, London: Bloomsbury.
Strømmen, Hannah and Ulrich Schmiedel, 2020, *The Claim to Christianity: Responding to the Far Right*, London: SCM Press.

11

Challenging Far-right Claims to Christianity: A Northern Irish Perspective

CHRIS WILSON

Introduction

The Claim to Christianity addresses an important question facing contemporary churches: how should we respond to far-right claims to Christianity? This crucial question provides the focus for this chapter. I offer my response as a Christian from Northern Ireland, whose research interests focus on systematic theology and theological responses to ethnic and religious conflict. As theologians in Ireland have been attempting to counteract a remarkably influential right-wing Protestant movement for more than half a century, I have framed this response as an attempt to bring Strømmen and Schmiedel's proposal into dialogue with the Irish experience.

This dialogue aims to highlight several important insights that Strømmen and Schmiedel have offered and to suggest how they might help churches in Northern Ireland respond to a legacy of nationalistic Protestantism. It also aims to allow the Irish scholarly conversation to raise critical questions about certain aspects of *The Claim to Christianity*. As this chapter includes several points of significant disagreement with Strømmen and Schmiedel, I want to begin by acknowledging that I write as one who shares their commitment to addressing far-right claims and who is grateful for their efforts to further an important conversation.

Investigating and Interpreting the Theologies of the Far Right

The Claim to Christianity engages with an impressive range of European contexts and scholarly disciplines. The book's core consists of three case studies that offer a critical analysis of the theology of far-right movements across Europe, including the terrorist right in Norway, the populist right in Germany, and the hard right in England. The multinational character of the study highlights several insightful parallels between these movements and the Church's responses to them. In addition, the work also draws on a diverse set of scholarly voices from different disciplines and manages to do this in a way that is both accessible and engaging.

This broad scope enables *The Claim to Christianity* to offer valuable insights for churches in Northern Ireland. More specifically, the work demonstrates that some of the challenges facing churches in Northern Ireland have parallels in other European countries: 'Culture Christianity', an ethnocentric conception of politics, manipulation of anxieties about cultural change, and appeals to biblical passages to support specific political ideologies. In so doing, Strømmen and Schmiedel show that Irish scholars have much to gain from entering conversations about the far right in Europe. For example, the affirmation that 'The Gospel is strong enough to stand on its own legs' (p. 57) might help to address an inclination of certain Protestant sub-groups to be excessively preoccupied with what they oppose.[1] The work also offers insights that may help to further our understanding of the connections between the legacy of inter-communal violence and other contemporary societal challenges, such as Islamophobia and antisemitism.

Another striking feature of *The Claim to Christianity* is its choice of interlocutors. That Strømmen and Schmiedel have taken the time to attend to Anders Brevik's theological blogging is one of several interactions that make this book very engaging. Reading it, I was struck by the contrast with Northern Ireland. During the Troubles, there were Protestant preachers and Catholic priests who were responsible for taking the lives of men, women and children (Bruce, 2009, pp. 240–1; Brewer, Higgins and Teeney, 2011, pp. 2–3; O'Leary, 2023). As yet, scholars have not shown much interest in attending to the sermons of these men. Strømmen and Schmiedel's work raises questions about whether these sources are not much more valuable than scholars have tended to assume.

While *The Claim to Christianity* engages with a fascinating set of interlocutors and an impressive range of European contexts, the broad scope of the work constrains its ability to undertake a detailed examination of any one context. This raises an interesting question: how much investigation is required for a response to the theologies of the far right? In considering this, the Irish scholarly literature provides an instructive example of the complexities that may need attention. In Northern Ireland, the conflict between 'Protestants' and 'Catholics' was part of a larger complex that included political, economic, cultural, colonial and religious dimensions. Early scholarship exhibited an all-or-nothing tendency in which the conflict was viewed, on one side, as essentially a religious war (Hickey, 1984) or, on the other, as an essential ethnonational war in which religion served only as an identity marker (McGarry and O'Leary, 1995). In recent years, there has been a consensus concerning the need to move away from reductionist explanations towards multidimensional theories that allow the role of religion in the conflict to vary across different times and groups (Ruane and Todd, 1996; Mitchell, 2006). Research has also demonstrated that despite its small size, Northern Ireland is home to several distinct Protestant sub-groups, which combine Protestantism and right-wing politics in quite different ways (Jordan, 2001; Mitchel, 2003; Ganiel, 2008). These groups consistently support a right-wing Protestant political movement but do so for different reasons.

In light of the Irish conversation, one question that needs to be asked is whether *The Claim to Christianity* allows 'insignificant religious factors' to overshadow 'significant non-religious factors' (Strømmen and Schmiedel, 2020, p. 13). While Strømmen and Schmiedel rightly contend that it is necessary to focus on religion, the Irish conversation primes us to acknowledge that the challenging question is not whether to focus on religion, but *how*? A weakness of the book's argument is that it moves swiftly from magnifying theological concerns to inviting the Church to intervene. There is no intermediate step in which the authors attempt to view these theological claims in the larger context of the far right's economic, political and cultural concerns. Because it neglects this step, the work lacks the necessary framework for evaluating the relative importance of claims to Christianity among other far-right concerns. While *The Claim to Christianity* demonstrates a commendable concern for addressing the theological claims of the far right, more research is needed to ensure that Christian interventions are attentive to the broader socioeconomic concerns of those they seek to address.

In so far as it highlights the problem of preaching to the choir, the Irish conversation suggests the need for a Christian response to the far right to reckon with the difficulties involved in addressing and persuading those who do not already share one's own political and theological views. Here, we might note that *The Claim to Christianity* lacks a detailed, grassroots analysis of far-right supporters within any national context. Instead, it seems to assume that an understanding of the theological claims made by far-right figures such as Anders Brevik or Nigel Farage provides an adequate basis for addressing individuals who are sympathetic to some of their concerns. Given the book's concern with helping large, national churches to make the right kind of statements in response to far-right claims, this focus on prominent far-right figures is understandable. However, it does limit the book's ability to offer guidance to local churches attempting to respond pastorally to individuals. For example, the pastoral task raises questions about whether Christians should offer a different kind of response to individuals who are deeply embedded in extremist ideologies and fiercely resistant to deradicalization versus those with comparatively less entrenched views. If we seek to help local churches to respond to these challenges, it will be necessary to go beyond *The Claim to Christianity* by offering detailed descriptions of the various cohorts of far-right supporters.

In summary, *The Claim to Christianity* rightly instructs us not to dismiss the role of religion in far-right claims. Considering the challenge of avoiding preaching to the choir, I contend that individuals seeking to respond to the far right must go beyond *The Claim to Christianity* in at least two ways. First, we need to develop a more detailed, multidimensional analysis that supplements theological analysis with greater attention to the political and economic concerns that are frequently exploited by far-right figures. Second, we need to invest more in understanding the various cohorts of people engaged by the far right, their involvement in the Church, and how they might best be approached and addressed.

Hijacking Christianity

The Claim to Christianity offers insightful criticisms of claims that the far right hijack Christianity or use it as 'a mere means to propagandistic and political ends' (Strømmen and Schmiedel, 2020, p. 6). On ethical grounds, it is problematic because it denies responsibility: when Christians 'characterize far right claims to Christianity as a hijacking, they characterize themselves as not responsible for these claims' (p. 6). On philosophical grounds, it is problematic because it engages in a 'No true Scotsman' fallacy, whereby any problematic form of Christianity is hastily brushed aside as a hijacked version. It is also problematic on historical grounds because it overlooks Christianity's deeply ambiguous history (p. 6).

These are insightful criticisms, and Christians in Northern Ireland should heed them. The work suggests the need to probe the connection between a tendency to view others as hijacking Christianity and the feelings of superiority and self-righteousness highlighted by other research on the Irish context (Liechty and Clegg, 2001, pp. 325–9). Although the next section raises questions about the anti-essentialist framework that undergirds this claim, Strømmen and Schmiedel can be profitably heard as calling for much greater self-criticism in any suggestion that Christianity is being hijacked or instrumentalized.

An Invitation to Intervene

The role of Christian theological convictions

What role do Christian theological convictions play in *The Claim to Christianity*? While Strømmen and Schmiedel appeal to both the Christian theological tradition and a postmodern understanding of different cultures and religions as 'complicated, complex and changing' (Strømmen and Schmiedel, 2020, p. 9), the latter criteria provide the driving centre of their argument.[2] Where the book diagnoses problems with far-right claims and church responses, it is usually because these involve conceiving a religion or a culture as being strong, stable, static or singular (pp. 25, 34, 35, 55, 153). When the book speaks of a 'theological trap', it uses this term to denote a concern that others are being essentialized in harmful ways (pp. 19, 21, 35, 147). When the book criticizes the 'distinction between hijacked and honest Christianity', it does so because this distinction 'operates through essentialism' (p. 138). The book's constructive proposals could be summarized by the claim that responses to far-right theologies should reflect the complex and contested character of national and religious identities.

That a postmodern account of religion provides the driving centre of Strømmen and Schmiedel's proposal can be seen in their emphasis on understanding Christianity as a 'project'. 'Christianity as a project' functions as a concise expression for Christianity understood through a postmodern lens; that is, as something that is 'complicated, complex and changing' (p. 9) and thereby cannot be 'fixed', 'frozen' or 'finished' (pp. 10, 144). The claim that Christianity is a project rather than a possession is a central motif of the book. It is announced in the Introduction: 'the identity of Christianity is a project rather than a possession' (p. 10). Although introduced as a claim about 'the identity of Christianity', by the end of the book it is repeatedly applied to Christianity as a whole (pp. 140, 141, 144): 'Christianity is a project and not a possession, because the call to follow Jesus Christ is neither fixed nor finished' (p. 144). Where Strømmen and Schmiedel treat 'Christianity as possession', they describe it as understanding Christianity as 'something we can own' (p. 120), as 'the possession of a particular people that demarcates and differentiates them from other peoples' (p. 118). This understanding that Christianity is a project and not a possession has implications that may surprise some readers:

Our proposal to characterize the identity of Christianity as a practical project, then, takes what is commonly considered a shortcoming – that Christianity can be interpreted and instrumentalized for a variety of political purposes, from the left and from the right – to be a strength. It can tackle the problems that became apparent in the comparison of the churches' strategies above. (p. 139)

How should we evaluate this? Strømmen and Schmiedel's argument that 'the identity of Christianity needs to be conceptualized in a new way' (p. 156) entails far-reaching claims about reconceptualizing the Christian faith. That this is the case can be seen in the way that the book shifts from making claims about 'the identity of Christianity' to making claims about 'Christianity' (pp. 140, 141, 144). Given that this claim is 'new' and far-reaching, it seems strange that it should be articulated in a few pages of a short, accessible book addressed to those members of the general public who are concerned about far-right claims to Christianity (p. 14). Surely, a claim of this magnitude deserves to be stated extensively and scrutinized by other theologians? The brevity of Strømmen and Schmiedel's argument makes it difficult to respond adequately, but I would nevertheless like to outline four criticisms.

First, Strømmen and Schmiedel's argument involves several problematic dichotomies. Their argument involves a contrast between categorizing religions as either 'changing' or 'fixed'. By obscuring a continuum of change, these binary labels distort perceptions of the relative stability of permanence of religious convictions. As Nick Spencer has rightly noted in Chapter 10 of this volume, the content of the Christian faith is 'always open to discussion and contestation', but this does not imply that 'that content has not proved enormously pervasive in and through British history and politics' (p. 145). In addition, the 'project and not possession' motif presents the reader with a stark choice between following Strømmen and Schmiedel – that is, allowing a postmodern account of religion to determine what Christianity can and cannot be – or adopting a problematic posture of possessing Christianity. This binary choice obscures a broad spectrum of possibilities and nuanced alternatives. For example, many Christian theologians – Karl Barth and Dietrich Bonhoeffer being prominent examples – have managed to combine a robust emphasis on the content of Christian teaching with a dispossessive account of revelation and a rejection of the idea that Christians can confidently demarcate the boundaries of the Church.

The 'project and not possession' motif in *The Claim to Christianity* also misleads to the extent that it presents 'project' and 'possession' as mutually exclusive alternatives. While it is admittedly a different sphere, it is perhaps helpful to consider a potential argument that a multinational corporation, such as Amazon, is 'complicated, complex and changing' (Strømmen and Schmiedel, 2020, p. 9), that it is a 'movement' rather than a 'monument or a mausoleum' (p. 156), and that it cannot be 'fixed', 'frozen' or 'finished' (pp. 10, 144). Would a persuasive argument that Amazon is a project establish the claim that it cannot be possessed? Rather than uncritically accept the motif, we should ask ourselves whether a persuasive argument that 'Christianity is a project' convincingly establishes that 'Christianity is not a possession'. This question is important because the dichotomy enables Strømmen and Schmiedel to repeatedly claim that 'Christianity is not a possession' without offering a substantial account of what it means to possess Christianity, or engaging with other theologians who have also attempted to disabuse the Church of the notion that it possesses Christianity. This neglect leads to one of the stranger characteristics of the work: while it relentlessly asserts that Christianity is 'not a possession', it simultaneously urges Christians to behave in a highly possessive way towards Christianity. This can be seen in Strømmen and Schmiedel's depiction of Christian activity – as 'laying claim to Christianity', deciding 'what Christianity should stand for', interpreting and instrumentalizing Christianity (p. 139). These terms express a far more possessive posture than a traditional Reformation understanding that depicts Christian activity in the idiom of hearing, trusting and obeying. While space precludes offering a fuller treatment of the problematically possessive character of *The Claim to Christianity*, I hope to have done enough to demonstrate that the 'project and not possession' motif is a misleading oversimplification that elides an important and complex set of questions about the pervasiveness of Christian theological convictions and what it means to possess or control a religious tradition.

Second, *The Claim to Christianity* does not discuss the costs of framing Christianity as a 'project'. This masks the fact that Strømmen and Schmiedel's postmodern account of religion does not provide a spacious and hospitable framework for the Christian faith but a procrustean bed that truncates and domesticates Christian teaching. One way this occurs is that the framing of Christianity as a 'project' deflates the significance of the content of scripture and the Christian tradition. As a result, it tends to depict Christians as well-meaning shapers of a relatively vacuous religious tradition. Nick Spencer's response in Chapter 10 of this volume has helpfully highlighted this issue: Christianity may be a project, but it is still a project 'about someone': 'we should not allow our understandable desire to avoid exclusionary theo-politics to lead us to a conceptualization of the Christian faith than empties it of content, even of content that risks being weaponized by others' (p. 146).

To understand the consequences of this deflation of the content of Christian theological convictions, it is helpful to examine the rôle accorded to Christ and the Spirit in *The Claim to Christianity*. While this conceptualization of Christianity stresses the importance of Jesus' teaching and practice, it treats questions about the incarnation, the resurrection and the activity of the Holy Spirit as being of little consequence for the shape of the Christian faith. This general pattern can be seen in the following observations. First, the book treats Jesus primarily as a religious teacher and – in contrast to some of the church responses examined (p. 106) – avoids appealing to the incarnation.[3] Second, some statements – for example, that Christianity's capacity to be 'instrumentalized for a variety of political purposes' is 'a strength' (Strømmen and Schmiedel, 2020, p. 139) – seem difficult to reconcile with the doctrine of the incarnation, in so far as the latter precludes the Church from treating Jesus Christ, and Christian teaching about him, as a means to its own political ends. Third, the work does not refer to the resurrection, the contemporary presence or the ongoing ministry of Jesus Christ. Fourth, Christianity is depicted as a collaborative human 'project' that can be adequately characterized, understood and lived without reference to the communicative presence of the risen Christ or the activity of the Holy Spirit. Finally, I have already noted the contrast between the Reformation idiom of hearing, trusting and obeying and the authors' depiction of Christian activity as 'laying claim', 'deciding', 'interpreting and instrumentalizing' (p. 139). One difference between these two idioms is that the latter dampens, if not eliminates, the sense that Christian action is human activity 'in correspondence to the self-bestowing, evocative presence and action of God' (Webster, 2001, p. 64). When considered together, these observations point to a problem with Strømmen and Schmiedel's one-sided emphasis on understanding Christianity as a project: it diminishes the significance of the content of Christian teaching, leading to a truncation of Christological and pneumatological convictions and an overly immanentist conceptualization of the Christian faith.

Third, Strømmen and Schmiedel's emphasis on Christianity's complex, contested and changing character invests heavily in a particular, postmodern view of religion. Consequently, this proposal raises questions about whether this anti-essentialist account of religion will stand the test of time. With one eye on current debates about gender and another on several major publications in systematic theology (e.g. Sonderegger, 2015, 2020), it is not clear to me that either the theological guild or the wider academy have reached a consensus on questions about essentialism. This, in turn, raises another question: why do Strømmen and Schmiedel persistently emphasize the contested and changing character of Christian theology while not acknowledging that the far more recent understanding of culture and religion that undergirds their entire analysis is also a complicated, complex and changing project? Drawing these together, a key problem with *The Claim to Christianity* is its insistence that Christians receive a set of recent and contested anthropological concerns as fixed and unquestioned givens while insisting that we treat scripture and 2,000 years of Christian tradition as shifting sand.

Finally, *The Claim to Christianity* insists that this 'new way' (Strømmen and Schmiedel, 2020, p. 56) of conceptualizing Christianity is required to open Christianity 'up to the other' (pp. 10, 141, 142). However, it is unclear whether Christians reconceptualizing themselves as well-meaning curators of a relatively vacuous religious tradition is necessary, or even beneficial, for enhancing relations between different faith groups. In this regard, we should not overlook Rabbi Deborah Kahn Harris's response to the book offered during the symposium: 'It seems to me to be the height of hubris to suggest that as a majority group with far more social capital than any other minority group in the UK certainly, that Christians need to be asking for help figuring themselves out.'

Despite the significant weaknesses in its ambitious attempt to outline a new way of conceptualizing the Christian faith, *The Claim to Christianity* nevertheless helps readers to think about responding in so far as it introduces and provides insightful commentary upon other valuable responses to far-right claims. I suggest that Christians in the UK seeking to respond to the challenges of the far right have much to learn from the response of Catholic bishops in Germany (Strømmen and Schmiedel, 2020, pp. 83–9). In addition, I suggest that it may be helpful to consult other Christian responses to nationalist and racist regimes, such as the Barmen Declaration, the Belhar Confession and the recent Declaration on the 'Russian World' Teaching by Orthodox theologians from around the world.[4]

What kind of intervention?

Having considered the role of Christian theology, this final part of the chapter explores the kinds of solutions that Strømmen and Schmiedel recommend. As it considers Christian responses to the far right, *The Claim to Christianity* concentrates on large, wealthy, mainline churches. One of the book's central concerns is that these churches make the right kind of statements in response to far-right claims. While such statements are not to be discounted, we should ask whether they deserve such a central place in a Christian response to the far right. As a British Christian, I'd like to ask whether British Christians are likely to change how they act or think as a result of the Archbishop of Canterbury making a suitably nuanced statement about far-right claims to Christianity. To put this more sharply, what fraction of the membership of the Church of England would even be aware that such a statement had been made?

Towards the end of their work, Strømmen and Schmiedel also appeal to Gordon Allport's contact hypothesis (Strømmen and Schmiedel, 2020, pp. 130–4) to contend that any Christian response to the far right 'has to create contact with Muslims' (p. 134). Here, we might note that Northern Ireland has been a testing ground for all kinds of contact initiatives. Scholarly evaluations have attended to the difficulties of implementing such projects. One problem is that those groups who are most likely to espouse hatred and bigotry are the least likely to participate in cross-community initiatives (Church, Visser and Johnson, 2004, p. 281). This may help to explain why some Christian efforts have been criticized for tending to achieve little more than middle-class people building bridges with one another (Brewer, Higgins and Teeney, 2011, p. 185). In light of this, Strømmen and Schmiedel's proposal raises the question of whether it is realistic to think that people with far-right sympathies will opt into church-led projects focusing on mutual encounter between Christians and Muslims. Will these efforts achieve anything other than generating new silos of middle-class people who have no relationships with, nor influence on, people with far-right sympathies?

Rather than invest intensively in nuanced statements that most people will not hear and interfaith encounters that people with far-right sympathies will not join, a Christian response to the far right needs to invest itself in two other areas. The first area concerns relationships with those engaged by the far right and those who provide potential target audiences. Recent reappraisals of the peace process in Northern Ireland have suggested that theologically sophisticated statements and an emphasis on mutual encounter were far less significant than the contribution made by church leaders who maintained relationships with paramilitaries and other hardliners. John Brewer has contended that 'the main religious carriers of change were not ecumenists but those from strong denominational positions ... who pioneered backchannel political dialogue' with illegal paramilitary organizations (Brewer, Higgins and Teeney, 2011, p. 215). These included Catholic priests who did not allow anxiety about personal complicity to break off all connections with illegal paramilitary organizations, even though this involved difficult situations about preaching at paramilitary funerals and responding to requests to deliver the last rites to individuals before executions. Scholars have also noted that an effective challenge to conflations of Protestantism and right-wing unionism came from the Evangelical Contribution on Northern Ireland (ECONI). This insider movement continued to identify with Northern Irish evangelicals and sought to engage this group from within using their own language and theological logic (Brewer, Higgins and Teeney, 2011; Power, 2011).

With this in mind, I suggest that a Christian response to the far right should consider where we invest our relational energies. More specifically, should we allow a preoccupation with personal complicity to distance ourselves from individuals with far-right sympathies? In saying this, I do not intend to portray an either/or choice between relations with the far right and relations with Muslim neighbours. Instead, I contend that the Church must be far more critical of its tendency to vacate working-class spaces and seek out middle-class enclaves. In the same way, Christian theologians who hope to respond to the far right need to supplement concerns about personal complicity with concerns about the vast chasm that renders so many of us unable to communicate effectively with individuals in working-class communities.

The second area concerns addressing the material conditions that provide fertile soil for far-right claims.[5] On Maria Power's analysis, a crucial shift took place in Ireland when an older emphasis on mutual encounter was combined with a new focus on addressing the challenges of violence and other problems faced by local communities (Power, 2007). In light of her work, I suggest that – without discarding or discouraging mutual encounter – a Christian response should focus on pursuing economic justice: fairness, social redistribution, quality housing, schooling and healthcare throughout the country. One advantage of such a strategy is that it addresses some of the economic frustrations that are easily exploited by the far right. Another is that it focuses on common challenges borne by working-class individuals of various ethnic and religious backgrounds. In this way, it may create opportunities for Christians and Muslims from these communities to work in partnership – for example, to pursue regeneration money, secure employment and adequate housing – without making this participation dependent on accepting a new and, as I have contended, problematic reconceptualization of the Christian faith.

In conclusion, *The Claim to Christianity* is essential reading for those interested in developing a response to far-right claims to Christianity. It may also be helpful for Christians in Northern Ireland as they continue to wrestle with a legacy of nationalistic Protestantism. Despite my significant reservations about the book's constructive proposal, Strømmen and Schmiedel's analysis undeniably provides many valuable insights for those seeking to navigate the challenges of responding to the theological claims of the far right.

Notes

1 'Orangeism (and Paisleyism to an even stronger degree) is an oppositional identity forged in and sustained by a hostile political and religious context' (Mitchel, 2003, p. 315).

2 I use the term 'postmodern understanding of cultures and religions' as a way of registering a shared concern with Kathryn Tanner's proposal that a 'postmodern modification of an anthropological notion of culture' characterized by 'a postmodern stress on interactive process and negotiation, interdeterminacy, fragmentation, conflict, and porosity' holds great promise for theology (Tanner, 1997, pp. x, 38).

3 Relatedly we might compare Strømmen and Schmiedel's affirmation that the image of God is 'confirmed in the preaching and practice of Jesus Christ' (pp. 121, 138) with the New Testament, which repeatedly affirms that Jesus *is* the image of God (Col. 1.15–20; 2 Cor. 4.4–6; Heb. 1.1–3) and does not present Jesus as explicitly addressing 'the image of God' in his teaching and preaching.

4 When interpreted together, these responses suggest a different approach that affirms Jesus Christ as the animating centre of Christian resistance to malignant forms of nationalism and racism. This can be seen in that the Barmen Declaration and 'A Declaration on the "Russian World" Teaching' express this in the way that each thesis begins with a citation from the New Testament, followed by a positive confession, followed by a repudiation of false doctrine (Barth, 1980, II/1, pp. 177–8; Bax, 1984; Gallaher and Kalaitzidis, 2022). In making this claim, I do not overlook the well-known weaknesses of the Barmen Declaration: it failed to address rising violence against Germany's Jewish population and its evangelical truths weren't explicitly directed against the Nazi regime. If Barmen was the only example of a Christocentric response to nationalism and racism, it might be contended that a Christocentric approach lacks capacity for political analysis and the ability to name the actions that the Church is called to side with the victims of the far right. However, these other examples refute this argument, in so far as they demonstrate that it is possible to take up Barmen's Christological emphasis while also speaking with a situational concreteness that names specific actions that Christians are called to in the face of nationalist and racist ideology.

5 See James Crossley, in this volume, 'Chapter 7: Encountering and Countering the Far Right in the UK Today'.

References

Barth, K., 1980, *Church Dogmatics*, Edinburgh: T & T Clark.
Bax, D. S., 1984, 'The Barmen Theological Declaration: A New Translation', *Journal of Theology for Southern Africa* 47, pp. 78–81.
Brewer, J. D., G. I. Higgins and F. Teeney, 2011, *Religion, Civil Society, and Peace in Northern Ireland*, Oxford: Oxford University Press.
Bruce, S., 2009, *Paisley: Religion and Politics in Northern Ireland*, Oxford: Oxford University Press.
Church, C., A. Visser and L. S. Johnson, 2004, 'A Path to Peace or Persistence? The "Single Identity" Approach to Conflict Resolution in Northern Ireland', *Conflict Resolution Quarterly* 21(3), pp. 273–93, https://doi.org/10.1002/crq.63 (accessed 5.4.24).
Gallaher, B. and P. Kalaitzidis, 2022, 'A Declaration on the "Russian World" (Russkii Mir) Teaching', *Mission Studies* 39(2), pp. 269–76, https://doi.org/10.1163/15733831-12341850 (accessed 5.4.24).
Ganiel, G., 2007, '"Preaching to the Choir?" An Analysis of DUP Discourses about the Northern Ireland Peace Process', *Irish Political Studies* 22(3), pp. 303–20, https://doi.org/10.1080/01629770701527043 (accessed 5.4.24).
Ganiel, G., 2008, *Evangelicalism and Conflict in Northern Ireland*, Basingstoke, New York: Palgrave Macmillan.
Hickey, J., 1984, *Religion and the Northern Ireland Problem*, Dublin: Gill and Macmillan.
Jordan, G., 2001, *Not of this World? Evangelical Protestants in Northern Ireland*, Belfast: Blackstaff.
Liechty, J. and C. Clegg, 2001, *Moving beyond Sectarianism: Religion, Conflict and Reconciliation in Northern Ireland*, Dublin: Columba Press.
McGarry, J. and B. O'Leary, 1995, *Explaining Northern Ireland: Broken Images*, Oxford: Blackwell.
Mitchel, P., 2003, *Evangelicalism and National Identity in Ulster, 1921–1998*, Oxford: Oxford University Press.
Mitchell, C., 2006, *Religion, Identity and Politics in Northern Ireland: Boundaries of Belonging and Belief*, Aldershot: Ashgate.
O'Leary, J., 2023, *The Padre*, Newbridge: Merrion Press.
Power, M., 2007, *From Ecumenism to Community Relations: Inter-church Relationships in Northern Ireland, 1980–2005*, Dublin: Irish Academic Press.
Power, M., 2011, 'Preparing Evangelical Protestants for Peace: The Evangelical Contribution on Northern Ireland (ECONI) and Peace Building 1987–2005', *Journal of Contemporary Religion* 26(1), pp. 57–72, https://doi.org/10.1080/13537903.2011.539842 (accessed 5.4.24).
Ruane, J. and J. Todd, 1996, *The Dynamics of Conflict in Northern Ireland: Power, Conflict and Emancipation*, Cambridge: Cambridge University Press.
Sonderegger, K., 2015, *Systematic Theology, Volume 1: The Doctrine of God*, Minneapolis: Fortress Press.
Sonderegger, K., 2020, *Systematic Theology, Volume 2: The Doctrine of the Holy Trinity: Processions and Persons*, Minneapolis: Fortress Press.
Strømmen, Hannah and Ulrich Schmiedel, 2020, *The Claim to Christianity: Responding to the Far Right*, London: SCM Press.

Tanner, K., 1997, *Theories of Culture: A New Agenda for Theology*, Minneapolis: Fortress Press (Guides to Theological Inquiry).

Thompson, J., 2003, 'Liechty and Clegg, Moving Beyond Sectarianism: Religion, Conflict and Reconciliation in Northern Ireland', *Studies in World Christianity* 9(2), pp. 280–2, https://doi.org/10.3366/swc.2003.9.2.280 (accessed 5.4.24).

Webster, J., 2001, *Word and Church: Essays in Christian Dogmatics*, Edinburgh: T & T Clark.

12

Taking Theology Out of the Trap: A Response to Nick Spencer and Chris Wilson

HANNAH STRØMMEN AND ULRICH SCHMIEDEL

The two theological responses to *The Claim to Christianity* are very different. In Chapter 10 of this volume, Nick Spencer offers two and a half cheers, reserving the space of half a cheer for criticism. And in Chapter 11, Chris Wilson offers half a cheer, reserving the space of two and a half cheers for criticism. We are grateful for both the cheers and the criticisms because they help us to think further about the role that theology might play in response to the far right. In what follows, we will concentrate on theology, because issues of ethics, politics and practice were already covered in our responses to Steinar Ims and Henrik Frykberg, Martin Accad and Shenaz Bunglawala, as well as James Crossley and William Allchorn. What about theology then?

The criticisms put forward by our respondents revolve around a suggestion that we have talked about throughout this book. In *The Claim to Christianity*, we suggest thinking of Christianity as a 'project' rather than a 'possession' (Strømmen and Schmiedel, 2020, pp. 135–42). Our respondents point out that Christianity is also about a 'person' which means that the turn from possession to project can only go so far (Spencer, Chapter 10 in this volume). Christianity revolves around the person of Jesus of Nazareth. So there can be no Christianity without Christ. We agree wholeheartedly. In fact, it comes as a surprise to us that our suggestion could be seen as a call for a Christianity without content. Re-reading what we wrote, we couldn't find any such call. Yet the fact that both of our respondents have heard it anyway means that we should dig a little deeper. After all, it's possible to say things by saying them and by not saying them. Once we dig a little deeper, we hit on a disagreement between our respondents. It's about the framing of the rise of the far right through the 'semantic struggle' for Christianity (Bednarz, 2009, pp. 7–9). As mentioned in our responses throughout this book, we maintain that claims to Christianity are framed in a struggle for the meaning of Christianity that is on-going.

Spencer concurs with our framing of the rise of the far right through the semantic struggle. His *The Political Samaritan* (2017) – a striking study of the uses and abuses of the parable of the Good Samaritan (Luke 10.25–37) in UK politics that has informed us immensely – presents the history of the interpretation of this very parable as a part of the struggle. As Spencer points out, the 'slippery samaritan' is evidence that 'the semantic struggle will always be with us' (Spencer, Chapter 10 in this volume). Spencer's own interpretation of the parable adds to the semantic struggle by stressing that the parable poses two questions about practice: it asks us whom we are prepared to help and whom we are prepared to accept help from. With these two questions in mind, Spencer follows our suggestion to think about Christianity as a practical project. What keeps him from the full-throated three cheers is that the characterization of Christianity as a project could lose sight of the significance of Jesus of Nazareth. According to Spencer, Christ is at the centre of Christianity, which counters any call for 'abolishing credal or confessional hurdles to membership' (Spencer, Chapter 10 in this volume).

We agree with Spencer. In *The Claim to Christianity*, we contend that a cooperation with Islam shouldn't mean that Christians become Muslims or that Muslims become Christians (Strømmen and Schmiedel, 2020, pp. 10–11, 140–2). This is why we found Mahmoud Ayoub's *A Muslim View of Christianity: Essays on Dialogue* so helpful. 'We must obey God as Muslims and as Christians,' Ayoub argues, 'not as Muslims who are also Christians or Christians who are also Muslims. We are different, and it is God's will that we be different' (Ayoub, 2007, p. 15; Strømmen and Schmiedel, 2020, p. 11). In accordance with Ayoub, then, our argument is anything but advocating for the abolition of credal and confessional hurdles to membership. We aren't asking Christians to get rid of Christ. On the contrary, our argument corresponds to the double commandment of love (Luke 10.27) that kickstarts the conversation in which Jesus tells the parable of the Good Samaritan (Strømmen and Schmiedel, 2020, pp. 7–8, 158–9). To cite Ayoub again: 'the best way to obey God is through care for our fellow human beings' (Ayoub, 2007, p. 15; Strømmen and Schmiedel, 2020, p. 141). Christians answer this call in their way, Muslims answer this call in their way, but we see no reason why these answers shouldn't come together.

As Spencer writes, Christianity is 'about a person' (Spencer, Chapter 10 in this volume). This person has inspired both the practices of Christians and the reflections on the practices of Christians that coagulated into creeds and confessions. Again, we agree. How we interpret the creeds and confessions that are inspired by the person of Christ, however, is not a given – which brings us back into the semantic struggle. Tradition isn't to be taken for granted. We cannot fall back on to it without thinking it through critically and self-critically.

Perhaps it is more in the consequences than in the conceptualization of the turn from possession to project that Spencer parts ways with us. Pointing to practical church politics, he finds that 'criticizing Justin Welby for reimagining a UK in which "Islam is welcome on Christian terms only" rather invites the question what other terms did you expect the Archbishop of Canterbury to use' (Spencer, Chapter 10 in this volume). There is no need to look too far for a response. Welby's predecessor, Archbishop Rowan Williams, offered terms that differed from those proposed by Welby. In a lecture delivered to open a debate on 'Islam in English Law' at the Royal Courts of Justice in London, Williams advocated for a 'transformative accommodation' in which Sharia would be allowed to transform the law of the land and the law of the land would be allowed to transform Sharia (Williams, 2008, p. 274). A lot of ink has been spilled about this dense and difficult lecture – we spilled some of it ourselves – so we won't dwell on it here.[1] What is crucial for practical church politics is that the criticisms of Williams came in fast and furiously. His lecture became known as 'Sharia Speech'. Headlines such as 'The head of the established Church on his knees before terror' and 'What a burkah: Archbishop wants Muslim law in UK' sum it up.[2] We are pointing to Williams's speech to show that it's possible for an archbishop to find ways of welcoming Muslims that go beyond 'on Christian terms only'. Of course, Williams is also speaking in Christian terms. It's arguably his apophatic theology, rooted in the doctrine of the Trinity, that allows him to say what he says (Schmiedel, 2021, pp. 233–45). He is calling neither for Christians to become Muslims nor for Muslims to become Christians. In a way, the criticisms of Williams confirm that he succeeded in challenging the construct of the clash of civilizations that cements the 'respectable racism' that Bunglawala presented and problematized in her response (Bunglawala, Chapter 5 in this volume). To us, there is more of Christianity and more of Christ in Williams's conceptualization of a transformative accommodation than in calls for Christianity to reign triumphantly as the religion that defines the terms of public and political debate in the UK. In any case, Williams shows that even Archbishops of Canterbury can surprise us with how they reimagine the UK.

Chris Wilson (Chapter 11 in this volume) concurs with Spencer's call to concentrate on the person of Jesus of Nazareth, but in contrast to Spencer he criticizes the framework of the semantic struggle that runs through both our methodology and our theology. Methodologically, Wilson suggests that we are moving from interpretation to intervention without offering sufficient intermediate steps. It's hard for us to see how Wilson reached this conclusion when you look at the steps we take throughout *The Claim to Christianity*. In each chapter, we evaluate the interventions of the mainline churches in the country that the chapter covers. Our own intervention is rooted in these evaluations. It is spelled out only in the final chapter, 'Challenging Churches: From Complacency to Critique' (Strømmen and Schmiedel, 2020, pp. 119–45). Although our approach opens us up to charges of 'too little' and 'too late', we waited with our intervention until the very end of the book because the comparison between the interventions is what guided our proposal for what might or might not work.

Of course, we can be criticized for our choice of countries and for our choice of churches. Wilson argues that the 'broad scope' of our book 'constrains its ability to undertake a detailed examination of any one context' (Wilson, in this volume). We found, though, that the comparison between the mainline churches in three countries was precisely what allowed us to pay attention to the specificities of each case. We can also be criticized for our concentration on theology, contending that any response to the far right should consider the social, the political, and particularly the economic factors that shape the context in which theology is conceptualized. We agree with Wilson that theology needs to be put into context. This is why we draw on studies that cover the social, political and economic factors that have contributed to the rise of the far right in Europe. However, to argue that contextual factors shape theology more than theology shapes contextual factors assumes that theology doesn't matter all that much. We're not convinced by this assumption.

Wilson points out that research on Northern Ireland has shown the significance of social, political and economic factors. There is a lot to be learnt from this research. We are grateful to Wilson for highlighting it. Given his expertise and experience of Northern Ireland, he is in a particularly promising position to push this research even further, thus contributing to the understanding of social and political conflicts. We agree with his argument that advocating for the pursuit of economic justice is crucial for people from different confessions and diverse churches to come together. This is spot-on. However, in the cases we covered, the concentration on Islam as the enemy creates connections between categories of race and religion that characterize the 'new racism'

(Chin, 2017; Strømmen and Schmiedel, 2020, pp. 18–21). This new racism, particularly in its Islamophobic pattern, is not what is at stake in Northern Ireland. As a consequence, arguments and analyses don't travel smoothly from one context to the other.

It seems to us that there is some misunderstanding when Wilson concludes that our 'constructive proposals could be summarized by the claim that responses to far-right theologies should reflect the complex and contested character of national and religious identities' (Wilson, Chapter 11 in this volume). As the conversations in this book clarify, his conclusion captures perhaps our point of departure. But it says nothing about our proposal for 'Challenging Churches' that stresses the significance of contact in solidarity with Muslims (Strømmen and Schmiedel, 2020, pp. 119–45).

Wilson recommends researching social, political and economic issues – which makes sense, given that he posits that statements of churches, such as the Church of England, matter very little because only a 'fraction of the membership would even be aware' of them (Wilson, Chapter 11 in this volume). However, it is *theology* that he focuses on. He asserts that the distinction between approaching the identity of Christianity as a project and approaching the identity of Christianity as a possession that we draw is neither explained nor elaborated enough. For Wilson, we counter the theology of the Reformation by making Christianity a 'human project' that cares little for God (Wilson, Chapter 11 in this volume). In particular, he is calling for more christological, pneumatological and soteriological engagement in conversation with theologians such as Karl Barth and Dietrich Bonhoeffer. While Wilson acknowledges in a footnote that the Barmen Declaration is not a straightforward resource given that it fails to mention Jews and Judaism, he recommends it together with similar statements by churches that followed it. It's left somewhat unclear, then, whether church statements do or don't matter for Wilson, unless he assumes that more than a 'fraction of the membership' is aware of the Barmen Declaration.

Finally, Wilson cites a comment that Deborah Kahn Harris made during our conversations. Given that her comment was made in conversation, it's a bit tricky to respond to it here, but since it has been cited we don't want to circumvent it. Kahn Harris noted that it 'seems to be the height of hubris to suggest that as a majority group with far more social capital than any other minority group in the UK certainly, that Christians need to be asking for help figuring themselves out' (Kahn Harris, cited by Wilson, Chapter 11 in this volume). Kahn Harris's call to caution is important and instructive. In all of the countries that we covered in *The Claim to Christianity*, Christians have access to power and privilege. Under these conditions, the call for help from communities who are in the minority rather than the majority can burden them in ways that Christians cannot even imagine. Hence, it's vital for Christians in these countries to reflect on both *when* to call for help and *what* help to call for (Strømmen and Schmiedel, 2020, pp. 57, 71–2, 100–3, 123–35). We have reflected more on the minority and majority positions of Christianity in response to Accad and Bunglawala (Chapters 4 and 5 in this volume). What is crucial here is that the charge of hubris cuts both ways: there can be hubris in a majority assuming that the minority can help them to figure themselves out and there can be hubris in a majority assuming that the minority cannot help them to figure themselves out – that there is nothing to learn from those who aren't in privileged and powerful positions. In our analysis, we have learnt a lot from Jewish and Muslim thinkers, such as Brian Klug, Ephraim Meir, Shadaab Rahemtulla and Mahmoud Ayoub. Neighbourliness, we agree with Spencer, has to do with whom one is willing to help and with whom one is willing to accept help from. Becoming someone's neighbour is far from straightforward.[3]

To come back to Wilson's theological recommendations (Chapter 11 in this volume), Bonhoeffer and Barth make sense when thinking about resisting the far right. Wilson isn't the only one who suggests we ought to take recourse to them.[4] However, there are reasons *not* to go to them when thinking about the rise of the far right in Europe today. This has to do with the connections between 'race' and 'religion' in the 'new racism' again. Of course, Barmen and Barth were not aware of such new racism. Could or should they have been?[5]

Barmen stands out among the Christologically focused statements that Wilson mentions in his response because it was meant to speak into a context where a contrast between Christians and non-Christians – in Barmen's case, Jews – was constructed. It is the construction of such contrasts that concerns us in *The Claim to Christianity*. A concentration on Christology can be problematic in these cases if it presents and pits 'the Christian' against 'the non-Christian' in a way that ends up confirming rather than criticizing the discriminations of the other in the name of Christianity. The fact that it didn't even mention the fate of the Jews, then, is a failure of Barmen, a failure that points to this potential problem of the Christological focus. In contrast to Barmen, the context of the Belhar Confession is concerned with a contrast between Christians and Christians rather than Christians and non-Christians. The very recent 'Declaration on the "Russian World" Teaching' comes closer to Belhar than Barmen in that regard. These cases differ significantly from the ones we are exploring in *The Claim to Christianity*.

Barth confirmed a core concept in the arsenal of anti-Muslim racism in order to respond to the rise of Adolf Hitler's regime – the concept of Islamofascism. In a lecture in which he called churches to resist Hitler, he presented 'national socialism' as the 'new Islam' (Barth, 1939, p. 27). Barth proclaimed: 'One cannot understand national socialism unless one understands it indeed as a new Islam' with 'Hitler as its prophet' (Barth, 1939, p. 27). In response to this 'new Islam', Barth argues that the Church cannot be neutral because Church is combating church here. He points to a prayer that calls for the destruction of 'the bulwarks of the false prophet Mohomet!' (Barth, 1939, p. 41). Barth falls for the theological trap of new racism that we described and discussed in *The Claim to Christianity* (Strømmen and Schmiedel, 2020, pp. 11–13, 20–1, 35–7). His call for resistance against fascism is rooted in a treacherous essentialization of Muslims as 'national socialists' and 'national socialists' as Muslims. It shouldn't come as a surprise, then, that we circumvented Barth in our response to the far right.[6]

In *The Claim to Christianity*, we go through a variety of cases that interpret and instrumentalize the construct of the clash of civilizations that Barth confirms here. Scholar of Islam Reinhard Schulze suggests that the trope of Islamofascism works as a tool to construct identity with a telling turn after 9/11 (Schulze, 2012). In the pre-9/11 world, the connection made between fascism and Islam is meant to exclude fascism from the identity of Christian Euramerica. In the post-9/11 world, the connection made between Islam and fascism is meant to exclude Islam from the identity of Christian Euramerica. The example of Barth shows that even the standard theological sources that we take to offer resistance against fascism – sources that are beyond a doubt in line with the concentration on the word of God, stressed by the Reformation – can fall for the trap of racism that they claim to forfeit. This is not a reason to abandon these sources, particularly in Wilson's case of Northern Ireland where Islam isn't identified as *the* enemy. However, it is a reason to consider the context and the content of all theology critically and self-critically so as to avoid falling into the same trap they fell for. All theological topics, including Christology, pneumatology and soteriology, need to be handled with care.

Interestingly, Schulze points to Paul Tillich to show that there are theologies that escaped the trap (Schulze, 2012, pp. 328–9). According to Schulze, Tillich countered fascism by connecting it to Christianity, thus disturbing any identity construction that could chime with the construct of the clash of civilizations. In a section on the 'History of Revelation' in his *Systematic Theology*, Tillich comments on how the so-called

German Christians attempted to 'cleanse' Christianity of everything that had anything to do with Jews and Judaism (Tillich, 1951, pp. 137–43). Countering these attempts, Tillich argues that 'the paradoxes of Jewish prophetism' and the 'the paradox of the Cross' go hand in hand (Tillich, 1951, p. 142). He continues: 'It is, therefore, not surprising that those who separated the New from the Old Testament ... lost the christological paradox, the center of the New Testament' (Tillich, 1951, p. 142). According to Tillich, the so-called German Christians are among those who lost the paradox of the cross because they attempted to 'cleanse' Christianity of Jews and Judaism. Crucially, Tillich contextualizes these attempts in the history of Christian anti-Judaism that harks back to the very inceptions of Christianity (Tillich, 1951, pp. 142–3). The difference to Barth, then, is subtle but significant. On the one hand, the rise of Hitler's regime *is* countered by externalizing it. Here, fascism is not Christian, but Islamic. On the other hand, the rise of Hitler's regime *is* countered by internalizing it. Here, fascism is not Islamic, but Christian – albeit a Christian heresy. Tillich's interpretation makes Christians as Christians responsive and responsible for countering Hitler's regime.[7]

Crucially, Tillich draws on what he calls 'the symbol of the cross' to make a case that comes very close to our turn from possession to project. In *Dynamics of Faith*, Tillich introduces the cross to distinguish between idolatrous and non-idolatrous interpretations of Christianity, arguing that 'in the picture of the Christ itself the criterion against its idolatrous abuse is given – the Cross' (Tillich, 1956, p. 104). Interpretations that put Christianity above Christ are idolatrous for him, as they assume that for a Christian it's more important to assent to doctrinally defined truths than to live by being ultimately concerned with Christ. Interpretations that put Christ above Christianity are non-idolatrous for him, as they assume that for a Christian it's more important to live by being ultimately concerned with Christ than to assent to doctrinally defined truths. In the terminology that we have used throughout *The Claim to Christianity*, Tillich's distinction could be captured as one between Christianity as a possession and Christianity as a project. If we approach Christianity as a project, we acknowledge and accept that we always stand under the cross. To put it in the terminology that Martin Accad has developed in his account of interfaith dialogue (Accad, 2020, pp. 25–6) – Helen Paynter takes it up in the Conclusion to this book – standing under the cross means that we are concerned with the 'kerygma' rather than the 'dogma', Christ rather than Christianity.

Of course, one can argue that Tillich's account of the symbol of the cross empties Christianity of its content. Many have made this argument about Tillich's theology, often with reference to Barth.[8] But one can also argue that approaching Christianity as a project allows for claims to Christianity that recognize that it is not Christians who own Christ, but Christ who owns Christians.[9] While the terminology of project and possession might be ours, this recognition is arguably at the very start of the movement of people who followed Jesus of Nazareth as their teacher.

It's a little strange to us, then, that our approach to Christianity is called 'postmodern'. Wilson signals that what he is getting at with the charge of postmodernism is our emphasis on process and porosity. Doubtless, we are influenced by thinkers who are associated with the treacherously slippery term of postmodernism. When we write about Christianity as complex and changing, though, there is no need to drag Jacques Derrida or Jean-François Lyotard out of the cupboard. It's simply a fact that Christianity is complex and changing. This has been the case from the very beginning of what we now call 'Christianity'.[10] As scholars have long been showing, what has tended to be labelled 'heterodoxy' and 'orthodoxy' are the results of claims to Christianity winning the day. While some might say that the Spirit was at work in these victories, it is undeniable that any consensus about what Christianity *is* has never been unanimous. If we also take into account everything we *don't* know about how people in the past practised Christianity because nobody cared except to coerce and correct them – slaves, women and children – then there are significant reasons for being careful about assuming historical continuities for some abiding 'essence' of Christianity.[11] If one wants to avoid process and porosity when doing theology, then the case needs to be made against history – not (just) against what has become the all-too-easy target of postmodernism.

We by no means want to erase all the good that has been done in the name of Christianity. But as one feature of the construct of the clash of civilizations is that Islam is characterized as lacking all of these goods, it was crucial to us to challenge this dichotomy. Although we pointed to scholars such as Jörg Lauster who charts the enormous impact Christianity has had on the cultures of Europe (Lauster, 2014; Strømmen and Schmiedel, 2020, pp. 34–5, 42–3, 147), Spencer may be correct that we might be oversensitive to claims to Christianity in public debate and political discourse. Given the material we have been working on, we are not sure that we would want to temper this sensitivity. That is not the same as saying it is always appropriate though.

Overall, the theology that runs through the turn from possession to project that we suggested in *The Claim to Christianity* ought to be contested. As with Christianity itself, we would suggest that such a contestation is a strength rather than a shortcoming because it opens ourselves up to the other. Our word, then, cannot be the last word. But a last word that we would like to say is thank you again for both the cheers and the criticisms offered by our respondents. They have helped us to think and re-think the significance of theology for countering the rise of the far right. Together, we can continue this re-thinking.

Notes

1 For a summary of the debate, including references to analyses of Williams's lecture, see Ulrich Schmiedel, 2021, *Terror und Theologie: Der religionstheoretische Diskurs der 9/11-Dekade*, Tübingen: Mohr Siebeck, pp. 233–45.

2 See Schmiedel, 2021, *Terror und Theologie*, pp. 233–4.

3 See the contributions to Marianne Bjelland Kartzow (ed.), 2021, *The Ambiguous Figure of the Neighbor in Jewish, Christian, and Islamic Texts and Receptions*, London: Routledge.

4 Peter Selby, 2020, 'Review of *The Claim to Christianity: Responding to the Far Right*' also points to the response of the German churches to 'national socialism' as a role model for responding to the far right, presumably referring to Bonhoeffer and Barth as well as the Barmen Declaration, *Church Times*, 6 November, https://www.churchtimes.co.uk/articles/2020/6-november/books-arts/book-reviews/the-claim-to-christianity-responding-to-the-far-right-by-hannah-stroemmen-and-ulrich-schmiedel. (accessed 5.4.24).

5 Bonhoeffer's striking statement that 'only the person who cries for the Jews may sing Gregorian chants' suggests that he was aware of the role that religion plays in the construction of antisemitism (Bonhoeffer, cited in Andreas Pangritz, 'Bonhoeffer and the Jews', in Michael Mawson and Philip G. Ziegler (eds), 2019, *The Oxford Handbook of Dietrich Bonhoeffer*, Oxford: Oxford University Press, p. 99).

6 Joshua Ralston, 2020, *Law and the Rule of God: A Christian Engagement with Sharī'a*, Cambridge: Cambridge University Press, pp. 199–252, shows how Barth can be retrieved for a comparative theology that is conducted in conversation with Islam.

7 Dorothee Sölle's concept of Christofascism pushes this even further, Dorothee Sölle, 1987, *Das Fenster der Verwundbarkeit: Theologisch-politische Texte*, Stuttgart: Kreuz Verlag, pp. 158–67. The English translation is available as Dorothee Sölle, 1990, *The Window of Vulnerability: A Political Spirituality*, Minneapolis: Fortress.

8 See, for example, Oswald Bayer, 2008, 'Grundzüge der Theologie Paul Tillichs, kritisch dargestellt', *Neue Zeitschrift für Systematische Theologie und Religionsphilosophie* 49(3), pp. 325–48. For a helpful overview of the arguments commonly made in connection with such a critique, see Gorazd Andrejč, 2019, 'Liberal Theology as a Slippery Slope: What's in the Metaphor?', in Jörg Lauster, Ulrich Schmiedel and Peter Schüz (eds), *Liberale Theologie heute – Liberal Theology Today*, Tübingen: Mohr Siebeck, pp. 215–26.

9 However, Tillich's theology is also problematic in as much as he draws on the symbol of the cross to single out Christianity, describing it as the only religion

that has the capability to critique itself. See Ulrich Schmiedel, 2022, 'The Legacy of Theological Liberalism: A Ghost in Public Theology', in Christoph Hübenthal and Christiane Alpers (eds), *T & T Clark Handbook of Public Theology*, London: Bloomsbury, pp. 127–45.

10 Bart D. Ehrman has emphasized the way alternative forms of Christianity in the early centuries wrestled over a number of major doctrinal questions, many of them unthinkable for contemporary Christians, such as how many gods there are, whether God created the world, and whether Jesus' death had anything to do with salvation. See Bart D. Ehrman, 2003, *Lost Scriptures: Books that Did Not Make It into the New Testament*, Oxford: Oxford University Press, and Bart D. Ehrman, 2005, *Lost Christianities: The Battle for Scripture and the Faiths We Never Knew*, Oxford: Oxford University Press.

11 To name a few famous examples: Mary Daly, 1973, *Beyond God the Father: Toward a Philosophy of Women's Liberation*, Boston: Beacon Press; J. Kameron Carter, 2009, *Race: A Theological Account*, Oxford: Oxford University Press; Gil Anidjar, 2014, *Blood: A Critique of Christianity*, New York: Columbia University Press. Dominant conceptualizations of Christianity have been critiqued for the impact their dominance has had.

References

Accad, Martin, 2020, 'View of Islam: Between Demonization and Idealization', in Martin Accad and Jonathan Andrews (eds), *The Religious Other: A Biblical Understanding of Islam, the Qur'an and Muhammad*, Carlisle: Langham Global Library, pp. 22–8.

Andrejč, Gorazed, 2019, 'Liberal Theology as a Slippery Slope: What's in the Metaphor?', in Jörg Lauster, Ulrich Schmiedel and Peter Schüz (eds), *Liberale Theologie heute – Liberal Theology Today*, Tübingen: Mohr Siebeck, pp. 215–26.

Anidjar, Gil, 2014, *Blood: A Critique of Christianity*, New York: Columbia University Press.

Ayoub, Mahmoud, 2007, *A Muslim View of Christianity: Essays on Dialogue*, Maryknoll: Orbis.

Barth, Karl, 1939, *Die Kirche und die politische Frage von heute. Vortrag gehalten an der Versammlung des Schweizerischen evangelischen Hilfswerks für die bekennende Kirche in Deutschland im Kirchgemeindehaus Wipkingen am 5. Dezember 1938*, Zurich: Verlag der evangelischen Buchhandlung.

Bayer, Oswald, 2008, 'Grundzüge der Theologie Paul Tillichs, kritisch dargestellt', *Neue Zeitschrift für Systematische Theologie und Religionsphilosophie* 49(3), pp. 325–48.

Bednarz, Liane, 2018, *Die Angstprediger: Wie rechte Christen Gesellschaft und Kirchen unterwandern*, München: Droemer.

Bunglawala, Shenaz, in this volume, 'Chapter 5: Beyond the Far Right: "Respectable Racism" and British Muslims'.

Carter, J. Kameron, 2009, *Race: A Theological Account*, Oxford: Oxford University Press.

Chin, Rita, 2017, *The Crisis of Multiculturalism in Europe: A History*, Princeton: Princeton University Press.

Daly, Mary, 1973, *Beyond God the Father: Toward a Philosophy of Women's Liberation*, Boston: Beacon Press.
Ehrman, Bart D., 2003, *Lost Scriptures: Books that Did Not Make It into the New Testament*, Oxford: Oxford University Press.
Ehrman, Bart D., 2005, *Lost Christianities: The Battle for Scripture and the Faiths We Never Knew*, Oxford: Oxford University Press.
Kartzow, Marianne Bjelland (ed.), 2021, *The Ambiguous Figure of the Neighbor in Jewish, Christian, and Islamic Texts and Receptions*, London: Routledge.
Lauster, Jörg, 2014, *Die Verzauberung der Welt: Eine Kulturgeschichte des Christentums*. Munich: C. H. Beck.
Pangritz, Andreas, 2019, 'Bonhoeffer and the Jews', in Michael Mawson and Philip G. Ziegler (eds), *The Oxford Handbook of Dietrich Bonhoeffer*, Oxford: Oxford University Press 2019, pp. 91–107.
Paynter, Helen, in this volume, 'Conclusion: The Church, the Far Right, and the Claim to Christianity: Towards Some Recommendations'.
Ralston, Joshua, 2020, *Law and the Rule of God: A Christian Engagement with Sharī'a*, Cambridge: Cambridge University Press.
Schmiedel, Ulrich, 2021, *Terror und Theologie: Der religionstheoretische Diskurs der 9/11-Dekade*, Tübingen: Mohr Siebeck.
Schmiedel, Ulrich, 2022, 'The Legacy of Theological Liberalism: A Ghost in Public Theology', in Christoph Hübenthal and Christiane Alpers (eds), *T & T Clark Handbook of Public Theology*, London: Bloomsbury, pp. 127–45.
Schulze, Reinhard, 2012, 'Islamofascism: Four Avenues to the Use of an Epithet', *Die Welt des Islam* 52, pp. 290–330.
Selby, Peter, 2020, 'Review of *The Claim to Christianity: Responding to the Far Right*', *Church Times*, https://www.churchtimes.co.uk/articles/2020/6-november/books-arts/book-reviews/the-claim-to-christianity-responding-to-the-far-right-by-hannah-stroemmen-and-ulrich-schmiedel (accessed 5.4.24).
Sölle, Dorothee, 1987, *Das Fenster der Verwundbarkeit: Theologisch-politische Texte*, Stuttgart: Kreuz Verlag.
Sölle, Dorothee, 1990, *The Window of Vulnerability: A Political Spirituality*, Minneapolis: Fortress Press.
Spencer, Nick, 2017, *The Political Samaritan: How Power Hijacked a Parable*, London: Bloomsbury.
Spencer, Nick, in this volume, 'Chapter 10: The "Semantic Struggle" against the Christian Far Right: Learning from the Good Samaritan'.
Strømmen, Hannah and Ulrich Schmiedel, 2020, *The Claim to Christianity: Responding to the Far Right*, London: SCM Press.
Tillich, Paul, 1951, *Systematic Theology*, Volume 1, Chicago: University of Chicago Press.
Tillich, Paul, 1956, *Dynamics of Faith*, New York: Harper.
Williams, Rowan, 2008, 'Civil and Religious Law in England: A Religious Perspective', *Ecclesiastical Law Society* 10(3), pp. 262–82.
Wilson, Chris, in this volume, 'Chapter 11: Challenging Far-right Claims to Christianity: A Northern Irish Perspective'.

Conclusion

The Church, the Far Right, and the Claim to Christianity: Towards Some Recommendations

HELEN PAYNTER

The colloquium that we convened was – for me – both inspiring and challenging in equal measure. It was inspiring to be in the same room as a group of people diverse in faith perspective, academic specialism, nationality and lived experience, who had all gathered to give their attention to a single question: how should the UK Church respond to the growing threat of the extreme right? It was also inspiring to be part of conversations that were gracious, truth-seeking and collaborative. But it was challenging to listen to those divergent opinions, sometimes strikingly so, and to seek to tease out practical applications and conclusions for a real Church in a real world. And it was challenging because these are not ivory-tower questions, but genuine, tangible issues for today and the years ahead. As I write this Conclusion in November 2023, incidents of both antisemitic and Islamophobic violence have taken a sharp upsurge here in the UK, as a result of the Israel–Hamas war that erupted with fresh ferocity a few weeks ago.

In this Conclusion I offer my own reflections on the question of how the Church should respond, in the light of the conversations that were held, and of the chapters that are offered in this book. I write as a Baptist minister with a pastoral concern for local churches, and as a biblical scholar who is deeply invested in combating the weaponization of scripture. Others might come to a different set of conclusions, but these are the stand-out learning points that emerged for me. I have here endeavoured to be highly applied and practical, leaning upon the best of academic research and practical experience. At the end of this Conclusion, the learning points are condensed further into a list of ten recommendations.

Facing up to the Problem

A core element of *The Claim to Christianity* is that it encourages the Church to face up to its occasional complicity with the far right, rather than disown the problem and seek to distance itself from it:

> When churches take on the strategy of challenge, they acknowledge particular periods and particular places in which such conflict existed, but they stress that such conflict is not necessary for Christianity to be Christianity. On the contrary, these periods and positions can be grounds for repentance. (Strømmen and Schmiedel, 2020, p. 100)

In an era when shady happenings within ecclesial contexts are being discovered far too regularly, it is imperative that the Church face square-on our own complicity in narratives that feed the far right.

This includes mainstream elements of our theology which can become weaponized. For instance, in his 'manifesto', the Norwegian mass-murderer Anders Breivik referred to the scriptural idea of God as a 'man of war'. The phrase, used in Exodus 15.3, 6 and Isaiah 42.13, was unremarkable in its original biblical context, and is uncontroversial in many parts of the Church today which would not dream of instrumentalizing it for contemporary violence. Nevertheless, Breivik used the phrase in support of his crusade, and even quoted the relevant scriptures (Breivik, 2011, p. 1332).[1]

These quotations are from the Old Testament, although by no means from obscure corners of it – Exodus 15.3 and 6 appear in the Revised Common Lectionary, for instance. It is true that, in many churches in the UK, the Old Testament is not read or preached from one month to the next. Even in the churches that use a lectionary, and therefore have a (curated) reading from the Old Testament every week, the preaching will generally relate to the New Testament text. But for the Church to ignore such scriptures and their potential for violent appropriation is an insufficient response that will only enable further such abuses. For this reason, the work of biblical interpretation for the sake of the Church, and in particular the work of faithful, careful hermeneutics of texts such as these, is more pressing today than it has ever been.[2]

This same spirit of honesty will also compel us to name and own contemporary and historical cases where the Church has been overtly complicit with racialized or nationalistic violence. There are always dissenters, of course, but the overwhelming support of Hungarian evangelicals for Viktor Orbán,[3] or of American white evangelicals for Donald

Trump,[4] should provoke the Western evangelical Church to deep soul-searching. Nor is the UK exempt, although happily widespread support of the Church for far-right groups is not yet in evidence.

However, a study that surveyed attitudes of Christians in 15 Western European countries, including the UK, showed that in response to the statement 'our people are not perfect, but our culture is superior to others', 54 per cent of church-attending Christians agreed, compared to 45 per cent in the overall population. A second statement, 'it is very/somewhat important to have a [British/English] family background to be truly [British/English]', generated a 72 per cent agreement from church-attending Christians, compared with 53 per cent in the overall population (Pew Research Center, 2018).

We need to be honest about the Church's historic and contemporary complicity with violence and othering, whether it is done through a theology we would wish to disclaim, or whether the rhetoric lies uncomfortably close to our own theological position. This non-defensive stance will be the indispensable first step in cultivating a faithful and useful response to the problem.

In exploration of the point above, the colloquium group spent some time debating the extent of the responsibility carried by the Church (or churches) to make public disavowal of aggressive actions or rhetoric offered under a 'Christian' banner. Our contributors from other faiths, particularly our Muslim participant Shenaz Bunglawala, reflected on the undue burden that such an expectation places on grassroots organizations, who may be repeatedly called upon to condemn (or criticized for failing instantly to condemn) Islamist attacks on British soil or around the world. None the less, as Martin Accad identifies (Chapter 4), more centralized and scholarly representatives of the Islamic faith have been commendably proactive in their response to recent atrocities:

> In the 18 months that followed [the emergence of *Daesh* in the summer of 2014], I collected with a group of colleagues the closing statements of over 30 conferences organized globally by Muslim authorities and organizations, which had clearly been convened in response to ISIS ...
>
> The themes that emerged from this introspection were not entirely new, but to my knowledge they had never been so broadly endorsed and vehemently affirmed. These included radically revisionist views of classical concepts of Jihad, the Caliphate, and the very notion of an Islamic state. (pp. 65–6)

We concluded that the Church has a responsibility to speak in clear condemnation of such misappropriations through its more central instruments. In the Church of England this might be from the top, such as the Archbishops' Council; in the less hierarchical traditions this responsibility may be delegated to spokespeople (such as the General Secretary of the Baptist Union of Great Britain). In both the established and dissenting churches, the importance of socially oriented think-tanks (such as Theos, Las Casas, or the Joint Public Issues Team)[5] and the theological work of scholars within those traditions is also vital. In other words, the thought-leaders within the denomination must take responsibility for the disavowal of violent actions in the Church's name, and for seeking to provide more faithful interpretations of instrumentalized texts.

However, notwithstanding this important public work, we should not anticipate that point-by-point rebuttals are likely to have any significant impact on those who are embedded within the often conspiracist narratives of the far right. There is a danger here of confusing two separate tasks. One is to help the Church to be, or to become, resistant to far-right narratives. This is a challenge that we can, and should, tackle. The other task is to help people who have already bought into these narratives to emerge from their influence. Such rehabilitation is likely to prove a highly specialized task and, depending on the degree of enmeshment and any criminal activity, it may amount to deradicalization, which certainly needs to be delegated to those with specific training in the field.

But in terms of the Church's public engagement, the non-defensive stance identified above must be combined with a refusal to remain silent about violent actions or speech conducted in its name. Silence is complicity. It is not necessary or plausible for every member to have a well-prepared statement of disavowal in hand for any eventuality, but it is the responsibility of the Church to make clear its refusal to collude. As Shenaz Bunglawala writes (Chapter 5), 'there is a notable difference between resisting the performativity inherent in demands to condemn, and displaying a lackadaisical attitude to violence committed by those purporting to act for or in the name of religion'. We walk the fine line between ignoring toxic rhetoric (which can make us complicit with it), and giving such rhetoric the oxygen of publicity through public and strident attempts to disavow it.

This leads us into a consideration of *how* the Church might publicly address the issues.

CONCLUSION

Whether to Dialogue, and How

The perceived threat posed by immigrants coming from certain stigmatized countries is that they represent a threat to the 'British way of life'. In the investigation into the Windrush scandal,[6] evidence provided to a British Parliamentary enquiry claimed that:

> [t]he infamous hostile environment agenda was not birthed out of thin air. It is the result of decades of antagonism towards immigrants and ethnic minorities. One of the most explicit examples of this was Enoch Powell's 'Rivers of Blood' speech in 1961. Here he accused immigrants of posing a threat to the way of life of people in Britain. (Osifo, 2020)

In our own day, the rhetoric of immigrants being at odds with 'British values' is promoted by the far-right party Britain First,[7] but also by mainstream politicians such as Suella Braverman, who was Home Secretary from 6 September 2022 to 13 November 2023.[8] The values under discussion might mean different things to different people, but a representative list was offered in 2014 by the then Prime Minister David Cameron: 'a belief in freedom, tolerance of others, accepting personal and social responsibility, respecting and upholding the rule of law'.[9]

It is therefore ironic that many of the measures suggested by far-right groups in response to the 'immigrant threat' are themselves intolerant and undemocratic. In some cases at least this emerges as a reaction to the liberal pushback against illiberal religious practices (Minkenberg, 2018, cf. Gushee, 2023, pp. 65–71).

In response to this, some churches work to promote democratic engagement and open dialogue. They host election hustings, or put on round-table discussion events, providing platforms for open debate in the hope that this will strengthen democracy.

Strømmen and Schmiedel offer words of caution around this practice. First, it presupposes that the Church should occupy a 'neutral' stance. In order to facilitate discussion and give an unprejudiced platform, the host or convener must express no opinion or, implicitly, occupy central ground. But this might come at the expense of advocacy:

> In a system of coordinates stretched out between left and right, churches claim to have the same distance from the left and from the right. Openness, however, is not neutrality. There can be no neutral position in the face of the persons who are turned into non-persons, whose dignity is

neither acknowledged. Unlike neutrality, openness can put the poor first. (Strømmen and Schmiedel, 2020, pp. 108–9)

Steinar Ims (Chapter 1) also offers caution around the idealization of neutrality. His Dialogue Pilots programme encourages the explicit 'ownership' of the Pilots' 'givens'; dialogue should be a 'mutual encounter between equal parties, *without hidden agendas*' (emphasis mine).

Strømmen and Schmiedel's second caution arises from the complex dynamics of hospitality and power. To convene such an event can reinforce the idea that the Church has a better grasp on democracy than others (such as Muslims) do; and that it – the Church – should have the privilege to determine who is included and excluded, who speaks and who is silent, and when and where the meeting should be convened:

> To decide about who can and who can't contribute to the consensus or the contestation – who is and who isn't 'in' the corridor, so to speak – requires a lot of power. Although this presumption is neither acknowledged nor argued for, it has consequences. One consequence is that the churches which assume they are neutral have a blind spot: Islam. If churches can make and maintain the corridor, then whose corridor is it? (Strømmen and Schmiedel, 2020, pp. 98–9)

There was brisk discussion of these issues during our consultation. Many of us felt the desire to 'talk with the bandits', to use Maria Power's term as she reflected on the parable of the Good Samaritan. Steinar Ims (Chapter 1) concurs:

> We need to find ways to invite these far-right voices ... into the churches for discussion and confrontation ... We need to call them out if they do not accept the invitation or are not willing to agree to the rules of encounter. (p. 26)

This is, however, a risky endeavour. Writing of the Northern Ireland context, Chris Wilson (Chapter 11) observes that:

> theologically sophisticated statements and an emphasis on mutual encounter were far less significant than the contribution made by church leaders who maintained relationships with paramilitaries and other hardliners. (p. 156)

However, some who have had direct dealings with far-right apologists caution both against platforming them and allowing them to waste our time in private meetings. In our conversation, James Crossley and Bonnie Evans-Hills advised that the far right instrumentalizes freedom of expression for its own ends. Many of its leading figures are masters at the tactic of endless fruitless dialogues, and of 'winding up' those who seek to reason with them.

On balance, surely conversation, careful listening and dialogue should be considered virtues. But the Church must not be naïve to the cautions offered: the risk of prioritizing neutrality over advocacy; the risk of giving credibility to harmful ideologies; the risk of allowing our good intentions to be cynically instrumentalized. Perhaps most importantly, the Church must be aware of the power relationships that lie in the background to any convening initiative, and that also lie within the room when such meetings occur. As a bare minimum, there must be advance agreement of rules for the conduct of the dialogue.

A related issue is the danger that in our enthusiasm to promote a non-racist agenda, we replicate the stance of those we seek to challenge. The human tendency to act in mimesis (imitation) of our adversaries is universal (Girard, 1977, pp. 143–68).

For example, one of the tropes of the far right in the UK and European context is to present Islam as a monolithic whole rather than a diverse faith tradition:

> Islam is taken in the dominant European imaginary to represent a collection of lacks: of freedom; of a disposition of scientific inquiry; of civility and manners; of love of life; of human worth; of equal respect for women and gay people. (Goldberg, 2006, p. 345)

Even if such essentialization is a key component of the far right's view of Muslims, we must not respond to it mimetically, by essentializing adherents of the far right. They, too, are diverse in age, ethnicity, motivation and the expression of their views (Butt, 2022). They are also diverse in the degree of their commitment to far-right ideology, and indeed in their previous political opinions. Nor should we speak as if everyone who is to our right on the political spectrum is 'extreme'. It is important to listen carefully and to seek to build bridges rather than demonizing those we disagree with.

The Church needs to model another way of disagreeing. We need to be bold truth-tellers, standing up unashamedly for the cause of all who are marginalized, but we also need to be gracious dialogue partners, with those who will dialogue in the same spirit with us. This entails listening carefully and well, and choosing not to reduce the political 'other' to a two-dimensional enemy. By modelling gracious, truth-seeking discourse, we can hope to turn the mimetic spiral in the other direction. At the very least, refusal to engage in the combative methods modelled by our antagonists moves the rules of engagement into more irenic territory.

One example of such 'othering' offered by several of the colloquium participants concerned the dangers of vilifying the white working class. The narrative that racism festers in white council estates, then finding its expression in far-right ideologies and campaigning, is a dangerously unhelpful stereotype. An anecdote shared by colloquium participant Bonnie Evans-Hills illustrates this. She describes being trapped in a train carriage, one of only two women, marked out by her clerical collar, and verbally baited by the other passengers. The rest of the carriage was occupied by well-to-do men returning from a social weekend away (and correspondingly well lubricated with alcohol), whose conversation indicated that they all worked in the finance sector in London, and that they were all members of UKIP or Generation Identity. In short, there are plenty of wealthy supporters of the far-right movements. In international terms, there is no shortage of evidence that enormous amounts of dark money are financing these movements.[10] Within the UK, the financing of Britain First appears to be obscured by a shell fund;[11] there may be Mafia links to certain far-right organizations;[12] and money from wealthy US funders is supporting the most right-wing of the mainstream political parties in the UK.[13] Far-right ideology is far from confined to the lower socioeconomic classes.

However, it cannot be denied that the ideology of the far right does find purchase in areas of socioeconomic deprivation and unemployment, a point made by James Crossley (Chapter 7) and Chris Wilson (Chapter 11). (See also Boon, 2010.) Henrik Frykberg (Chapter 2) points out the danger of collapsing racism to the individual rather than seeing it as the consequence of structural issues. Those who feel 'left behind', and experience fear, insecurity or a sense of alienation from the democratic process – what Nietzsche would term *ressentiment* – prove more susceptible to far-right ideologies (Salmela and Scheve, 2017).

Unfortunately, well-intentioned responses by the Church, or by individuals, can exacerbate this problem, particularly the sense of alienation. Those who mobilize within the Church on these issues are frequently those from the so-called 'metropolitan elite' – people who have been educated at university level, are politically liberal, and enjoy moderate affluence. The consequence of this is that the Church may be perceived to talk down to working-class people (and indeed this may be no misplaced perception), lecturing them on their 'bigotry'. Far better to 'kick upwards' (to use Steinar Ims's expression), calling to account those whose systems, structures and policies have driven deprivation and marginalization. This point is powerfully made by James Crossley (Chapter 7), and, as Chris Wilson points out (Chapter 11), any theological issues around the mobilization of far-right ideologies need to be held in the wider economic, political and cultural context.

The problems raised by conflating political liberalism with theological orthodoxy are manifold. In missional terms it introduces or reinforces the sense of a gulf between the Church and the reality of life for working-class people: the Church is 'out of touch'; its theology is of the 'ivory tower'; it is a religion for the 'haves' rather than the 'have-nots'. In political terms it is also counter-productive. Opinions formed in the context of life's harshest realities are not reshaped when those who do not share those realities shout at the people who hold them.

Strømmen and Schmiedel seek to mitigate this danger by the use of liberation theology (Strømmen and Schmiedel, 2020, pp. 101ff.), an approach forged in the favelas of Latin America, which privileges the perspective of the most marginalized. Significantly, this theological move was developed by indigenous theologians living among the most marginalized of Latin America. It is a theology driven by solidarity and incarnationalism. Is the UK Church attending sufficiently to the theological articulations of confessing Christians living at the margins of our society? We should beware of making this an exclusively middle-class project.

Further, as Chris Wilson writes (Chapter 11), suspicion towards the white working class runs the risk of reinforcing the divisions between 'natives' and 'immigrants' by casting hardship relief and even inclusion as a zero-sum gain. The Church needs to find ways of embracing the hardships of all – *simultaneously*. No one can fairly accuse the UK Church of being indifferent on matters of – for instance – food poverty, fuel poverty, human trafficking and refugees. But projects working largely for the relief of what we might call 'indigenous deprivation' and those working for the benefit of the immigrant have tended to be managed by separate interest groups within the Church; interest groups that can tend to pit their priorities in opposition to one another. We need to find better ways of joining up these equally valid concerns. As Crossley says (Chapter 7):

> Where churches act as hubs of community support, they have individuals better equipped than most to deal with, or act as a point of contact for, disillusioned and isolated individuals attracted to far-right ideas, particularly in their Christianized forms. (p. 101)

Prevention is Better than Cure

But reaction is always less preferable than prevention. Here, another anecdote may help. In May 2019, I attended the first annual conference of the Centre for the Analysis of the Radical Right, whose former director William Allchorn was a participant in our colloquium and has contributed Chapter 8 to this book. In addition to a range of stimulating and disturbing paper presentations were interviews with two 'Formers': people who have exited violent right-wing movements through a process of deradicalization. Both of the interviewed men had been radicalized in their teens; one of the strong take-home messages for me was the consistent message that they had no deep right-wing ideology in the first instance, but were drawn into these movements by a group who showed them respect, affection and community. I was left wondering what might have happened if they had encountered a thriving church youth group instead.

The UK Church has seen a gradual decline in youth worker training and youth worker positions over the last decade. This is a trend that has many causes, of which funding decline in the wake of austerity measures is a significant one (Howell, 2022). This has many consequences, but one that should not be overlooked is the risk that we are abandoning to the mercies of hard-right extremists young people who might otherwise be drawn into the Church and into healthy relationships.

Another form of prevention, again particularly relevant to young people, is found in programmes that train them in non-disputatious dialogue, and courteous and curious listening to those who are different from them. This facilitates respect across religious and cultural divides. There are a number of creative projects that model replicable good practice. One example is offered by Steinar Ims (Chapter 1), where he describes the 'Dialogue Pilots' programme; a similar example in the UK can be found in 'The Feast' youth project, a programme that facilitates dialogue between young people of different faiths.[14] The contributor of Chapter 4 to this book, Martin Accad, is the Director of Action Research Associates,[15] which seeks to build resilient societies through exploring the divergent narratives around painful moments in a community's past, using the model developed by South Africa's Truth and Reconciliation project:

> The Truth and Reconciliation Lebanon project seeks to address this situation, not by seeking a unified national history, but by recognizing the legitimacy of each community's perspective and weaving them

into a common national tapestry. The goal is to cultivate understanding and empathy across sectarian lines by facilitating conversations about opposing perspectives on contentious events. In the long term, this is meant to foster reconciliation and a vision for the common good.[16]

A further preventative action, perhaps optimally aimed at young people, but with wider benefit if applied effectively, is providing training in critical thinking. A key part of this is the need to equip our young people with the tools that they need to handle social media wisely, due to its enormous capacity to polarize by the amplification of extreme rather than moderate voices, and by the production of echo-chambers.

While critical thinking skills might properly be considered the purview of schools, church youth work should reinforce such proficiencies. Sadly, sometimes, the catechizing of young people – where this takes place in church youth work – may be done in a way that stifles rather than promotes questioning, debate and the discussion of hard topics. This may also be reinforced within the mainstream education system. Anecdotally, as the mother of three daughters who took GCSE Religious Studies[17] between 2014 and 2018, I was appalled by the way that nuanced Christian and Muslim theological positions were collapsed into simplistic – and inaccurate – proof-texting. (I should add that this was driven by the curriculum and exam mark schemes, and not by local teachers.) Teaching young people that believers from the major faith traditions unthinkingly regurgitate trite and decontextualized scriptural texts neither models good practice nor promotes cross-religious respect.

This discussion of secondary education leads on to tertiary and vocational education, particularly as it relates to theological and biblical literacy within the churches. There are many pressures on ministerial training (or 'formation') programmes today. Where once aspiring clergy were trained in biblical languages, scripture and patristic theology, now an enormous range of concerns press upon us – I speak as one who is heavily involved in the training of Baptist ministers at the Bristol Baptist College. Rightly, we now provide space in our ministerial formation programmes for safeguarding training, leading change, pastoral counselling, church planting and a thousand more things. Our colloquium discussions highlighted the importance of basic competence in social sciences for our training programmes, too.

But if we are tempted to water down the theological and biblical training of ministers and priests, we do so at great risk. This is one of the challenges that theological colleges are facing in the current UK climate, where previous funding models are being trimmed, and where the much-quoted line 'we've had enough of experts'[18] is finding approval in parts of the Church. But there is clear evidence that those in our congregations who are regularly exposed to biblical teaching are less likely to show signs of radicalization and violence (Billiet, 1995; see also William Allchorn (Chapter 8)).[19] Further, it is clear that the theological trajectories that lead to autocratic shifts among Christians require wise and careful handling by those who have deep roots in the scriptural and theological traditions of our faith.

The Prophetic Church

If we, the Church, are to respond faithfully to this challenge, our engagement must be attentive to the spiritual dynamics that are at play. The Church is not simply another social organization, but – we who are Christians believe – the dwelling place of the Living God (Eph. 2.22); the first-fruits of the eschaton (2 Thess. 2.13); and the mystery of unity that God concealed in ages past and then revealed in his Son (Eph. 3.3–6). Here, I concur with Chris Wilson's critique (Chapter 11) of *The Claim to Christianity*, that:

> the work does not refer to the resurrection, the contemporary presence or the ongoing ministry of Jesus Christ ... Christianity is depicted as a collaborative human 'project' that can be adequately characterized, understood and lived without reference to the communicative presence of the risen Christ or the activity of the Holy Spirit. (p. 154)

Practical solutions, such as the ones proposed above, will only take us part of the way, because at heart this is a spiritual problem. (This is, of course, not at all saying that we should view those we disagree with as demonized![20]) We all live in, and are products of, a world that is broken, and some key features of that brokenness are inhospitality, suspicion and violence. Understanding political realities in the light of this theological framework invites us to look at the distinctive role that the Church can play in the situation. One way to express this is to understand the Church as having a prophetic calling:

> The Church is called into being by God to be a prophetic community that both points to and incompletely manifests the life of the world to come. The Church's role is not identical to that of the [Old Testament] prophets, but our calling is in continuity with theirs – to represent the

truth of God by word and deed ... [W]e are to witness by word and action to the peaceful, just, and holy world that God is inaugurating. (Paynter, 2023, pp. 243-4)

What does a prophetic Church look like in this context? Nick Spencer (Chapter 10) urges us to move from semantics to praxis; from the lawyer's technical, perhaps even casuistic, question of who a neighbour *is*, to Jesus' insistent words about what a neighbour *does*. 'Go and do likewise' (Luke 10.37). The faithful response must always be more than words *about*, more even than words *to* – important as truth-telling and gospel proclamation are. As we have discussed above, it will involve hard grassroots work to relieve material conditions that can prove an active seedbed for the far right.

It may also involve prophetic action and disruptive practice. Henrik Frykberg (Chapter 2) describes the creatively disruptive actions taken by some Swedish Christians in response to the planned burning of the Qur'an in a public place. They were also joined on some of those occasions by local Muslims, who made their own peaceful protest.

This exemplifies one of the themes emphasized by Strømmen and Schmiedel: that contact with those who are 'other' can be a positive way of reducing cross-cultural tension, especially when that contact is meaningful, prolonged and in the pursuit of a shared goal (Strømmen and Schmiedel, 2020, p. 120).

For some Christians, the call to make common cause with Muslims is troubling. Aren't they the 'religious other' whom we should be seeking to convert? A helpful perspective on this question has been offered by another of our colloquium participants, Martin Accad, who developed the SEKAP model of five positions Christians take as they engage with Muslims. These positions are:

- Syncretistic – affirms all faiths and makes no truth claims about one's own faith.
- Existential – seeks common ground on ethical or practical matters, and disregards theological differences.
- Kerygmatic – see below.
- Apologetic – defends the Christian faith when challenged, affirming it as the superior religion.
- Polemical – seeks to use Islam's sacred texts to undermine their plausibility.

At the centre of this range is the kerygmatic approach:

The kerygmatic approach is rooted in the proclamation – the Greek word kerygma means to proclaim – of the values, character and model of Jesus Christ as the heart of the gospel. In this approach, the kerygma is not Christianity but Christ ... [T]he kerygmatic approach is respectful and loving toward Muslims, and it is prophetic, scientifically honest, supra-religious and centered on Christ. (Accad, 2020, pp. 25–6)

Christians will differ on where they wish to position themselves on this spectrum, and which, if any, they would rule out (Accad commends the kerygmatic stance). However, it should be clear from this spectrum that cooperation with Muslims on ethical and practical matters is not incompatible with authentic Christian belief and expression.

Another way in which the Church can exercise a prophetic role is when it unites to offer an ecumenical statement of principle.[21] Three such statements have left a particular mark upon the global Church in the last 100 years. In 1934 the Theological Declaration of Barmen was made by the Confessing Church in Germany, in response to National Socialism's attempt to co-opt the Christian churches to its own ideology. In 1985 an ecumenical group of ordained and lay Christian theologians in South Africa produced the Kairos document in response to the ongoing crisis of apartheid in South Africa. In 2009, on the seventy-fifth anniversary of the Nakba, a group of Palestinian theologians produced the Kairos Palestine document. Each one of these three declarations, in its own distinct voice, speaks boldly and courageously:

'But speaking the truth in love [we] may grow up in every way into him who is the head, Christ, from whom the whole body [is] joined together' (Eph. 4.15, 16). The Christian church is the congregation of brothers in which Jesus Christ acts presently as the Lord in Word and Sacrament through the Holy Spirit. With her faith as with her obedience, with her message as with her order, in the midst of a sinful world, as the church of pardoned sinners, she has to testify that she alone is his property, and that she lives and wants to live only from his comfort and from his instruction, in the expectation of his appearance. We reject the false doctrine! As if the church is allowed to abandon the form of her message and her order to her own pleasure, or to the changes of prevailing ideological and political convictions. (Barmen Theological Declaration, 1934, Article 3)

Both oppressor and oppressed claim loyalty to the same Church. They are both baptized in the same baptism and participate together in the breaking of the same bread, the same body and blood of Christ. There we sit in the same Church while outside Christian policemen and soldiers are beating up and killing Christian children or torturing Christian prisoners to death while yet other Christians stand by and weekly plead for peace. The Church is divided against itself and its day of judgement has come. (Kairos Theologians, 1986, p. 2)

The mission of the Church is prophetic, to speak the Word of God courageously, honestly and lovingly in the local context and in the midst of daily events. If she does take sides, it is with the oppressed, to stand alongside them, just as Christ our Lord stood by the side of each poor person and each sinner, calling them to repentance, life, and the restoration of the dignity bestowed on them by God and that no one has the right to strip away. (Kairos Palestine, 2009, 3.4.1)

The time may come when the European churches will once again need to unite in this way, holding tenaciously to the good news of the kingdom of God in the teeth of those who would undermine all these goods – and some of that opposition may come from within our own congregations and denominations.

The Baptist Distinctive

Finally, I would like to offer some remarks from my own position within the (European[22]) Baptist tradition. Since one of the things that defines the state is the claim to a monopoly of force within its territory, Baptists believe that the Church's purview is entirely separate from the state's. We consider the New Testament principle of Christian churches being formed on the basis of voluntary association to be incompatible with the state promotion of Christianity (Lusk, 2017, p. 89). A key Baptist distinctive is therefore the separation of Church and state, and the eschewing of political power by the Church. This is a long-standing Baptist conviction:

> The rejection of sacred power hierarchically administered in favour of consent-based patterns of government espoused by [the early] dissenters led to the development of 'a pluralistic society in which men [sic] would learn to live in peace with others with whom they disagreed without resort to the scaffold or firing squad'. After all, if the enforcement of religion was taken out of the hands of the secular power, the role of that power shifted towards the more modest one of providing the conditions

within which people could negotiate their own religious convictions. In particular ... democracy represent[s] the social application of the priesthood of all believers and [is] the political analogy of the 'democratic' religious congregation. (Wright, 2005, p. 205)[23]

This is, of course, not at all the same as saying that individual Christians should not be involved in politics, or that churches and other organizations should not seek to persuade in the public arena. Indeed, James Crossley (Chapter 7) points to the role of nonconformists in the great labour movements of the twentieth century. But the Baptist shape of that political engagement is distinctive, as Paul Lusk describes:

> The state can be run by anyone who is competent and honest, whatever they believe. The Christian enters public life not to make the state more Christian, but to give glory to God by doing the job well. The state is there not to uphold any particular version of goodness, but to protect the freedom of all to pursue goodness. (Lusk, 2017, p. 98)

The principle does, however, stand firmly against the Church – or any other faith or non-faith organization – having a privileged position within the leadership of a nation. While I want to commend my brothers and sisters from the non-dissenting traditions when they also eschew religious power in the public arena, it seems to me that the dissenting traditions have a distinctive contribution to offer.

Towards the end of his book *Defending Democracy from its Christian Enemies*, David Gushee offers a list of resources that the Baptist democratic tradition can bring to democratic politics (Gushee, 2023, p. 184). I abbreviate and paraphrase his list as follows:

- A rejection of authoritarianism, because Jesus Christ alone is Lord.
- A rejection of state religion.
- Belief in the sovereignty of God over human consciences.
- A robust tradition and conviction of human rights.
- Belief in the right to equal political participation.
- Understanding of the Church as a training ground in democratic self-government.
- Respect for individual conscience and dissent.

Again and again during the conversations of our colloquium, I found myself doodling the word 'Baptists' on my notepad. Ours is not the only faithful tradition, of course; nor is it the only ecclesiology that has resources to resist the rise of far-right-wing and nationalistic politics. But it does contain deep dissenting traditions, and the principles of the eschewing of power, which we might usefully draw upon. We who dissent would do well to rediscover our history and tell it afresh to a new generation.

Conclusion

At the end of our two days together, I invited each participant to draw out in the moment a final concluding thought. Many of them have been reflected in this discussion or in the papers that precede it, but I will here conclude with my own.

Jesus said:

> The kingdom of heaven is like a mustard seed that someone took and sowed in his field; it is the smallest of all the seeds, but when it has grown it is the greatest of shrubs and becomes a tree, so that the birds of the air come and make nests in its branches ... The kingdom of heaven is like yeast that a woman took and mixed in with three measures of flour until all of it was leavened. (Matt. 13.31–33, NRSV)

This fundamental truth is often overlooked by those who seek to employ power for their own theological agenda. That applies both to those who are promoting the ideologies of the far right, and to those who seek to counter them. But it is not by force or coercion that the kingdom of God grows, and it is not by force or coercion that positive change will be realized. We cannot challenge the authoritarian tendencies in ideologies we deprecate by ourselves employing heavy-handed 'top-down' measures that belittle, de-platform or intimidate. But change is possible, when it is prayed in by the faithful, whispered in by the Spirit, and patiently nurtured by the Church.

To this end, it is grassroots actions that will count the most: slow, patient contact and long-term investment in cross-cultural relationships, such as those in communities like Easton, Bristol. In the middle of that thriving Muslim-majority area, St Mark's Baptist Church has attained a well-deserved reputation for generosity, service and community participation. And the warmth goes in two directions. When I turned up there with a group of students recently, we were charmingly and generously 'kidnapped' by the leader of the local mosque, which stands directly opposite the church, to visit his premises and enjoy his hospitality.

Patience will be required, too, for the necessary work of shaping the hearts and minds of future ministers and priests by the process of theological education. It is needed for the nurturing of generous, open-hearted young people who are secure in their own faith and warm towards those who do not share it, or whose culture is different from their own. The week-by-week formation of the character of God's people through the faithful preaching and exposition of God's word is a slow, patient business, too.

By patience and through small things, this is how the kingdom goes, and this is how the kingdom grows. And God, by his Spirit, continues to breathe his life in the Church he is calling to be a prophetic presence in the world, no less today than ever.

Recommendations

1 The Church must own up to, rather than attempt to conceal, its own historic or contemporary complicity with the far right or entailment with its rhetoric. We must demonstrate due humility in this regard.
2 Disavowal of violence perpetrated in the name of the Church is an important public act, but the responsibility lies with denominational leaders and other thought-leaders, rather than with every individual church member.
3 The Church should be wary of reinforcing far-right stereotypes of Muslim illiberality by positioning itself as the primary upholder of democratic dialogue.
4 When churches hold dialoguing events between dissenting voices, they should be attentive to the possibility of their good intentions and neutral space being hijacked by bad actors. This can partly be countered by agreeing rules of engagement in advance.
5 We need to seek and propagate rich and nuanced understanding of the causes of far-right movements, and avoid demonizing certain demographic groups as pervasively racist.
6 At the same time, we need to be more attentive to the factors that can drive far-right ideology among deprived groups, and find ways of mitigating such deprivation without setting this in conflict with aiding immigrants. As part of this initiative, we need to facilitate the theological equipping and amplify the theological articulations of those Christian believers who live and operate within situations of marginalization in the UK.
7 We should seek to be faithful to the prophetic calling of the Church,

and be open to expressing radical love and welcome and, conversely, to standing against hatred and divisiveness in creative, non-violent ways.
8 We should attend to the risk of radicalization of young people by investing in youth work and youth programmes that enhance dialogue across religious and cultural boundaries.
9 Theological education matters. We should invest unashamedly in the high-quality theological education of those who will lead churches, and promote biblical and theological literacy in church by a range of means. We must invest in and promote the work of biblical scholars who are working to address themes and passages that are readily weaponized by the likes of people such as Anders Breivik.
10 Churches in the dissenting traditions should seek creative ways to draw on the deep values of dissent and democracy that they embody, and to articulate these in fresh ways to their congregations of today and tomorrow.

Notes

1 Breivik's manifesto was previously freely available on the internet but now appears to have been taken down from mainstream sites. No doubt it is still available on the 'dark web'. In preparation of this chapter I have consulted a previously downloaded version.

2 The Centre for the Study of Bible and Violence has a preachers' blog: *Sunday Sermon, Monday Mourning*, which aims to help preachers identify the violent potential of texts they may preach on, https://www.csbvbristol.org.uk/blogs-sunday-sermon-monday-mourning/ (accessed 5.4.24).

3 See https://www.christianitytoday.com/news/2022/april/orban-hungary-evangelical-election-voices-choice-conservati.html (accessed 5.4.24).

4 https://www.pewresearch.org/short-reads/2021/08/30/most-white-americans-who-regularly-attend-worship-services-voted-for-trump-in-2020/ (accessed 5.4.24).

5 Information about Theos can be found here, https://www.theosthinktank.co.uk/ (accessed 5.4.24). For information about Las Casas, see https://www.bfriars.ox.ac.uk/research/las-casas-institute-for-social-justice/ (accessed 5.4.24). The Joint Public Issues Team website is https://jpit.uk/ (accessed 5.4.24).

6 The so-called 'Windrush scandal' broke into the British news in 2017, with a group of stories concerning people who had legally moved to the UK from the West Indies in the 1950s and 1960s, usually as children with their parents. Many had never formally applied for British citizenship, as they had been led to believe they had automatically naturalized. When the Home Office's 'hostile environment' came into effect under Prime Minister Theresa May, they found themselves unable to work, unable to claim benefits, criminalized, detained and deported.

7 https://www.britainfirst.org/race_immigration_and_demographics (accessed 5.4.24).

8 Braverman was briefly forced to resign from the role by Prime Minister Liz Truss on 19 October 2022, but reappointed less than a week later by Truss's successor Rishi Sunak. For an example of her rhetoric on 'British values', see https://news.sky.com/story/suella-braverman-criminal-behaviour-by-people-arriving-illegally-at-odds-with-british-values-12866871 (accessed 5.4.24).

9 https://www.gov.uk/government/news/british-values-article-by-david-cameron (accessed 5.4.24).

10 https://www.radicalrightanalysis.com/2020/08/19/the-dark-money-that-fuels-radical-right-ideology/ (accessed 5.4.24).

11 https://www.vice.com/en/article/43jzbp/britain-first-donations-shell-company-investigation (accessed 5.4.24).

12 https://www.journalismfund.eu/mafias-and-far-right (accessed 5.4.24).

13 https://www.theguardian.com/politics/2019/nov/29/wealthy-us-donors-gave-millions-to-rightwing-uk-groups (accessed 5.4.24).

14 https://thefeast.org.uk/ (accessed 5.4.24).

15 https://actionresearchassociates.org/ (accessed 5.4.24).

16 https://truthandreconciliationlebanon.org/en/about.html (accessed 5.4.24).

17 GCSEs, more properly known as General Certificate of Secondary Education examinations, are national exams taken by the vast majority of 16-year-olds in England, Wales and Northern Ireland.

18 These words were spoken by Michael Gove in an interview with Faisal Islam for Sky News on 3 June 2016.

19 A similar phenomenon has been noted in the study of domestic abuse trends, where regular rather than nominal church attendance appears to reduce the risk of perpetration (Wilcox, 2004, pp. 181–2).

20 This should go without saying, but sadly doesn't.

21 It should be noted that not all participants were wholly enthusiastic about this approach. Chris Wilson, although commending the Barmen Declaration in our conversation, cautions in Chapter 11 of this volume about the dangers of simply 'preaching to the choir'. Hannah Strømmen and Ulrich Schmiedel pointed out in our conversation that the Barmen Declaration omitted any specific reference to the plight of the Jews.

22 I here refer to the British and Continental Baptist tradition, which has very clear distinctives from many of the Baptist streams in the USA.

23 Wright's quotation is from Michael R. Watts, 1978, *The Dissenters: From the Reformation to the French Revolution*, Oxford: Clarendon Press, p. 2.

References

Accad, Martin, 2020, 'View of Islam: Between Demonization and Idealization', in Martin Accad and Jonathan Andrews (eds), *The Religious Other: A Biblical Understanding of Islam, the Qur'an and Muhammad*, Carlisle: Langham Global Library, pp. 22–8.

Barmen Theological Declaration, 1934, https://creedsandconfessions.org/barmen-declaration.html (accessed 5.4.24).

Billiet, J. B., 1995, 'Church Involvement, Individualism, and Ethnic Prejudice among Flemish Roman Catholics: New Evidence of a Moderating Effect', *Journal for the Scientific Study of Religion* 56(3), pp. 303–26.

Boon, M., 2010, *Understanding the Rise of the Far Right: Survey Results*, Equality and Human Rights Commission Research Report 57, https://www.equalityhumanrights.com/sites/default/files/research-report-57-understanding-the-far-right-survey.pdf (accessed 5.4.24).

Breivik, Anders, 2011, '2083 – A European Declaration of Independence' (no longer online).

Butt, S., E. Clery and J. Curtice, 2022, 'Culture Wars', in S. Butt, E. Clery and J. Curtice (eds), *British Social Attitudes: The 39th Report*, London: National Centre for Social Research.

Girard, R., 1979, *Violence and the Sacred*, Baltimore: Johns Hopkins University Press.

Goldberg, David Theo, 2006, 'Racial Europeanization', *Ethnic and Racial Studies* 29(2), pp. 331–64.

Gushee, David, 2023, *Defending Democracy from its Christian Enemies*, Grand Rapids: Eerdmans.

Howell, David, 2022, *Longitudinal Research into Student Numbers on Higher Education Programmes in Christian Youth Work/Ministry Programmes and Children's Work/Ministry Programmes – 2011–12 to 2022–23*, Christian Youth Work Consortium, https://cte.org.uk/app/uploads/2022/08/Student-Numbers-Report-to-Training-Agencies-Jul22.pdf (accessed 5.4.24).

Kairos Theologians, 1986, *Challenge to the Church: A Theological Comment on the Political Crisis in South Africa. The Kairos Document*, 2nd edn, Johannesburg: Skotaville Publishers.

Kairos Palestine, 2009, 'A Moment of Truth: A Word of Faith, Hope and Love from the Heart of Palestinian Suffering', https://www.kairospalestine.ps/index.php/about-kairos/kairos-palestine-document (accessed 5.4.24).

Lusk, Paul, 2017, *The Jesus Candidate: Political Religion in a Secular Age*, London: Ekklesia.

Minkenberg, Michael, 2018, 'Religion and the Radical Right', in Jens Rydgren (ed.), *The Oxford Handbook of the Radical Right*, Oxford: Oxford University Press, pp. 366–93.

Osifo, Faith, 2020, 'Immigration, as Highlighted by the Windrush Scandal', written evidence presented to the UK Parliament's Joint Committee on Human Rights for its enquiry into Black people, racism and human rights, 7 October, https://committees.parliament.uk/writtenevidence/12263/html (accessed 5.4.24).

Pew Research Center, 2018, 'Being Christian in Western Europe', https://www.pewresearch.org/religion/2018/05/29/being-christian-in-western-europe/ (accessed 5.4.24).

Salmela, M. and C. von Scheve, 2017, 'Emotional Roots of Right-wing Political Populism', *Social Science Information* 56(4), pp. 567–95.

Strømmen, Hannah and Ulrich Schmiedel, 2020, *The Claim to Christianity: Responding to the Far Right*, London: SCM Press.

Wilcox, W. B., 2004, *Soft Patriarchs, New Men: How Christianity Shapes Fathers and Husbands*, Chicago: University of Chicago Press.

Wright, Nigel, 2005, *Free Church, Free State: The Positive Baptist Vision*, Eugene: Wipf and Stock.

Afterword: Lived Theology

HANNAH STRØMMEN AND ULRICH SCHMIEDEL

This book starts with a 'Christian Crusade'. In the Introduction, Helen Paynter sets the scene for our conversation by stressing how Muslims in the UK have been harassed in the name of Christianity. The attitudes that animate the crusaders in this scene, Paynter suggests, can be found in the extremist margins as well as the established mainstream of societies across Europe. While it's difficult to capture the far right and the not-so-far right in any clear-cut definition, it's clear that Islamophobic campaigns have been successful. Scholars have started to talk about 'The Christian right in Europe', showing how it has been shaped by 'a global exchange of ideas', networked in a way that allows for communication and collaboration beyond borders (Mascolo and Stoeckl, 2023, p. 13). But how can these terms hang together, the 'right' with the 'Christian' and the 'Christian' with the 'right'?

We wrote *The Claim to Christianity* because we were fed up with the standard story that has been told to answer this question. This is the story of a Christianity that has been 'hijacked'. According to the story of the hijacking, Christians have little to do with the far right and the far right has little to do with Christians. The relationship between them is instrumental. The far right might use or abuse Christianity for its aims, and Christianity might use or abuse the far right for its aims; but according to what theologian Jan Niklas Collet calls and criticizes as the 'instrumentalization thesis', the relation between them cannot cut to the core of what Christianity is (Collet, 2021, p. 180, our trans.). Of course, there are cases in which Christianity is interpreted and instrumentalized in a superficial way so that one could say it was hijacked by the far right. But spinning a story out of these cases to capture the rise of the far right ignores how shaky the assumptions are on which it stands.

The standard story assumes that we can draw distinctions that allow us to ask whether the Christian right wing is a religious movement that became politicized or a political movement that became religionized

(Mascolo and Stoeckl, 2023, pp. 15–16). Any scholar who has looked even a little into debates about the category of religion will rub their eyes at such an assumption. Analytically, it is impossible to say *this* is where religion ends and politics begins or *that* is where politics ends and religion begins. The categories aren't stable. Take the movement that revolved around Jesus of Nazareth. Was it religious rather than political? Was it political rather than religious? And how would one tell the difference? Asking questions like these, we aren't even talking about the research that suggests that the category of religion is a modern invention that would not have made sense to anybody in Jesus' time.[1] If we perceive the rise of the far right in Europe through such simplistic categories, we won't be able to see what is going on. And if we aren't able to see what is going on, we will have no chance of understanding or undermining the rise of the far right.

As the conversations in this book clarified, our critique of the instrumentalization thesis connects to the conceptualization of Christianity as a project rather than a possession. The standard hijacking story assumes that there is no need for Christians to resist the rise of the far right. According to the instrumentalization thesis, Christianity will not be swayed by far-right politics and far-right politics will not be supported by Christianity because their relationship is only superficial. There is no special responsibility for Christians to respond to far-right claims to Christianity. On the contrary, Christians can assume that Christianity is immune and immunizing against racist discourse and religious discrimination. We disagree. We argue that we need to let go of the standard story in order to see how Christianity relates to the rise of the far right in Europe. There is no need to repeat our argument here. But it's important to note that the critique of the instrumentalization thesis connects to the conceptualization of Christianity as a project. The story of the hijacking suggests a strong and stable definition of Christianity. One needs such a definition to say what constitutes the 'honest' Christianity and what constitutes the 'hijacked' Christianity. We suggest that the matter is not so simple. 'Christianity' is a slippery concept. If it has been claimed in different ways throughout history, then it is key to address these claims critically and self-critically, regardless of whether we find them palatable or unpalatable. Christians, then, are responsible for countering the claims to Christianity in far-right politics.

In her Conclusion of this volume, Paynter offers a succinct summary that outlines the challenges that our argument poses to churches in Europe. These churches must not remain neutral in the face of the far right, which means that they have to acknowledge their own complicity and their own complicity with racism past and present in order to offer a convincing critique of the far right. Any such acknowledgement cuts to the core of what Christianity is. The stakes, then, are high. Precisely because the stakes are high, we are so grateful for Paynter's initiative, along with Maria Power, to convene the conversations collected in this book.

Paynter and Power brought together the analysts and the activists whose responses to *The Claim to Christianity* confirm and challenge our argument in critical and constructive ways. Like anyone who writes anything, we had hoped that our book would be read. But we didn't anticipate that the reception would result in such inspiring and instructive conversations. These conversations introduced us to courageous people and creative practices that counter the rise of the far right, often at a very high personal cost. We are grateful for the opportunity to learn from them.

Paynter points to the reception of *The Claim to Christianity* by churches in the UK that prompted her to convene our conversation. While there were responses in all of the countries that we covered, Sweden was probably the country in which our book was met with the most interest, resulting in invitations to speak about it in churches and communities. This was a little surprising to us as Sweden isn't covered in the book. Neither of us was working in Sweden at the time. The fact that *The Claim to Christianity* seems to have hit a nerve none the less shows that the rise of the far right is a challenge that churches in many countries have to confront. Sweden is its own case, with its own problems and its own potential. The then Archbishop of Uppsala, Antje Jackelén, had to tackle the rise of the far right during her tenure as primate of the Church of Sweden.[2] Sweden, then, also confirms that the far-right claim to Christianity connects countries, continents and confessions beyond the characteristics of each case. Any response to the rise of the far right needs to reach across the borders of countries, continents and confessions as well.

The conversation that Paynter and Power convened sketches pathways for how to create coalitions beyond borders. To us, this is a very promising point of departure. Such coalitions can revolve around 'churches [that] act as hubs of community support' (Crossley, Chapter 7 in this volume). There needs to be diversity in these coalitions. There needs to be disagreement in these coalitions. In fact, 'the Church', as Paynter argues in her conclusion, 'needs to model another way of disagreeing' (Paynter, Conclusion, in this volume).

Disagreeing well is particularly difficult when it is about faith. Concurring with Chris Wilson (Chapter 11 in this volume), Paynter cautions us

AFTERWORD: LIVED THEOLOGY

that there is too little Christological, pneumatological and soteriological reflection in our book. 'Practical solutions', she contends, 'will only take us part of the way, because at heart, this is a spiritual problem' (Paynter, in the Conclusion of this volume). In many ways, we agree. We wrote *The Claim to Christianity* because we wanted the *theology* of the far right to be characterized, captured and countered. But we are hesitant to pit theology against practice or practice against theology in any straightforward way, which is why we concentrated on what could be called 'lived theology' throughout our book.[3] As we pointed out in our response to Wilson, there is no innocent theology. Even the theologies of liberation from which we have drawn in *The Claim to Christianity* are not beyond critique.[4] Each and every Christological, pneumatological and soteriological statement needs to be checked critically and self-critically. Paynter's discussion of what she calls 'the Baptist distinctive' offers such a check (Paynter, in the Conclusion of this volume). It presents the problems of an ecclesiology that seeks political power for the Church and the potentials of an ecclesiology that shuns political power for the Church. This discussion goes beyond a call for more ecclesiology because it shows what difference that ecclesiology can make in contemporary society. The call for more Christological, pneumatological and soteriological reflection remains a self-referential assumption unless it can showcase the contribution that such reflection can make.

Given that the discussion about theology cannot be closed, we suggest that the trick is to move from practice into theology and from theology into practice *without* arriving at a conclusion that pretends to have reached closure – a bit like we have aimed to do in the conversations collected in this book. Our agreements and disagreements demonstrate that Christianity is open and open-ended because the God whose call Christians claim to hear and heed is greater than anything that we can think or talk about. 'God is greater' was the motto of Jackelén's tenure as Archbishop of Uppsala (Jackelén, 2020), causing controversy because it was perceived to come too close to the takbir *Allāhu 'akbar"* (الله أكبر). But God *is* greater. As a consequence, any Christianity that is called by God needs to be more a project than a possession. It cannot be fixed. There is no closure, at least not in this life.

For Christianity to counter the far right, 'grassroots actions will', as Paynter argues, 'count the most' (Paynter, in the Conclusion of this volume). The ten succinct recommendations into which she skilfully condensed the conversations that are collected in this book are spot-on. They bring theology into practice and practice into theology so that the rise of the far right can be resisted both inside and outside churches. We are convinced that they have the potential to empower communities to resist racist discourse and religious discrimination, both where it is easy to see and where it is not so easy to see. Resistance is needed in the established mainstream and in the extremist margins that come to the fore in the crusade of Britain First with which this book started. We are grateful to the convenors and to the contributors who made the conversations collected in this book happen. Knowing that *The Claim to Christianity* might have helped a little to spark a conversation about the motivations, the meanings and the means of such resistance is more than we could have wished for. Thank you!

Notes

1 See the classic by Tomoko Masuzawa, 2005, *The Invention of World Religions: Or, How European Universalism Was Preserved in the Language of Pluralism*, Chicago: University of Chicago Press. The debate has grown significantly since. A succinct summary is provided by Jayne Svenungsson, 2020, 'The Return of Religion or the End of Religion? On the Need to Rethink Religion as a Category of Social and Political Life', *Philosophy and Social Criticism* 46(7), pp. 785–809.

2 See the report about the Archbishop in *Le Monde*, Anne-Françoise Hivert, 2003, 'Antje Jackelén, l'indignée de l'Eglise suédoise', *M le magazine du monde*, https://www.lemonde.fr/m-le-mag/article/2023/06/14/antje-jackelen-l-indignee-de-l-eglise-suedoise_6177510_4500055.html (accessed 5.4.24).

3 In *The Claim to Christianity*, we draw on the classic conceptualization of lived religion by Robert Orsi, 2005, *Between Heaven and Earth: The Religious Worlds People Make and the Scholars Who Study Them*, Princeton: Princeton University Press. There is a growing discussion about the category in the study of religion, including theology. See the contributions to Charles Marsh, Peter Slade and Sarah Azaransky (eds), 2006, *Lived Theology: New Perspectives on Method, Style, and Pedagogy*, Oxford: Oxford University Press, for a variety of theological takes.

4 As Paynter points out, liberation theology started in the favelas of Latin America, but did not stop there. The debate about the potentials and the problems of liberation theology is on-going. See the contributions to Christopher Rowlands (ed.), 2007, *The Cambridge Companion to Liberation Theology*, Cambridge: Cambridge University Press. A lot of the concerns are taken up in postcolonial theologies today. See Catherine Keller, Michael Nausner and Mayra Rivera (eds), 2004, *Postcolonial Theologies: Divinity and Empire*, St Louis: Chalice Press.

References

Collet, Jan Niklas, 2021, 'Rechte Normalisierung und kirchlich-theologische Normalität: Möglichkeiten und Folgen einer Inanspruchnahme "orthodoxer Kirchlichkeit" durch rechte Christ*innen für Prozesse rechter Normalisierung', in Jan Niklas Collet, Julia Lis and Gregor Taxacher (eds), *Rechte Normalisierung* *und politische Theologie: Eine Standortbestimmung*, Regensburg: Friedrich Pustet, pp. 159–81.

Crossley, James, in this volume, 'Chapter 7: Encountering and Countering the Far Right in the UK Today'.

Hivert, Anne-Françoise, 2003, 'Antje Jackelén, l'indignée de l'Eglise suédoise', *M le magazine du monde*, https://www.lemonde.fr/m-le-mag/article/2023/06/14/antje-jackelen-l-indignee-de-l-eglise-suedoise_6177510_4500055.html (accessed 5.4.24).

Jackelén, Antje, 2020, *God is Greater: Theology for the World*, Minneapolis: Fortress Press.

Keller, Catherine, Michael Nausner and Mayra Rivera (eds), 2004, *Postcolonial Theologies: Divinity and Empire*, St Louis: Chalice Press.

Marsh, Charles, Peter Slade and Sarah Azaransky (eds), 2006, *Lived Theology: New Perspectives on Method, Style, and Pedagogy*, Oxford: Oxford University Press.

Mascolo, Gionathan Lo and Kristina Stoeckl, 2023, 'The European Christian Right: An Overview', in *The Christian Right in Europe: Movements, Networks, and Denominations*, Bielefeld: Transcript, pp. 11–42.

Masuzawa, Tomoko, 2005, *The Invention of World Religions: Or, How European Universalism Was Preserved in the Language of Pluralism*, Chicago: University of Chicago Press.

Orsi, Robert, 2005, *Between Heaven and Earth: The Religious Worlds People Make and the Scholars Who Study Them*, Princeton: Princeton University Press.

Paynter, Helen, in this volume, 'Conclusion: The Church, the Far Right, and the Claim to Christianity: Towards Some Recommendations'.

Rowlands, Christopher (ed.), 2007, *The Cambridge Companion to Liberation Theology*, Cambridge: Cambridge University Press.

Svenungsson, Jayne, 2020, 'The Return of Religion or the End of Religion? On the Need to Rethink Religion as a Category of Social and Political Life', *Philosophy and Social Criticism* 46(7), pp. 785–809.

Index of Names and Subjects

Action Research Associates 182
A Common Word between Us and You 78–9, 86, 88n13
Adams, Peter 114
Affect 47–8
Ahmed, Rumee 67
Ahmed, Sara 48
Ahmed, Shahab 66
Ali, Makram 101
Allport, Gordon W. 18, 40–1, 47–9, 77, 86–7, 116, 156–7
Alternative für Deutschland 136
Anderson, Benedict 79
Anti-Fascism 114, 116
Anti-Muslim racism, *see* Islamophobia
Antisemitism 4, 5, 12n11, 12n12, 52, 95–7, 148, 170n5
Authoritarian Reactionary Christianity xii, 6
Archbishop
 of Canterbury 145, 156, 163
 of Uppsala 52–3, 196–7

Ball, John 103
Baptist distinctives 187–9
Bangstad, Sindre 27n5, 67, 84
Barmen declaration xi–xii, 155, 158n4, 165–6, 170n4, 186, 192n21
Barrow-in-Furness 98, 99, 103

Barth, Karl 152, 158n4, 165, 166–9, 170n4, 170n6
Bat Ye'or 67, 84
Bednarz, Liane 46, 161
Benn, Hilary 136
Bible, *see also* Scripture
 Interpretations of 6, 8, 53, 65, 68, 83, 85, 122, 137, 140, 174
 of North-Sámi 52–3
 Slavery Bible 121–2
 Used by far right groups 1, 69, 110, 125
Biblical literacy 183–4, 191
Black Lives Matter 7, 96
Blair, Tony 95
Braverman, Suella 4, 96, 177, 192n8
Breivik, Anders 17, 67, 75, 106, 110–11, 134, 134, 174, 191
Brexit 102–3
Brexit Party 4
Britain First 1, 93, 99 100, 106–7, 110, 112–15, 122, 125, 177, 180
British National Party 1, 106, 110, 112–13, 115
Brubaker, Rogers 109, 123–4

Caliphate 66, 175
Cameron, David 76, 95, 145, 177
Cantle, Ted 141

INDEX OF NAMES AND SUBJECTS

Catholics, Catholicism 7, 63, 67, 113, 135, 148, 155, 156–7
Census data 78, 133
Challenging Church 25, 50, 122, 165
Chin, Rita 81
Christian-Muslim relations 8, 10–11, 18, 20–1, 29, 35, 38, 54, 61, 64, 156, 162–3, 185–6, 189
Christian Nationalism 6
Christian theological convictions 20–1, 26, 151–5, 184, 187–8
Christianism xii, 109, 112, 123–4
Christianity as a project or possession 68, 135–6, 144, 151–5, 165
Church, as prophetic community 65, 184–6, 190–1
Church of England 1, 8, 103, 156, 165, 176
  General Synod 1
Church of Norway 17, 19, 22–3, 25, 27, 47, 50, 54, 75
Church of Sweden 30, 33–7, 38–9, 41–2, 52, 196
Citizens UK 142
Civil Society 30, 33–8, 40, 42
Civilization
  Christianity as 124
  Clash of 2, 47, 51, 81, 82, 94, 97, 100, 127, 163, 167, 169
Colonialism 148
Common good 39, 42, 63, 183
Communism 96
Condemnation
  of the far right 81–3, 94–6, 113, 115, 127, 175–6, 190
  of Islamist terrorism 73–7, 81–3, 175

Conservative Party of the United Kingdom 4, 96, 101–2, 137, 141
Consolidating Church 25, 50, 66, 122
Conspiracy theories 4, 98, 100, 106, 109, 116n2
Contact hypothesis 18, 29, 40–1, 48, 77, 86, 156
Cooper, Rosie 101, 104n1
Corbyn, Jeremy 95–6, 101, 104n1, 137
Cox, Jo 100, 104n1
'Cultural Marxism' 12n10, 96, 97
Culture 151, 155, 158n2
Culture Christianity 69–70, 73, 78, 79, 109, 111, 115, 123–4, 148
Crusader Christianity xii, 70, 73, 76, 78, 79, 110, 111, 115, 123, 134, 194

Daesh, see ISIS
Dempsey, Eddie 102
Deprivation, see Socio-political-economic factors
Dialogue
  Interfaith, see Christian-Muslim relations
  with the far right 18, 26–7, 156–7, 178–9
Dialogue Pilots 20–1, 25, 50, 178, 182
Difference, see Multiculturalism and elitism 5
Disavowal of violence, see condemnation
Diversity 21, 24, 28, 42
Dowson, Jim 110

INDEX OF NAMES AND SUBJECTS

English Defence League 5, 93, 94, 95, 97, 102, 103, 106, 107, 114, 117n4, 117n5, 122
Essentialization
 of Muslims 67, 167, 179
 of Christians 8, 65, 151, 154–5, 179
Essentialism, *see* Essentialization
European Union 96, 102, 103

Face-to-face 18, 26, 82
Faith and life-stance 17–19, 21, 24–5, 27
Fascism 96, 98, 101, 103, 112, 167–8
'Formers' 182
French New Right, *see* Nouvelle Droite

Generation identity 180
Germany xi, xii, 51, 64, 66, 67, 109, 134–5, 148, 155, 158n4, 186
Golding, Paul 110, 114
Good Samaritan, parable of 85, 86, 116, 122, 136–40, 142, 143, 162, 178
Green, Alan 113, 122
Griffin, Nick 94, 127

Hermeneutics, *see* Bible, interpretation of
Heseltine, Michael 102
Hijacking of Christianity 64, 123–5, 136, 144, 150, 151, 194–5
Hitler, Adolf 3, 96, 100, 167–8
Hope not Hate 1, 4, 110

Identity 17, 63–5, 86, 110, 141, 143–4, 149, 167

Christian 6, 17, 135
 Communal or national 63–4
 English 103
Identity politics 111, 116, 141
Instrumentalization thesis 7, 64, 150, 152–4, 167, 179, 194–5
Insurrection, 6 January 2020 2
ISIS 65, 66, 70, 80n7, 175
Islam and Muslims 24, 34, 37, 61–8, 69–80, 81–7, 9–101, 133–5, 156–7, 162–3, 175, 178, 185
 Christians making common cause with, *see* Christian-Muslim relations
 Stereotypic/essentialization of 70–3, 179, 190
Islamic Law, *see* Sharia
Islamist extremism 66, 76, 74, 107, 111, 134, 175
Islamofascism 167
Islamophobia 5–7, 30–2, 39–40, 42, 68, 69, 93, 95, 109, 113, 126, 148, 167, 194
Israel 12n11, 62, 65, 95, 97

Jackelén, Antje 196, 197, 198n2
Jesus Christ 115, 134, 138, 144, 151, 154, 158n3, 158n4
Jews 64, 65, 70, 86, 88n10, 125, 128n3, 166, 168, 170n5, 192n21
Jihad 66, 110, 175
Johnsen, Tore 22–3, 25, 27–8, 27n10, 27n11, 54
Johnson, Boris 4, 96
Judaism 85–6, 88n10, 88n12, 165, 168

Kairos document 186–7
Kairos Palestine document 188–7

203

Klug, Brian 75–6

Labour Party of Great Britain 94, 96, 97, 102, 106, 141
Lebanese, Lebanon 10, 61, 62, 63, 64
Liberation theology 67, 181, 198n4
Local organizing 30, 33–7, 38–9, 40, 42
Luther, Martin 52, 125
Luton 79n1, 106, 107, 114–15, 122
Lynch, Mick 102

MAGA, see Make America Great Again
Make America Great Again 2
Maronite, Maronitism 62, 63
Marxism 12n10, 96–7
May, Theresa 145, 191n6
McFarland, Ian 140
Million Programme 31–2
Ministers, training of, 183, 190
Mosley, Oswald 100
Multiculturalism 42, 141–3
Muscular liberalism 76
Muslims, see Islam
Muslim-Christian relations, see Christian-Muslim relations
Mutual encounter 19, 156–7, see also Contact hypothesis

National action 101
National Front 98
Nationalism 63, 158n4
Neighbour 2, 138–40, 142, 143, 144, 157, 166, 185
Neighbourliness 31, 142, 143, 166

Neutrality 8, 17, 19, 21, 25, 50, 51, 116, 177–8, 179
New Racism 24, 63, 69, 81, 164–5, 166, 167
Northern Ireland 147–50, 155–8
Norway, Norwegians viii, 10, 17–28, 64, 67
Nouvelle Droite 108
Nuttall, Paul 69

Openness 26, 49–51, 70, 77, 86, 126, 141, 144, 177
Orbán, Viktor 2, 174
Overton Window 4, 11n9

Palestine, Palestinians 62, 65, 98, 186
Patriotic Alternative 5, 93, 98, 100
Partij voor de Vrijheid 2
Party for Freedom, see *Partij voor de Vrijheid*
Pegida 66, 134, 135
Pew Research Center 175
Prejudice 29, 41
Polyphony 18, 22, 24–5
Protestants 63, 67, 147–9, 153–4, 157–8

Qur'an 66, 68, 69, 77, 85
Burnings 19, 29–34, 39, 43n1, 47

Racism 17, 24, 63, 81, 95, 98, 102, 121, 123, 127, 155, 158n4
Anti-Muslim 18, 69, 73
Church and racism 40–5
Structural 30, 31–2, 40, 41
Race 50, 63, 81, 87n1, 95, 98, 108, 115, 164

INDEX OF NAMES AND SUBJECTS

Religion 17–19, 24, 61, 63, 64, 65, 66, 68, 149–55, 158n2
Rigby, Lee 95
Riots 30, 31, 32, 35–7, 40
Robinson, Tommy 5, 93, 94, 95, 99, 114, 127

Samaritan 85, 86, 116, 136, 137, 138, 140, 142, 143, 146n7, 162, 178
Sámi 22–3, 25, 27–8
 Cosmology of 22–3
Scripture xii, 53, 68, 83, 85, 88n8, 107, 121, 153, 155, 173, 183
Sectarianism 63
Secularization 7, 19, 43
SEKAP model 185
Self-critical/Self-criticism 17, 24–6, 28, 150
Semantic struggle 19, 29, 135–6, 137, 140, 144
Sharia 67, 106, 117n2, 163
Shiite, Shiism 62, 63
Slavery 121, 122, 169
Socio-political-economic factors 30, 31–2, 107, 149–50, 157, 180–1, 190
Spencer, Robert 67
Straw, Jack 94
Sunni, Sunnism 62, 63

Taef, accords of 62
Takfirism 75–6
Thatcher, Margaret 137
Theological education 190, 191
Tillichs, Paul 167
Theos 141, 176, 191n5
Tower Hamlets 107, 112–14, 122
Trump, Donald xi, 2, 4n9, 50, 96, 175
Truth and Reconciliation project 182

UKIP 1, 4, 69, 74, 80n6, 180
United Kingdom 1, 4, 122, 155

Vaccination effect 111

Wilders, Geert 2, 11n5, 117n8
Williams, Eleanor 99
Working class 97, 101, 102, 109, 112, 157, 180, 181, *see also* Socio-political-economic factors

Young people
 Radicalisation 182–4, 191
Youth work 182–4

Zionism 12n11, 65
 Christian Zionism
 Zionist 65
Žižek, Slavoj 94

www.ingramcontent.com/pod-product-compliance
Lightning Source LLC
Chambersburg PA
CBHW022054290426
44109CB00014B/1097